BOOKS BY MARY MACCRACKEN

A Circle of Children
Lovey: A Very Special Child
City Kid

by Mary MacCracken

LITTLE, BROWN AND COMPANY   BOSTON — TORONTO

This book recounts the essence of my experience and in that
sense is a true story. However, it is not intended as a literal
account, and it is not to be taken as a portrayal of any living
person. All names (except for my family's and mine) of
individuals, places, and institutions are fictitious.

FIRST EDITION

Library of Congress Cataloging in Publication Data
MacCracken, Mary.
   City kid.
   1. Juvenile delinquency—United States—Case
studies. 2. Teachers, Training of—United States—
Case studies. 3. Urban schools—United States.
I. Title.
HV9104.M189   371.93′092′4   80–26547
ISBN 0–316–54186–9

MV

Designed by Janis Capone

Published simultaneously in Canada
by Little, Brown & Company (Canada) Limited

PRINTED IN THE UNITED STATES OF AMERICA

FOR CAL:
who believed in me.

1

"Which one is Luke?" I whispered.

"There, next to my desk," Lisa answered. "The one not working, of course. He doesn't even answer when his name is called. Listen, I've got to go. Talk to you later."

Lisa walked to the front of the classroom to continue the math lesson I'd interrupted. I sat on a radiator cover and studied Luke.

I couldn't believe it. When they had told us at college that we'd be working with children who were socially maladjusted juvenile delinquents, I conjured up images of burly kids with bulging muscles and perpetual sneers. And now here was this little boy in second grade who couldn't be more than seven years old.

I peered at him intently, saying his name under my breath, "Lucas Brauer, Lucas Brauer," trying to make him real. He shifted slightly in his seat and I could see that his brown hair curved around his cheeks, so that from this angle he looked almost like a girl.

There must be some mistake, I thought. How could this child have a record of twenty-four arrests for arson, theft, and truancy? I shook my head. Something was wrong somewhere.

But if something was wrong, something was also right. For the first time in months, I felt the beginnings of the familiar, soaring, ridiculous excitement that came with teaching — a feeling I'd almost forgotten since I'd become a student at the state teachers' college.

I had entered in September, full of hope and determination. By February I was full of disillusionment. In fact, until that day when I found Luke, I wasn't sure I could make it through one year, much less two.

So now I memorized him — the scruffy sneakers half the size of mine, the faded jeans torn at the knees, a plaid shirt with one button missing, and each inch of his small profile. I could help Luke, now that I'd found him. I knew I could, and he would help me, too. He would make me remember there was some reason for the endless empty courses, the meaningless assignments, and the foolish terror of exams.

★

I had known it wouldn't be easy, going back to college at age forty-four. In 1970 the movement for continuing education had not yet become popular and ninety-nine percent of the members of the junior class at Union State College were under twenty years old. They walked the campus in pairs or clumps, ate in noisy groups at the student union, shouted cheerfully at one another over the blare of rock that poured from speakers mounted in the ceiling. I walked alone, ate my cheese and apple in my old convertible, and tried to learn to be heard over the sounds of the Grateful Dead.

That was all okay. I was there to get a degree, to get certified so that I could continue teaching, not to develop my social life. I had remarried in June and the excitement of living with Cal and trying to blend our combined seven kids, aged fifteen to twenty-seven, into some kind of homogeneous group was challenging and absorbing. None of the children lived at home full time, but they arrived in bunches on weekends and vacations and filled our apartment or country house with excitement, laughter, and dirty laundry.

It would be difficult to give up teaching and go back to college after a twenty-five-year interval between sophomore and junior years, but it was also the one way I could continue to teach. What I hadn't expected was the stifling boredom, the frustration of hours spent taking courses that had nothing to do with teaching, and most of all, the overpowering, unending longing for the troubled children I had taught.

I had been teaching seriously emotionally disturbed children full time for more than six years, when the school where I taught became "state approved" and its teachers had to be fully certified. I had no certification, only two years at Wellesley and some night-school education credits. Not enough. I had to leave because the only way I could continue to work as a teacher was to get a bachelor's degree in education, and certification. I could get my degree and dual certification in elementary and special education in two years going full time during the day; it would take six years at night school. At my age there was no choice.

But where were the children? Children had been the warp and woof of my life for years. Without ever really asking, as an education major I had assumed that my days would be filled with children. Not so. They saved the children until senior year, and then only for six weeks of student teaching.

I railed inwardly at the poor preparation the young teachers-to-be were getting. How could they learn to be teachers without children, without the models of experienced teachers, without being in a classroom?

I remembered Helga, the wonderful teacher I had

worked under as a volunteer when I had first started, and all she had taught me. Where would these young people learn about commitment and involvement and communicating with children? Not in my courses in Background of Mathematics I, Adapted Physical Education, Integrated Techniques, Current Methods and Materials for the Mentally Retarded, and Teaching Reading to the Mentally Retarded.

Of all my courses, Background of Mathematics I was the worst. Not only did it have nothing to do with children, it was also couched in a foreign language. Math to me meant addition, subtraction, multiplication, division, fractions, decimals. Maybe word problems and a few math concepts. Not so to Mrs. Kaiser, our professor. She talked of sets and union and commutative properties.

Each morning she said coolly, "Good morning, class. I will explain the work to be assigned. Follow now." With that she turned her back to the classroom and the tight blond braid that ran across the back of her head bobbed up and down as her chalk made numbers, arrows, circles with overlapping circles, equations resting between and below her drawings. She talked rapidly to the figures on the board, never turning her head. She covered one, two, sometimes three of the blackboards that surrounded the room.

Then, "Volunteer?" she demanded more than asked. Five hands in the front row shot up. She chose two and sent them to the unused portion of the board. Then she read a problem out loud and the race was on. Who would finish first? Who would get it right?

I watched from the back of the classroom, never volunteering and hoping only for invisibility and sudden insight.

Ian Michaels, the boy in the seat next to mine, attended

only every other day and never volunteered. Instead he silently scratched out the problem on a back page of his notebook. He was always right, always ahead of the blackboard people.

I decided I would try to do the same. I was beginning to understand some of the vocabulary now — matching sets, equivalency, the commutative property — but usually I got lost about halfway through the problem.

One morning Ian's hand reached lazily across my paper, underlining the place where I had gone wrong, putting it right, then finishing the problem. After several days of this, I began to follow it through, while Ian dozed beside me, coming awake just before the end of class to circle those I had gotten right.

Dr. Kaiser was a believer in unexpected quizzes. She would sit wearing the same bland expression as we arrived each day, but twice a week, always on different days, after her "Good morning, class," the scribble on the board was put there for us to solve on paper and hand in.

I began to wake in the middle of the nights from the sound of chalk on blackboard rattling in my dreams. My stomach was queasy on the morning elevator rides from the apartment to our cars.

"Are you all right?" Cal asked.

"I don't know," I said. "I've got a sixty-eight average and I dream about Mrs. Kaiser."

Now Cal, too, studied the associative, distributive, and commutative properties, shaking his head, saying almost inaudibly, "This is math?" Cal was an engineer and inventor with over eighty patents. If he had trouble understanding Background of Mathematics I, how could I ever hope to get it straight?

I was okay in my other courses, averages in the nineties,

but I wasn't at all sure I would pass Background of Mathematics I.

I said so to Ian Michaels.

He opened his eyes slightly and looked at me through half-raised lids. "No problem," he said between yawns. "Just copy my answers on the final. Then go back and mess up enough to get you what you need."

He closed his eyes again.

Cheating. He was suggesting that I cheat.

I knocked my sneaker on his boot. "That's cheating," I said.

His eyes stayed closed. "No shit," was his nearly inaudible comment.

I wasn't sure how to interpret this. I sat silently drawing circles on my notebook, watching the others file into class.

★

Everybody cheated. This was my first exposure to the marketing of papers. All the various societies and clubs on campus had a file of papers for every course, going back over several years. This was supposed to be a secret, but unless you were considered the type that would rat, the availability and cost of papers were discussed openly. Students mocked professors for giving an A to a paper that had earned only a B two years before. Copy machines made it possible simply to "rent" a paper for a day, copy it, return it, and then, depending on audacity and/or willingness to risk, either retype it or simply hand in the copy, saying you were keeping the original for your files.

Did anybody ever get caught? Not that I knew. Did the professors know what was going on? Again, not that I knew. But somehow the fact that it was happening contaminated the atmosphere. There was an "I'll get away with as much as I can" philosophy among a large group of students.

The environment was so impersonal that the students often reminded me of little children with their hands in the cookie jar, wishing desperately that someone would catch them, just so they'd know someone cared.

★

Adapted Phys Ed was a two-credit course, which meant that we met only three times a week. As if to make up for this, Mrs. Hogan assigned twice as much work as any other teacher. Each class ended with a lengthy new assignment, and a moan from the students. Mrs. Hogan had graduated from Union State five years earlier. It was as if she were saying, "In my class, you're going to work for those two credits."

I admired her spirit, but wished she had a subject closer to my work. One of her favorite assignments was to ask us to write twenty abstracts on twenty different physical education articles. I spent hours in the library. Locating the article was a major problem in itself; often the one needed issue was missing from the stack. Then I spent more hours reducing articles on wheelchair volleyball and adapted jungle gyms to short abstracts, and still more hours typing them up. Where were the children? What was I doing here?

We were assigned to demonstrate before the class a "phys ed technique" that would be useful with "special children." I could not do this. I had taught Rufus to swim, Hannah to ride a bike, Brian to climb a mountain, but I could not bring myself to stand before those forty nineteen-year-olds and put on a demonstration.

An old shyness returned, and for the hundredth time I thought, "I cannot do this. I cannot stay here in these classes for two whole years, while the children are out there."

Cal put his arms around me in the middle of the night, and then wiped my tears. Neither of us spoke.

★

The next morning I wrote a letter to Mrs. Hogan asking if I could substitute a paper or else more abstracts for the demonstration. Perhaps because of my age, the letter came back. "Permission granted for substitution of twenty abstracts for class demonstration." Back to the library.

If only I had known about Luke then.

Our final math exam was on December 20. I was later than usual and I could feel nervousness building as I inched the car along the highway. It was snowing lightly and snow combined with Christmas shoppers made travel slow. I finally reached the college parking lot, found a spot heading downhill, and then walked rapidly across campus, quiet and beautiful under the fresh cover of snow.

For once, Ian Michaels was in his seat before I was. We always sat in the same seats. I don't know why, but it was the same in all my classes. There was some slight juggling and changing the first week. After that we returned as though programmed to the same seat each day.

I hesitated inside the doorway for a minute. Maybe I should take another seat. Maybe I couldn't resist looking at his paper, with the problems worked so simply, so elegantly, so clearly once I saw him do it. Ian, I thought, whatever I have learned in this class, I've learned from you.

I sat down in my regular seat next to him. He opened his eyes to half-mast and winked at me.

"Listen," I said, the wink catapulting nervousness into annoyance. "Keep your answers to yourself. I can do this on my own."

The eyelids lowered. "Sure, lady."

Thirty minutes later, Ian had handed in his paper and was gone. Forty-five minutes later, everybody was gone but me. On the hour, Dr. Kaiser announced, "Time's up. Pass the papers to the front, please." There was no one there to pass to. I carried my paper to her desk.

A week later, Dr. Kaiser stood in front of us. "I will announce both your exam grade and your final grade. Anyone who wishes to see his paper may request it after class. Barker, Frank — exam eighty-six, final grade eighty-two. Cavaluso, Florence — exam sixty-five, final grade seventy-eight."

I studied my notebook, wondering how far Dr. Kaiser would go. Would she read the failures?

"Mann, Anita — exam forty-eight, final grade fifty-two."

She would. She was — and she was already to the M's. Could my stomach really churn like this over a math grade?

"Michaels, Ian — exam ninety-eight. Congratulations, Mr. Michaels. Final grade ninety-six."

What was the matter? Where was MacCracken? Mac-Cracken came before both Mann and Michaels.

"MacCracken, Mary. I always leave the Mc's and Mac's till the end of the M's."

She pinned me with her eyes. The others turned to look. Ian Michaels's eyes were closed. My stomach rumbled beneath my jeans. Say it. Would you just say it and get it over with?

"MacCracken, Mary — exam eighty-eight, final grade, eighty."

I passed! I not only passed, but a B! Exultation flooded through me. How could I care so much about a math grade? I felt foolish, but anyway, I wouldn't have to take this course again. I did it! We did it!

Ian Michaels's boot nudged my sneakers. Eyes half-opened, he gave me his accolade before lowering his lids once more. "Way to go, MacCracken."

★

The second half of my junior year was still filled with required courses, but the ordeal of scheduling and registration was a little easier the second time around. I was getting to know most of the professors in the special ed department by name and/or reputation and that helped.

"Have you had Bernstein yet? Well, don't if you can help it. He's a pig."

"Jones? A good lady. Marks hard, but knows her stuff."

"Telker? Terrific if you need an easy B. Never gives anything lower."

I wondered if the teachers knew their reputations were graven into oral history and available to anyone who listened.

Still, registration was always tedious, sometimes traumatic. We were classified like so many potatoes. With us, the identifying characteristic was the first initial of our last names. On the first day of registration names beginning with A through F were admitted; on the second day, G through L; on the third, M through R; and on the fourth, S through Z. The following semester the order would be reversed. Patiently we lined the walks and stairs and halls of the student union, where various rooms and floors had been partitioned into cubicles representing different courses. The faculty took turns at the adviser's desk.

To actually get in the front door, an hour process in itself, took two things, your student identification card and your social security number. Nobody cared what your name was, only what letter it began with, to make sure you were with the right potatoes. After that you were known by your social security number. I wondered, as I stood waiting in boredom, if I could find my numerical relatives by adding up my digits and matching the total results. If I was a 46, who were the other members of my clan? Were there 42's and 48's around me? I contemplated the girl ahead of me, her hair combed into a high Afro; maybe she was a generic 40.

Behind me a red-haired woman in her twenties shifted from foot to foot. "What's taking so long? Christ! If Statistics is filled by the time I get there, I'll kill myself. I only need six more credits, but that one's required. I'll have to come back to this hole again next semester if I can't get that course." I understood. I had some required courses myself. If I didn't get them I could quit, I told myself. I could stop taking these inane courses . . . but what about teaching? What about the children?

Inside, we raced frantically from booth to booth, checking our catalogs against our schedules.

Working with schedule sheets and catalog in hand, I was trying to keep to my plan of double certification (in both elementary and special ed), which meant I had a lot of courses to fit in. Trouble came when the course planned for 10:40 or 11:40 turned out to be filled; then there was a scramble for the catalog. What else have they got at that hour that's required? Teaching math. Great. Nope — turned out it wasn't allowed.

"You don't have the prerequisite. You have to complete Background of Math Two first. Sorry, it's the rule," said the graduate student manning the booth.

The rules! I was beginning to understand the frustrations of some of my natural-born children and their friends. It had been different in a small private college like Wellesley, where students were honestly seen as individuals, or at least they had been twenty years ago. But in a state college like the one I was attending, there were no exceptions. As long as it came out right on the computer, it was okay. (Computers don't make exceptions.)

Well, Statistics and Orientation to Psychological Testing didn't have a prerequisite — and what's more, it was required and met only once a week, on Thursdays from 4:00 to 6:30. I signed up.

Finally, my spring schedule was complete: Counseling and Guidance for the Handicapped; Current Methods of Teaching Mentally Retarded Adolescents; History of Education in the United States; Background of Mathematics II; Statistics and Orientation to Psychological Testing; and a Practicum in Teaching Reading to the Mentally Retarded. All required courses.

Schedule and course sheet in hand, I headed for Professor Foster's office. I had discovered at registration that he had been assigned as my adviser and his signature was required on my completed course schedule. A stroke of luck to get him, I was told. He was considered one of the best.

Foster's office door stood open and he sat with his feet on the desk, chair tipped back against the wall.

"Professor Foster?" I asked from the hall. "I'm Mary MacCracken. Could I see you for a minute about signing my course schedule?"

"Mary MacCracken? Where the hell do you keep yourself? I've been trying to locate you for weeks. Ever since I discovered you'd been a teacher at Doris Fleming's school and have over six years' experience with emotionally disturbed kids. Is that right?"

I nodded.

"Well, come in. Sit down." He lifted a pile of journals from a chair beside the desk. "Do you ever hear from Doris? I've been out to that school several times. Damn good reputation, even before it got state approval. Those are tough kids. When did you teach there?"

"Until last year."

"What the hell are you doing here?"

"Trying to get certified."

"Ah, I get it. Last year is when the state approval came in, right? No tickee, no job, eh?"

I nodded.

"Well, Doris is a tough old war-horse, but she kept that school alive when no one else could."

"Yes, she taught me a great deal." Glad that I could say it. That the hurt of having to leave was easing.

"Okay now," Foster said, "let's get down to business. We have come up with a terrific idea."

"We?"

"Yeah. Bernie Serino and me and the Falls City Mental Health Clinic. You know Bernie?"

"Yes. He was supervisor of special ed when I was teaching and helped me get one of my kids back into a regular class in junior high."

"Yeah. Well, Bernie and I have lunch every Wednesday. A little business, a little pleasure. We've known each other a long time.

"In some of the districts they're having a hell of a time with the younger kids. Not just truancy, you expect that, but stealing, setting fires, drugs — you name it. So what happens, they call the school social worker or psychologist, she adds a name to her list. Then the truant officer, they call him something fancier, but I don't remember what it is, checks in. Nine times out of ten he comes back and says it's a 'broken home,' either the father's skipped or nobody knew who he was. All they got is uncles, Uncle This and Uncle That. Every time Mom gets a new boyfriend, the kids get a new uncle. Convenient, but unstable.

"So they have a conference and call up Bernie and tell him they need 'special services.' Well, about the only 'special services' Bernie's got any connection to where he might get help for these kids is the Mental Health Clinic. They're a good bunch, working hard in the community, but they got an even longer waiting list than the school social worker."

He paused and I asked what he knew I would ask.

"What happens?"

"What happens?" Professor Foster banged his feet to the floor and leaned toward me.

"Same damn thing happens every time. By June the kid has moved up to number thirty on the waiting list. He's been picked up by the police, taken to court, warned and fined, and released. The school year ends and the whole thing begins all over again the next fall."

I said nothing. I sat looking at my hands, feeling the old familiar sadness as I heard about the children. What sense did it make? Any satisfaction I had felt at completing registration faded. What was I doing here in this college memorizing the commutative, associative, distributive mathematical properties and the content and study skills of reading?

I was so deep in my own thoughts that I missed the first few words or sentences of Professor Foster's next statement, tuning in when he got to ". . . the Mental Health Clinic has gotten a grant to put 'therapeutic tutors' into one of the schools in Falls City on a trial basis. Bernie's agreed and picked the school and I've offered to supply the therapeutic tutors."

16

"What's a therapeutic tutor?" I interrupted.

"Somebody who's good with kids. What else? You can hear it in fancy words later. So what do you say?"

"It sounds like a good idea from what you've told me."

"No. Not that. Will you do it? Be a tutor?"

"Me?" I couldn't believe it. I answered instantly, before he could change his mind. "I'd love to. Where do I go?"

Professor Foster smiled at me. "Don't you want to know about credits — hours?"

I looked down, embarrassed and immediately shy. I had been too eager, revealed too much. I nodded.

"Well, first there'll be training sessions at the clinic. Then you'll see your child three times a week for about fifty minutes each session. Eventually you'll have three children."

In my mind's eye, I could see the schedule of courses that I had just completed. Falls City was about twenty minutes from the campus; that would mean another forty minutes each time I went down. There wasn't a day when there was a block of time long enough. Wordlessly I handed Professor Foster my schedule.

He studied it briefly, then whacked it down on the table.

"What the hell is this? How could you sign up for classes before you checked with me? Am I your adviser or not? Why didn't you ask for advice?

"Never mind," Foster said after a minute, picking up my schedule. "Sorry. Didn't mean to yell. Let's see what we can do." He studied it closely and then grinned at me. "At least you've got good taste, picking 'Counseling and Guidance for the Handicapped' — that's mine. Unfortunately, it's only a two-credit course, but at least that gives us a couple of hours to play with. Mmm-de-dum-dum."

Professor Foster hummed to himself as he flipped through catalog pages, checking them against course requirements and my own schedule. Finally, he looked up at me and said, "That'll do it. Drop History of Ed and take Independent Study in its place and spend the time of my course at School Twenty-three and you'll be all set."

"What's Independent Study? And what do I do about History?"

"Independent Study is whenever I want you to do something. I just write up a slip and send it to the dean. You'll get your three credits."

"Power," I said.

"What was that?"

"Nothing."

"Okay, now. Go on back to registration before it closes and drop that history course. You can always take it next year, there are plenty of sections. Here's a note if you need it.

"Thank you," I said as I stood up. "When, where will I start?"

"Well, the other two tutors are both seniors with much more freedom in courses, so scheduling will be a lot easier for them. Let's see your schedule again. Okay. You've got some time on Monday afternoons. We'll meet down at the clinic at two." He glanced out his door. Four pairs of blue-jeaned legs could be seen below the hall bench.

"Ah. Gotta rush now, way behind. See you next Monday. Call the clinic to get directions down there. Sorry I can't talk longer." He was already standing, tucking in his shirt, smoothing back his hair.

The line was still long at the student union. I went up to the guard at the door. "I've already registered. I just want to drop one course. Is it all right if I go in?"

"Name, please."

"Mary MacCracken."

"MacCracken. M. That's all right. Social security number?"

"No. Look, I've already done this. I don't need to regis —" It wasn't any use. I was just wasting time. I sighed. "One four seven —"

"All right. Step to the back of the line. No exceptions."

I went back. Six new people in line since I arrived, but I should have known better than to ask the guard. There were no exceptions on the lines, only in professors' offices.

But if the system bothered me, it couldn't snuff out the small bubbles of excitement surfacing inside me. What kind of children would they be? What were we going to do together? Who would be my child?

3

It was cold, even for the end of January, and the fact that there was no snow made it worse. The campus looked bleak and bare, and the contrast with the remembered warmth of Christmas made it even more difficult for me to return.

We had spent most of vacation and winter break at our house in the country. We cut our own tall, wonderful, scraggly Christmas tree and carried it up from the woods. We hung eleven stockings in front of the stone fireplace, ours and the children's and the grandparents' and friends'.

The house was not meant to be a winter house. Cal's parents had built it for summers fifty years before. It took days to warm the stone walls and floors. The small furnace worked valiantly, shedding soot as well as heat. Gusts of wind and small mice scurried through chinks in the stone walls to the inside warmth of the house.

In the mornings we lay in bed and blew smoke rings of warm breath into the frosty air and then rushed from bed to shiver by the window as we watched deer leap across the meadow. We ate simple meals and trudged along unplowed roads, chopped logs and read and talked quietly to each other. Happiness was almost visible that week.

Vacation over, spring courses began. I wondered if every one had as hard a time coming back to school as I did. But I did have seventy-six credits now — five A's and a B — and fifteen more credits coming up this semester. If I could just get through Statistics and Orientation to Psychological Testing and Background of Mathematics II, I'd have ninety-one by May. And now, thanks to Professor Foster, there would be children.

★

Many of the faces in Background of Mathematics II were familiar, but instead of Dr. Kaiser, the teacher was a man in his thirties, wearing black horn-rimmed glasses — and there, sleeping beneath a grubby tennis hat, was Ian Michaels. My spirits lifted.

I stepped over several pairs of blue-jeaned legs and settled beside Ian, who continued to sleep, or to pretend he did.

On the board was written Background of Math II. Beneath this was the statement:

A denumerably infinite set is one that can be put in a 1–1 correspondence with the set of counting numbers.

Oh, no. Here we go again. I had thought we'd at least be to something like fractions.

I opened my notebook and copied the statement down anyway; I could puzzle over it later.

A familiar hand reached lazily across the page and scrawled an example.

Ex: The set of multiples of 5 is a denumerably infinite set.

1, 2, 3, 4, 5, ... n ....

5, 10, 15, 20, 25, ... 5n ....

I looked at what Ian had written. Okay, I see that. I smiled at Ian's tennis hat.

"Thank you," I said, settling back in my chair. "The one thing I'm good at in math is knowing how to pick the right seat."

★

If classes at college were as frustrating as ever, our training sessions at the clinic were fascinating.

The Mental Health Clinic was in the center of Falls City on the second floor of the Logan Building, and although the streets were littered and the surrounding buildings shabby, there was a lingering ambiance of power and elegance.

In earlier years Falls City had been a leading manufacturing center. Its chief industries were the dyeing and finishing of textiles and the manufacture of silk. But with the rising popularity of synthetic fabrics, business declined and companies closed. Although pockets of culture remained, the downtown area had become drab and rundown and the population was predominantly lower middle class.

Inside the Logan Building, shabbiness was more evident. Water stains marked the ceilings, walls needed painting, floors were bare, furniture was folding metal. But there was a lot of space, a large waiting room, several secretarial offices, and a half-dozen rooms for therapists to meet with clients. Some rooms were furnished with chairs, table, and couch; another had low furniture and toys for children. We met in the children's room.

The other two tutors were both seniors, Shirley Hayes

and John Hudson. Shirley was quiet, with a soft sure voice and dark smooth skin. Hud was tall, slender, red-haired, filled with vitality. Shirley was going on to graduate school next year, and was working now as a clerk in a department store after her college classes to earn tuition. Hud was job-hunting, hoping to teach teenagers with emotional problems. I liked them both. Hud had worked with multiply handicapped children at summer camp. Shirley with disadvantaged children at a day care center.

Jerry Cotter had been put in charge of the program and conducted our training sessions. He was small, with a brown-gray beard and a gentle handshake. His official title at the clinic was psychiatric social worker.

At our first meeting Jerry said, "This program could be the beginning of a revolutionary change in the treatment of emotional problems in children. The central idea is to expand and intensify mental health services in the schools themselves, instead of letting kids vegetate on waiting lists. We are going to try to do this through therapeutic counseling and tutoring at the school — and you are the ones who are going to do it."

At later sessions Jerry stressed again that help would go to the child in a familiar place, his school, rather than the child going, or waiting to go, to a clinic. He also said we would not be asked to work with psychotic children, the ones who were so disturbed that they would be considered autistic or schizophrenic. He smiled at me. "These children are not as out of touch with reality as the children you've worked with, Mary. Instead, they take their anger out on society, stealing, burning, destroying, and earn the label of 'socially maladjusted' or 'juvenile delinquent.' "

I smiled back but didn't reply. Labels meant little to me. In fact, as far as I could see, their only use was to give a name to a program so it could be funded. Nobody funded anything without a name.

The next four sessions focused on diagnostic tests and teaching procedures. Jerry demonstrated the administration and scoring of various tests given to screen for emotional or neurologically based impairments. We, of course, did not have the skill to score the tests ourselves, but we were all amazed at how much information he was able to obtain from such seemingly simple devices.

Our last session was on observing and charting behavior. Jerry gave us stopwatches and taught us how to use observation charts, marking down the number of incidents of a child's disruptive behavior during short intervals carefully timed by the stopwatch.

At the end of this session, Jerry said, "That's it. I, of course, will be at the school scoring tests and supervising from time to time. The grant covers the rest of this year and I'll get over as much as I can, but we're short-handed here and you're going to be more on your own than originally planned.

"Anyway, good luck. I've enjoyed our sessions together and I'll see you all at School Twenty-three on Wednesday."

How could I wait till Wednesday?

4

School 23 was a half-hour drive from the college, just off one of the main streets of Falls City. It was old, like most of the city's buildings, its dark red brick packed with city grime. The gray cement steps, worn smooth by thousands of children's feet, dragging in, rushing out, descended directly to the sidewalk of the small street. There was no front yard or back yard, only a macadam side lot that evidently served as teacher parking lot and play yard.

Small, rundown houses surrounded by yards consisting of brown dirt and cracked cement lined the rest of the short block.

I parked across from the school and started across the street. A large white dog came off the steps of one of the houses, snarling and hurling himself against the chain-link fence that surrounded the house. I shivered involuntarily and then ran back and locked the car doors before I climbed the steps to School 23, not realizing I was holding my breath until I reached the door.

"Remember," Jerry Cotter had warned us at the beginning of the training sessions, "the kids you'll be working with are different than most. We call them 'socially maladjusted with an overlay of emotional disturbance.' What we mean is — they are tough, street-wise, and don't give a damn."

The warmth inside the school was unexpected. Steam radiators clanked cheerily. Mrs. Karras, the principal, was waiting in the hall. Her handshake was strong, her smile warm, and I liked her immediately.

Jerry arrived next and then within minutes of each other, John Hudson and Shirley.

Mrs. Karras poured us mugs of steaming coffee and we carried them across the hall to the music room and sat down around a long folding table that had been set up in the back of the room.

"This will be your room," Mrs. Karras said cordially. "Fortunately, or unfortunately, we don't seem to have a music teacher this year, so the room is all yours. I've had those file cabinets over there cleaned out for you. I know you said you needed room for some materials."

Jerry nodded his thanks and then we all listened intently as Mrs. Karras described her school, kindergarten through fifth grade, twenty-eight to thirty children in each room. Many of the teachers were on the far side of fifty and tired of teaching unruly kids, but money was short and jobs hard to come by. Tenure assured these teachers their jobs at School 23, though they longed to be elsewhere.

Mrs. Karras again added her welcome and delight we were there and then said, "Let's not waste any more time."

She turned toward Jerry. "I understand you feel it's best for each tutor to begin working with just one child at first and then gradually take on two more. Right?"

Jerry nodded, and Mrs. Karras continued. "Here's a list of the youngsters we've selected for the program. They've been given an intelligence test by the district psychologist. The tests are in the file in my office. Just ask the secretary for the key, their records are open to you. That's been made clear to their families. You do understand that in ninety percent of the cases, family means a mother and, of course, other brothers and sisters. Almost all of the kids live in the low-income project, and the reason they live there is that there's no father around to provide adequate income.

"Norm Foster called and asked me to pick three young-sters for you to start with. I don't know if it's fair to you, but I picked the three worst. Seemed to me they needed help the most. Of course, it's up to you to decide who gets who.

"So here are my three candidates. Vernon Schofield, Lucas Brauer, and Milton Green. Vernon's in fifth grade, Mrs. Jacobson's class — eleven years old. He's black, dis-ruptive, been in several knife fights, picked up by the police for shoplifting. Has a younger brother who's on the list as well, but Anthony isn't as bad yet.

"Lucas Brauer's in second grade. German background. Luke's hard core. Nobody gets through to him. He's got a list of arrests as long as your arm. Been picked up twenty-four times. He's set over a dozen major fires, stolen over fifty dollars' worth of goods from the stores on Main Street. He's got a hundred and two average IQ, but he's a truant and even when he does come to school he doesn't do any work. Just sits at his desk drawing pictures. Actually, he's one of the lucky ones that made it off the waiting list into the clinic last year. They worked with him for six months and then discontinued, said they just couldn't get through to him.

"And then there's Milt Green, black, one of eight kids. He's in third grade, quiet, except he cries all the time and then climbs on the desk and swims like a fish."

"I'd like him," Shirley said.

"And if you don't mind, Mary, I'd like Vernon Schofield," said John Hudson. "I think I'd do better with a fifth grader."

If I had been asked, I would probably have picked Milt. It took a certain amount of something to swim like a fish on a desk in a third-grade classroom, but it didn't really matter. I could never tell anything anyway until I saw the child.

"Fine. I'll work with Luke."

Jerry glanced at his watch. "Suppose I take each of you down to the classrooms. Let's see, Vernon is in Mrs. Jacobson's class, you say? That's on the second floor, isn't it?"

"Yes," Mrs. Karras responded. "And Luke is in Miss Eckhardt's class and Milt in Miss Fuller's, both just down the hall. I'll show you."

Miss Eckhardt's class was first, a jumble of confusion and noise that was instantly quiet when Mrs. Karras walked in.

"Miss Eckhardt, would you please go out to the hall for a moment? I'll take the class. All right, class. Get out pencil and paper and copy these five words that I dictate.

"*Hen.* The hen laid an egg. *Hen.*"

A boy in the third row laughed out loud.

"I'd like to see you in my office at three o'clock, Jimmy," Mrs. Karras said. The room was absolutely silent as Mrs. Karras said, "*Hen.* Do you have that? All right. Your second word is *ran.* The dog ran after the ball. *Ran.*" One thing was obvious. You didn't fool around with Mrs. Karras.

Miss Eckhardt walked through the room, which was now absolutely silent.

In the hall, Jerry held out his hand. "Lisa, do you remember me? Jerry Cotter from the Mental Health Clinic. We met at Bernie's a couple of months ago."

"Of course, Jerry. I'm glad to see you." Lisa Eckhardt's voice was warm and deep dimples appeared by the corners of her mouth when she smiled. Her brown hair was cut short and it curled in disarray around her pretty face.

Jerry introduced me as the tutor for Luke Brauer and Lisa immediately invited me into her classroom. Jerry pressed a data sheet and stopwatch into my hand. "Good luck."

Lisa and I went back together, and it was then that she pointed Luke out to me. He was just a little kid, I thought once again, as I watched him from my seat on the radiator.

As Lisa took over from Mrs. Karras, she said, "Class, we're lucky to have a visitor today. Mary MacCracken is here."

The kids paid no attention. A boy in the back wadded the paper he'd been writing on into a ball and, as soon as Mrs. Karras closed the door, threw it at the girl across the aisle. She yelled and the others immediately joined the fracas.

Except Luke. He turned and looked at me as though from a million miles away, and then turned back to his desk. It was as though he looked but didn't see me, any more than he heard the shouts and yells around him.

At his desk, small and alone, Luke drew something on a paper. I put the stopwatch and data sheet in my pocket and moved to a windowsill near his desk.

What was he drawing? Horses? I couldn't quite tell.

"The first two rows go to the board."

Eleven bodies crowded along the blackboard at the side of the room, grabbing chalk from one another.

"Luke," Lisa said, "aren't you in the first row? Go to the board."

Reluctantly, Luke stuffed his picture in his desk and walked to the blackboard.

By the time he arrived, there was no chalk left and almost no space. He wedged himself in between two other boys, looked up and down the chalk rail and then, seeing no chalk, just stood silently.

"All right, now," Lisa said. "I'll call out a problem for each of you. You write it on the board, figure it out, and then we'll check it. John, nine plus five. Ed, seven plus six. Luke, eight plus six."

Luke had no chalk. He could easily have asked to borrow some, or told Lisa. He did neither. He just stood, doing nothing, and then returned to his seat.

"Luke," Lisa called sharply. "Where are you going? I told you to write your problem on the board. Eight plus six. Go on now."

But Luke's head never turned. He hunched down in his seat, turning his picture over and over.

A boy at the board hit his neighbor with an eraser.

"John! Stop that! Now read your answer to the class and see if they agree." As Lisa talked she went toward Luke, then stood in front of his desk. "What's the trouble, Luke? Don't you feel well?"

28

Luke shrugged without looking up. A boy in the back row yelled, "John's hittin' Ed again. Lookit him, Miss Eckhardt."

"John, get back to your seat, since you can't behave at the board."

As soon as Lisa turned away, Luke pulled out his picture and spread it on the desk, his head bent down so that it almost touched the paper.

I edged closer, trying to make out what he was drawing. Maybe they were lions. One large one lying down and three little ones on the far side of the paper.

I squatted beside Luke's desk. "Hello," I said. "I'm Mary. Will you come with me for a minute? Bring your picture.

"Luke and I are going to do a little work," I said to Miss Eckhardt. "We'll be back in about a half hour."

I knew I shouldn't be doing what I was doing. I could feel the stopwatch pressing on my thigh in the front pocket of my jeans. I knew both Luke and I should still be in his classroom while I "charted" his behavior. But I couldn't stand to waste the time. It was already clear that he did no work and his behavior was negative. What I had to know was why and I couldn't find that out with a stopwatch. I had to listen to Luke, even when he wasn't talking, and I couldn't do that in a roomful of thirty kids.

I walked down toward the music room, Luke beside me, hoping that Jerry had gone back to the clinic.

I was glad to find the music room empty, filled only with a musty, unused smell.

"Let's sit here," I said to Luke. He wiggled onto a chair at the long table and I sat beside him. He kept his picture under the table.

"I think," I said, "that those were tigers on your paper. Very, very tired tigers."

Luke's round eyes stared at me.

"They probably got very tired because of all the noise in the zoo and had to lie down," I said.

Luke turned away and we sat silently for three or four minutes. I concentrated on Luke — the ring of grime on the back of his neck, the sharp points of his elbow bones. What went on in his head when he set fires? What was he thinking right now? I felt, rather than saw, Luke move, and then slowly he brought his piece of paper up from under the table.

"Nope," he said in a voice so soft I could hardly hear him. "They're lions. They got no stripes."

"You're right," I said. "I should have noticed."

Luke got a little stub of a pencil from his pocket. "And this one's got fur around her face," he said, drawing whirls around the lion's face.

"It's a her," I said.

"Yup. Even though she's got fur like a beard."

"It must be a pretty big cage," I said. "Those little lions are so far away from the big lion."

"It's not a cage. It's Africa. It's the mother lion and her babies in Africa, and then a zoo keeper came to Africa and they got caught and he put them in a big field with a big, BIG, fence around it."

Luke was on his knees on the chair drawing a fence around the lions.

"There are three babies . . . and —" Luke stopped suddenly, obviously surprised at himself. He wasn't ready to trust me with any more. "That's all."

It was enough for one day.

"That's a good story," I said.

We sat silently looking at the lions.

I had no materials with me. What to do? What to do? Suddenly I remembered the stopwatch. We were supposed to use the stopwatch. I took it out of my pocket and laid it on the table.

"Do you know what this is?" I asked Luke.

He nodded without expression.

"This one works like this. Press the thing at the top to make it go. See, there are sixty seconds in a minute. Press it again to make it stop. Now this little thing on the side makes the hands go back to the beginning when you press it. Try it."

I nudged the stopwatch toward Luke.

Luke stared at it, then touched it tentatively with one finger. Suppose he threw it, dropped it, broke it. Suppose he did? I wanted him to know I trusted him. And I did trust him. More than that. Already more than that.

Luke picked up the stopwatch and held it carefully in his left hand, pushed the button on the top with his right index finger. Tick, tick, tick. The stopwatch and my pulse beat together. Five, ten, fifteen, twenty.

"Okay," I said. "Time me. Give me something to do and see how long it takes."

Luke pushed the top button and then the side button. The hands returned to the top. He looked at me steadily. "What can you do?"

I shrugged. "I don't know. Think of something."

"Can you do dition?"

"Dition?"

"Like pluses. Add."

"Oh. Sure. Addition. I think so."

"All right. One million dollars plus two million dollars. Write it down here. Go."

Luke snapped on the stopwatch and turned over the lion picture. I wrote it down.

"Ten seconds. Twenty seconds," Luke counted off the seconds.

"Three million dollars. There." I pushed the paper back.

Luke clicked off the watch and put it down carefully on the table away from the edge. He studied my face and then, never saying anything, turned back to the paper and wrote 100 beside my 'dition and turned back to me.

"You can keep it if you want," he said.

"Thank you, Luke," I answered. "Listen, we've got to go back now, but I'm going to come down here every week, a couple of times a week or more, and see you. If that's okay with you."

Luke nodded and we walked back to class without talking.

Just outside the door, he stopped. "When you comin'?" he asked.

"Tomorrow," I said, without thinking. "I'll be down again tomorrow."

Time dragged the next morning. It was harder than ever to sit through Current Methods of Teaching Mentally Retarded Adolescents and Practicum in Teaching Reading to the Mentally Retarded. This was a practicum with no practice, only mimeographed sheets. Finally the clock buzzed its muted signal to freedom and I was out and on my way to School 23.

I thought about Luke as I drove. I'd talked to Cal the night before. I didn't understand it. Luke just didn't seem that bad to me. Was it because I had taught such seriously disturbed children before that now Luke seemed easy in comparison?

Partly, perhaps. Or was it his environment that didn't give him a chance? It seemed as if people didn't listen to him. Did Luke realize this and so didn't bother to talk? Maybe his resistance grew into refusal to do work and he escaped into the fantasy of his drawings. I would have to get into the office and read his records carefully.

I arrived at ten to one, and the yard at the west side of the school that served as parking lot and playground was jammed with kids. A heavy woman, with a plastic kerchief tied over her gray hair and black galoshes on her feet, stood in the center of the yard blowing short shrill blasts on a whistle. The children cheerfully ignored her, pushing, shoving, moving like a tidal wave from one side of the yard to the other, back and forth, swirling around the teacher almost without noticing her.

Occasionally something would distract them. A fight would break out between two boys, and a small group of ten or twelve children would form a protective circle around the combatants, their cheers drowning out the agitated whistle blasts.

A long loud bell rang inside the school and the wave of children rearranged itself.

"Line up. Line up. We're not going in till I see straight lines."

The children separated themselves into a dozen or so groups.

"Straighten up those lines" — a few more whistle blasts.

The children didn't move at all, except to dart from their clusters to pick up a forgotten glove or book.

"All right. Kindergarten first." No one seemed to expect to have to form lines as they had been instructed to do, and one group after another tramped through the side door. Once again, words were meaningless.

Lisa Eckhardt was mixing paint when I walked into her second grade.

"Hi," she said cheerfully. "I didn't expect to see you so soon. Come on in."

"I know," I said. "I didn't mean to be here so soon. I think we're only supposed to come twice a week in the beginning."

"Well, feel free. Come whenever you like. You know, Luke actually said something to me yesterday. Didn't do any work, of course, but he did say good-bye when he left. And that's something. I wasn't sure he even knew I existed."

The door burst open and the kids poured in. Lisa yelled, "Put your boots in the closets or else wipe off your feet. The floor's getting too wet to paint on."

"Okay, Miss Eckhardt."

"We gonna paint. All *right!*"

In between pokes and yells and boots tossed across the classroom, the children managed to find a pile of men's shirts and help one another button them up.

I watched, liking what I saw. Obviously they had all done this before and knew what to do. It was noisy and chaotic, but there was a sense of unity, almost of a family. The bickering was part of their communication.

Remembering Luke's pictures, I knew this was not the time to take him out of class. During art, at least, he could be doing the same thing as the rest of the class.

Luke came in last. No boots. No gloves. His hands rough and red, nails black with dirt. I stood beside him as he hung his jacket on a hook in the closet.

"I'm going to come back for you in about a half hour," I said. "I have to go down to the office right now. Okay?"

Luke nodded without expression. He stood by the coat closet, alone and silent. I wanted to get him a shirt, help him button it, find a paintbrush. Instead, I walked to the door. It would not help to treat Luke like a baby in front of the other children.

Mrs. Karras was nowhere in sight when I walked into the office, but the secretary willingly gave me the key to the file and in a minute I had lifted out Brauer, Lucas. The file was thick and the folder smudged and bent. It had obviously been in and out of the drawer many times. I took the file to the music room and sorted the contents on the long metal table.

There were four piles of pink absence slips signed by the truant officer. Twenty-five slips in three piles, twenty-eight in the fourth. One hundred and three altogether. Luke had been enrolled in school for two years. One hundred and eighty days to a school year. Two years and half of this one. Four hundred and fifty days altogether and Luke had missed over a hundred of them — over half a year. Had he been out more days this year than last? I tried to read the dates, but the carbon print was smudged and illegible. I sighed and put the pink slips back in the folder.

There was another large pile of white typewritten pages. I began to leaf through these and realized they were descriptions of Luke's arrests. Twenty-four pages, a separate sheet for each arrest. Last November he had stolen over ten dollars' worth of toy guns and army men from the five-and-ten. The previous April, a woman's purse and gold earrings from the local department store, and before that, a cigarette lighter and aspirin and cough medicine from the drugstore.

The accounts of fires were more numerous. Luke had set both small and large street fires, and there was one major episode on the hills on the edge of the city during a dry spell. The fire had gotten out of control and it had taken the entire Fire Department two days to put it out.

My stomach felt queasy. The reality of the folder hit me harder than the report Mrs. Karras had given us the day before. But the mismatch between this file and Luke of yesterday was the hardest to understand. How had all this started? Why? I searched the folder for a social history or background information, but there was none. Only a signed permission slip from Luke's mother, agreeing to his being part of the program, and the intelligence test Mrs. Karras had mentioned.

I studied the test form closely, trying to decipher the psychologist's handwriting and remember what Jerry had explained about the WISC (Wechsler Intelligence Scale for Children). He had felt that there was some bias against culturally deprived children on all verbal sections of intelligence tests, but that the performance sections, made up of puzzles, pictures, and mazes, were more accurate. I could see that there was a great deal of difference in Luke's subtest scores. He had given mainly one-word answers or no answer at all to verbal questions, but on the performance part of the test, where he had to arrange pictures sequentially or build block designs from patterns, his score was far above the mean of ten. I made a mental note to discuss all this with Jerry at our next meeting.

I glanced at my watch. I'd spent over twenty minutes going through Luke's file. No more time to think about the past. Now I needed to think about today.

I took the file back to the office and hung my jacket and scarf in the closet in the music room and then stood looking around the room. We were not going to have much in the way of books, or any kind of equipment; at least I wanted to keep my coat in our room. It was going to be difficult to work in a room that wasn't mine. For the past six years I had tried to build a room for children where they could feel physically and emotionally safe. I was convinced that all children needed a safe place somewhere in their lives in order to grow. A place where they knew they were listened to, accepted, and cared for.

I had filled my room at school with books, records, pictures, and plants, with scraps of bright carpet sewn together for mats, old pillows covered in soft prints, fish tanks, and homemade games. There would be none of this in the bare, drab music room of School 23, only cold metal furniture and an old piano.

Yet somehow I was sure Luke could grow. The pink truant slips and typed arrest sheets faded from my mind. That was last week, last month, last year. Now the image of yesterday's Luke hunched over his lion picture filled my mind. Suddenly I knew what to do. I took Luke's lion picture from the file cabinet where we were to keep our records, data sheets, and tests on the children and wrote down his story as nearly as I could remember it; then I went back to the office and typed it on a white unlined piece of paper. I wrote the title in capitals.

THE LIONS

There were four lions. A mother lion with fur around her face and three baby lions. They lived in Africa. A zoo keeper caught them and put them in a big field with a big, BIG fence around them. They lived happily ever after.

by Luke Brauer

As I typed, I thought of Luke's picture. Was there any relationship between the baby lions and Luke and the large space between the lions and their mother?

Careful, I warned myself, don't read in too much.

In the music room, I cut a file folder in half to make front and back covers, punched the picture, the story, and the covers with a three-hole punch. I put Luke's story and lion picture between the two halves of the folder and laced them all together with some red yarn from the materials drawer. With Magic Markers, red, yellow, and blue, I wrote LUKE'S BOOK on the front cover.

Painting was over by the time I got back to Lisa's room. They were cleaning up, to use the word euphemistically, accompanied by Lisa's shouts. ". . . Dump the water in the sink, for Pete's sake. Not on the floor. Pick up the papers!"

Lisa looked up at me. "I swear I don't know why I do it. It's not worth the mess." Then she smiled. "Well, maybe it is. Look at this." She pointed to what was obviously a picture of School 23, grimy red bricks outlined in black, gray stone steps, even a lady with a whistle in the yard beside the school.

We smiled together. "It's worth it," I said. "How about Luke? What did he do?"

"God! You know, I don't know. He's so quiet. The other twenty-nine are so noisy, it's like he's not there. But I know he did something — I would have noticed that at least."

Lisa wiped her hands with paper towels at the sink.

"Luke," she called. "Come here."

Luke's body crouched lower over his desk.

"Luke Brauer. Do you hear me? Come over here."

Lisa's voice was not mean. Just loud.

Reluctantly, Luke stood up as the class watched with interest.

"Come on over here. Now what did you paint?"

Oh, Lord, I thought. Why had I asked? I never wanted him to be singled out like this.

Luke stood in front of Lisa. Paint was smeared on his shirt, his face, his hair.

"Well," she said, "what did you paint?"

Luke shrugged.

"See," Lisa said. "That's all he ever does." She hunched her own shoulders in imitation.

"I'll ask you once more, Luke. What did you paint?"

Luke kept his eyes on the floor.

"All right. All right. I give up. Go on with Mary." She shook her head at me. "Maybe you can get something out of him."

Lisa turned to the class as Luke and I headed for the door.

"Get out your phonic workbooks." The class groaned and then shouted its objections as Luke and I left.

I walked down the hall toward the music room with Luke beside me, not talking, wanting only to give him some space to let the humiliation dissolve a little.

When we got to the music room, Luke crawled up onto the same metal chair of the day before. I sat beside him, turning a box of crayons in my fingers.

After a while I said, "I thought maybe you might be tired of drawing or painting. I wasn't sure, but I thought maybe we could read a little."

Luke's expression never changed, his eyes stared straight ahead. He had yet to speak to me today. Still, I might as well try; there certainly was nothing to lose.

I pulled the file folder toward us and turned it over.

"I made this while you were painting. The cover isn't too good, because I made it very quickly. You can make another one sometime, if you want."

"Luke's Book," Luke said.

You are wonderful, Lucas Brauer, I wanted to say, remembering my other children and how it often took months to get a single spoken word. You talk. You read. But I'm sure you startle easily. I kept myself silent, my body still, not even turning the cover.

Luke looked at me and reached for the book at the same time.

"Luke's Book?" This time it was a question and there was surprise in his voice.

"Mm-hm. Remember how you drew the lions yesterday?"

Good! He can't resist. Luke opened the cover, then turned the book sidewise to study the lions. Then he looked at me. "I can make better lions," he said. "Do you want me to make better ones?"

"I like these," I said. "But you can make more if you want." Will he look at the story? Can he read more than his name?

Luke turned the book back and easily, as easily as anything, he read, " 'The lions. There were four lions. . . .' " When he'd finished he said, "You forgot to say they were lying down." He said it softly, without accusation.

"Yes," I answered. "I thought that was all right because anybody who looked at the picture could see they were lying down."

Luke turned the book around again and studied the picture.

"I guess," he said. "But next time put in about how they're lying down."

Next time! There was going to be a next time. Luke might set fires and lie and cheat and steal, but there was no doubt that he could be reached.

Now I was the one who leaned back and stared out across the room, wanting the moment to last a little longer. Where was the arsonist and thief of the file folder? Where was the rebellious truant? It didn't make sense.

Luke squirmed beside me and rubbed his nose, leaving new smears of red paint across his face.

There was a sink in the back of the room and I nodded toward it and smiled at Luke.

"How about washing up? You've got red paint from here to here." I touched my own face to show him.

40

I turned the faucets back and forth — hot, cold, a little more hot. Making it the right warmth, as I had for my own children.

"Okay," I said. "Here's a piece of soap." I wanted to mix the soap between his hands, wash his face, but I knew better. I moved back and sat on the table, watching him from across the room.

Luke rewarded me with a question.

"Know how I got so much paint?"

"Unh-unh. How?"

"From the kangaroo. I made him all red."

"The kangaroo you made during art?"

"Yup. I could tell a story about it, but you write it down so you don't forget stuff this time. It's called 'The Kangaroo.'"

There was a long pause. Then Luke said, "How'll I start?"

"Lots of good stories begin 'once upon a time.'" If pretending made it easier for him to talk, it was okay with me.

"Okay. Once upon a time there was a kangaroo, and he hopped very high. He was funny and he was a boxing kangaroo. One day he hopped into a bucket of red paint. That was bad. The kangaroo was sad. A zoo keeper put a fence around him. But then he remembered how high he could hop and he hopped right over the fence."

Luke stopped. "Do you think a kangaroo could hop that high?"

I nodded, still writing. "A good young boxing kangaroo could definitely hop that high," I said.

Luke nodded. "Write 'The End by Luke Brauer.'"

★

Friday night Cal and I drove up to the country. The snow was gone, but there had evidently been a heavy windstorm and broken branches lay across the road and path into the house.

Before breakfast the next morning, Cal was out prowling around, inspecting the damage.

"There'll be a lot of clean-up work to do in the spring. A couple of big trees are down in the meadow. Must have had a wet snow before the wind."

I poured our coffee and Cal talked to me as I cooked the eggs.

"You know, my father used to tell a story about President Roosevelt. After he had finished his first term in office, he went to register to vote. In those days you had to write down your occupation. You know what he wrote? 'Tree Grower.' I was thinking about that this morning. When I'm here in this place, I think if I couldn't describe myself as engineer or inventor, I'd say 'grower of trees.' Not very good trees, maybe, but certainly lots of them."

I put our eggs on the table and climbed in on the bench next to the stone wall. "Yes," I said. "I can see that. You are a grower."

"And you," Cal asked. "If you couldn't say teacher or writer, what would you say?"

I watched the sun glimmering through the small window panes, highlighting a pale brown spider who was beginning to spin a web in the far corner of the room. Cal was one of the few people who knew about the journals I kept and the occasional poems and articles I'd published. He teased me sometimes about my diaries, but it was an old habit. From the time I was a little girl, things stayed brighter, clearer for me if I wrote them down. After I began to teach, I kept a small black and white notebook for each child I taught. My version of a lesson plan, I suppose.

A montage of the children I'd known imposed itself upon the spiderweb and I smiled at Cal.

"I know what I would think, but I'm not sure I could tell other people."

"What?"

"A lover of children."

This time Cal smiled at me as he got up to pour us more coffee. "That sounds very nice. You should get used to saying it."

6

We no longer had our meetings at the clinic on Mondays. Now that we were with the children at School 23, it didn't seem natural to meet in any other environment. We had unanimously agreed that our meetings would be at the school.

Each week we discussed one child in depth and shared opinions, ideas, and suggestions about things we should eliminate, continue, or increase. We alternated discussions of children and this time it was Luke's turn.

I was eager to talk about Luke with Shirley and Hud. Luke was so different from the seriously emotionally disturbed children I had known. I thought perhaps at the day care center or camp they might have had other children similar to Luke.

Most of all, I wanted to talk to Jerry. He had promised to check the records at the clinic for background information about Luke. He had also asked me to copy Luke's subtest scores from the WISC test and to give Luke two other tests: the Bender Gestalt, in which a child copied designs to test visual perception, motor and memory abilities; and the House-Tree-Person, in which drawings often revealed to a trained examiner how a child felt about himself and his world. Luke had enjoyed copying the nine design cards of the Bender and doing the drawings. I also had asked Luke to draw a picture of his family, and now I spread his tests and stories and my notes on the table for Shirley and Hud to inspect and Jerry to score and interpret.

"Well, he's not dumb, that's for sure," Jerry commented as he examined the WISC. "His scores in information and vocabulary are low, but look at this sixteen in Block Design and a fourteen in Picture Arrangement. This kid knows how to plan, organize, and then carry out his thoughts, and he's socially aware and alert to detail. Whatever the reason for his acting-out behavior and poor school performance, it is not because of lack of intelligence."

Shirley commented in her soft voice as she leafed through Luke's book, "His stories seem to be mainly about animals. Does he talk about other things?"

I shook my head. "No, not much, although he didn't object when I asked him to draw the House-Tree-Person — or even to drawing his family. I really feel he's trusting me an awful lot when he talks at all. Do you think I should ask him more?"

"Not yet," Jerry answered. "The records at the clinic show he didn't talk at all while he was there. Just poured the sand back and forth from bucket to bucket. I'd go slow for now. Besides, he's telling us a lot with his drawings.

"See how tiny the door is on this picture of a house? Now I don't feel you should try to read an entire psychoanalysis into children's drawings, but if you treat their pictures as one more piece in the puzzle, they can be helpful."

"What's the matter with a little door?" Hud asked. "I

bet I'd put a little door on a house if I drew one. I'd probably draw my camping tent with a very little door."

"I doubt it," Jerry said. "In any case, don't put too much weight on any single drawing. But still, studies do show that a door like this one often means the child is reluctant to share his thoughts and tries to keep a lot inside."

"That certainly fits Luke," I said.

"Notice how small his picture of a person is?" Jerry continued. "How over in the family picture there is no father, the mother is positioned a great distance from the three children, who are huddled together?" Jerry talked further, pointing out evidence of anxiety, depression, and hostility.

"Are there three children?" I asked.

Jerry nodded. "Luke has a younger brother and sister. The parents are divorced. His mother was described by the clinic social worker two years ago as having physical and emotional problems, and much of the care of the two younger children was left to Luke, but the social worker added that it was hard to get much information as Mrs. Brauer was very guarded."

I sat silently, trying to put together all Jerry had said. What did it mean? How would it help Luke? Finally, I asked the last question out loud.

Jerry shook his head. "Tests can only give so much information. The rest you have to get from personal interviews and interaction. Let me ask you about that, Mary. What's your impression of Luke?"

Again I sat without speaking, thoughts tumbling through my head. Impression of Luke? I shook my head, trying to answer.

"I don't know, Jerry. I guess the main thing is he just doesn't seem that bad to me. He is not spitting or biting himself, or talking in weird gibberish, or refusing to eat.

Besides, the way he acts in the music room just doesn't fit with the boy described in the folder."

"Well, don't let him fool you," Jerry interrupted. "Remember the fires, remember the thefts. Those weren't accidents. Those were planned destructive acts."

I nodded. "I'll remember. But why? Why did Luke do those things? And how can we help him not do them?"

Jerry shrugged. "Your guess is as good as mine. Remember he spent six months at the clinic without making any progress and he was a year younger then and supposedly more reachable."

"Listen," I said. "I know he can be reached. Sure, he's reticent and suspicious, but you give him half an opening and he's off and running. My God, Jerry, he can walk, he can talk, he can even read. Maybe he doesn't use what he's got, but maybe he's never seen anyone use words effectively, so he hasn't bothered to try. If his mother's 'guarded' and his father's not there, maybe he's never learned that you don't have to set fires to show how you feel. Maybe he's never had anyone he could trust."

I stopped abruptly, realizing I had been speaking with too much emotion. "Sorry. I didn't mean to sound off."

Jerry smiled. "Don't worry about it. Maybe that's one thing nobody's tried. Just caring about the kid."

I collected all the tests carefully and put them back in Luke's folder. I would return to them many times in the next months, remembering, studying, searching for clues that would help me reach Luke. But usually it was not until I was with him that I had a real feel for what we should do that day.

★

Lisa Eckhardt made my times with Luke successful. She was far from a model teacher; she might not be able to

46

keep thirty seven-year-olds in perfect order; she might yell and scream in frustration; she might not always be sensitive to an individual child's problem; but she loved the kids and set me up for success with Luke, and I blessed her for it.

Each time I arrived in her second grade she would greet me with "Hello, Mary. Okay, Luke. No more work for you for a while. You get to go with Mary now." And Luke came with increasing eagerness as his classmates shouted, "That's not fair, Miss Eckhardt! Luke went last time." "He always gets to go." "When's it gonna be my turn?"

How smart of you, Lisa. Finally, Luke had something that the others wanted, even if it was only an out from work.

7

I arrived at school one Tuesday in March and even though it was still cold, the sun was so bright that the air seemed warm, and as I walked up the gray stone steps, I knew it was ridiculous to stay inside on a day like this. Luke and I had been working together for several weeks, gradually building rapport, but we had not moved outside of School 23. It was time to expand our world.

Mrs. Karras gave immediate permission for Luke and me to go out for a walk. The groans and complaints from the other second graders were louder than ever as I told Luke to bring his jacket.

"Hey, Mary. I wanna go. Why don't you ever take *me?*" A small bevy of second graders crowded around us. I smiled down at them and then at Lisa. Thanks to her, we at least didn't have to worry about stigma.

47

Down the hall and out the door. The white dog set up his uproar, throwing himself against the fence, as if to tear holes in the wire links.

Luke picked up a small stone and threw it at the dog. Instinctively, my hand went out and pulled his hand down so that the stone fell short and landed on the sidewalk.

Luke looked up at me inquiringly.

"It must be hard to be fenced in like that," I said. Ah, Luke. That's the first time I've touched you. I wouldn't have planned it like that. Never mind. Let it go. I jogged out into the sunlight. Luke ran beside me.

I didn't know the town very well. Where should we go? What would be the right thing to do? Easy. Ask Luke.

"Where'll we go, Luke? We have forty minutes."

Luke knew. "The doughnut shop," he said without hesitation.

I nodded. "Okay, you show me."

Luke quickened his pace so that he was slightly in the lead. Down the side street to one that was a little wider, but still quiet in the early morning. A grocer was piling grapefruit and oranges in the front window of his store and he waved to Luke as we went by. Luke waved back and I thought, this is what I need. A feel of Luke's world.

He slowed down as we went by the five-and-ten. Was this the one where he had stolen the jewelry and toys? Probably. He stopped and stared at a red fire engine. I moved away a little and studied a sale of wicker baskets. Nobody likes to be rushed when they're window-shopping.

In a few minutes Luke was back, nosing around like a small puppy, his body urging me down the street. We waited for a light at the corner and then stopped in front of a shabby-looking movie theater.

Luke read the coming attractions out loud to me. "*Godzilla and the Hairy Monster; Big Foot and Dracula.*"

"Scary," I said.

"Yup. I saw Big Foot. His foot's as big as that whole building." Luke pointed to the bar and grill we were passing. "He could step on you and just like that you'd be dead."

I shook my head. "I don't think I'd like that."

"It's okay, it's just a movie."

We rounded a corner and there was Dunkin' Donuts. Luke stood close to the window and inspected everything going on inside, his breath making steamy patches on the window. "See," he said, pointing to the waitresses in their white uniforms, the shiny steel coffee maker, the rows and rows of doughnuts lining the wall.

"Let's go in," I said.

Luke hesitated. He obviously hadn't planned on this, but he followed me through the door.

Counter or table? Counter. Better view of the doughnuts. Luke and I sat silently admiring them.

A waitress swished a wet rag in front of us. "What'll it be?" she asked.

Should I go first? Had Luke ever ordered?

"Do you have a menu?" I asked. That would give us a little time.

"A menu? Uh — yeah, I guess so." She was back in a minute and handed me a pink and white cardboard menu.

"Thank you." I spread it out between Luke and myself. We read in silence the information inside. THE HEARTY WESTERN (two eggs any style, bacon, hash browns, and muffins), THE PICK ME UP (tomato juice, one egg, cottage cheese), THE CONTINENTAL (orange juice, Danish, and coffee).

"Where are the doughnuts?" Luke whispered.

"There, I guess." I pointed to the bottom. DONUTS — 35¢.

"Oh," was all he said, but I could hear disappointment behind his voice.

Suddenly I remembered Howard Johnson's, and how I had loved hearing the flavors of ice cream.

I looked at the waitress. "Could you tell us what kind of doughnuts you have?"

"Cinnamon, sugared, raised, potato, chocolate, jelly, cheese, or plain."

It was wonderful. Almost like a litany. I wished she'd do it again.

"Cinnamon, chocolate, raspberry . . ." I said, making the mistakes easily, purposely.

"Cinnamon, sugar, raised, potato, chocolate, jelly, cheese, or plain."

Wonderful, wonderful.

I looked at Luke. He was smiling. I had never seen him smile before.

"Jelly for me," I said, "and coffee."

"Me too," said Luke.

"Two jellies. Two coffees. Be right back."

Luke poured two containers of cream and four spoonfuls of sugar into his coffee and held it between his two hands. Nutrition experts would have a stroke, but sometimes there are more important things than too much sugar.

It was nice, sitting there in the sunlight, sipping our coffee, nibbling at our doughnuts, and licking jelly from our fingers. I wished we could have stayed all morning, but the wall clock said 10:00. We had already used up thirty-five minutes and I wanted to be back on time so we could get out again.

On the last block before school, Luke stopped beside a telephone pole and dug deep in his pocket. He brought up his fist closed tight. He looked up at me and then opened his hand. A shiny gold shell lay in the center of his palm. My stomach lurched. A bullet shell?

But Luke was talking to me. "See? I got it at the factory and shined it. You can see your face if you want."

"The factory?" I asked.

"Yup. The lipstick factory. I go by it on my way home. I got a secret place there."

An empty lipstick tube. Not a bullet after all. But I still couldn't find my voice.

Luke touched me this time. He put his hand into mine and turned it upside down. "It's a secret place. But you can keep this one if you won't tell. I got more. Look. See if you can see your face."

I peered at the gleaming shell, and sure enough, there I was, distorted and oval around the empty tube.

"Thank you," I said. "It's nice. Lucky, too. I can tell."

"Yup," said Luke. "It's luckier than anything."

March meant midterms at college. Background of Mathematics II. Not too bad. We were studying probability.

$$P\,(E) = \frac{\text{no. of favorable elements sample space}}{\text{tot. no. of elements sample space}}$$

Current Methods of Teaching Mentally Retarded Adolescents was easy. A take-home exam, plus an interview with someone who was willing to hire a mentally retarded educable person. I interviewed Cal. He had several people, good people, in his plant with IQ's in the seventies.

Counseling and Guidance. Even easier. Lunch with Norm Foster to report on the Special Education Independent Study Project. My project, of course, was Luke.

Reading practicum. The exam read, "Discuss causes of reading disability in four categories." I knew those. I even knew five. Meeps: mental, emotional, educational, physical and social.

But Statistics and Orientation to Psychological Testing was not so easy. We had spent an inordinately long time on bell curves and standard deviation. The curve I understood. Its normal distribution curve did seem normal △ — it seemed right that there would probably be more average people than other kinds. Professor Frye said that a random sample of a thousand people in Times Square yielded 68.26 percent ($\frac{2}{3}$) with IQ's between 85 and 115. However, the curve wasn't always normal; sometimes it skewed to the right, sometimes it skewed to the left. Then beware the mean and trust only the median.

Worst of all was σ. This simple little sign stood for standard deviation, and Professor Frye was determined that we all be able to figure out standard deviations mathematically, although there are perfectly good charts in the test manuals that are readily available.

But day after day we memorized the formula and did the computations. If I did them carefully, two or three pages of numbers and many minutes later it was possible to arrive at the measure of the variability of a group of scores independent of the mean.

Where was Ian Michaels? And what did all this have to do with helping Luke?

My head steamed like an overheated teakettle.

I wrote everything on index cards and laid them on the floors through our apartment. Then I walked through my carpet of cards picking up the ones I thought I knew, piling them on the dining room table, then picking up the others and studying them once again. The steaming in my head turned out to be mostly due to the flu, and I staggered from bed to exams and back to bed again. I called School 23 Monday morning to explain to Mrs. Karras that I was ill and couldn't come until Friday. Mrs. Karras was out, but her secretary said she would relay the message to Lisa, Luke, and Mrs. Karras.

I finished my last exam on Thursday afternoon. My temperature was down, and on impulse I drove to School 23.

John Hudson was in the music room with Vernon when I arrived. They were playing catch with a tennis ball over the piano.

Hud said, "Christ. I'm glad it's you. Come on in."

Hud and I hardly ever saw each other anymore. Our schedules at the school were on different days and our group meetings were dwindling.

Vernon pegged a hard ball at Hud's stomach. Hud dug it out with his left and sent it looping back.

"Nice," I said to Hud.

"You know him?" Vernon asked.

"Yes," I said.

"Kin he bat? He say he bat as good as he throw. That true?"

"I don't know."

"Hey, Vernon," Hud said, "come on, man. You gotta have faith."

Vernon threw the ball hard, harder than ever.

"We'll see, man. We'll see . . ." he said.

Hud grinned. "What do you think, Mary? Am I convincing?"

"*I* believe you," I said. "I'll leave you two. I just came down to see Luke for a minute."

John pocketed the ball.

"They didn't tell you?"

"Tell me what?"

"Vernon, set up the checkerboard, will you? I'll be with you in a minute."

Hud came over and stood close to me.

"Luke's not here."

"Why? Where is he?" My stomach plummeted down.

"They can't find him. At least the probation officer can't, although they think he comes home at night and his mother just doesn't let on."

"Why?" I asked again, not understanding. "Why would he do that?"

Hud shrugged. "Because of the fire, I guess."

I sat down, suddenly nauseated, remnants of the flu rolling in my head and stomach.

"You know about the fire, don't you?" Hud asked.

I shook my head.

"Oh, Christ. I'm sorry. Tuesday afternoon some cosmetic factory caught on fire. No one was hurt, but they lost a back storage shed. The police are sure it was set by kids, but they can't prove it. They got one kid, Wendell Higgins, who had been involved in a lot of other fires and grilled him. (He's on our waiting list, too, I hear.) According to him, he didn't have anything to do with it. It was all Luke."

"What does Luke say?"

"That's just it. Nobody can find Luke."

Vernon began pitching the checkers in our direction. I got up. "Thanks, Hud. I'll talk to you later."

"Listen, Mary. I can stay when Vernon goes back to class. If I can help . . ."

Again I nodded my thanks and headed for the office.

The door to Mrs. Karras's office was closed. I looked inquiringly at the secretary, who smiled sympathetically.

"She's in conference, one of the board members. Probably be awhile."

I nodded and asked for the file keys.

Brauer, Lucas. I lifted out his folder, but there was nothing new except absence slips for Tuesday afternoon, Wednesday, and Thursday. I put it back and handed the key to the secretary. "Have you heard how much damage there was at the fire?"

"Not much. Didn't really amount to a lot. Just a storage shed for extra lipstick tubes, from what I heard. Fire Department got there fast. Kept it under control."

"Do you know where the factory is? Is it close by?" My face felt as if it were frozen. Lipstick tubes.

"Sure. It's right over on Jefferson. Just three blocks down. We could see the fire from the steps."

"The steps? Oh, yes. The front steps."

It was all like a bad dream. I headed for the door. "Tell Mrs. Karras —" I stopped suddenly. "She did get my message — I mean, Luke — uh, Miss Eckhardt knew why I haven't been in this week, didn't they?"

A look of confusion passed briefly over the secretary's pleasant face. "Not in? Let's see, you're Shirley, aren't you? Let me see, here in my notes . . ."

I didn't wait for her to finish. Obviously, the secretary had been confused. Nobody had gotten my message. Nobody knew I was home sick. Luke must have thought I just hadn't bothered to show up. One more person in his life he couldn't count on.

I walked across the street to my car. Not really thinking yet, just ordering my stomach to be still. I drove straight ahead. There it was, Jefferson. I parked my car and got out and walked down the street. Most of the buildings were

55

empty, or else the windows were covered with grimy sheets concealing whatever went on behind them.

The factory was immediately recognizable. There was an unpleasant acrid smell and then the sight of burned grass and piles of blackened tubes. Automatically I touched the outside of my front jeans pocket. I could feel the tube that Luke had given me for luck. I had carried it to each exam.

I looked at my watch. Three-fifteen. Nothing to do now. I felt better, though. The walk had cleared my head and I went back to the car to wait.

By four o'clock the last of the school kids had passed. At four-thirty the factory whistle blew and a dozen or so workers poured out. A few minutes later, what were evidently secretaries or bookkeepers or office personnel left and the plant seemed empty. I waited a few more minutes and then opened the car door and walked back toward the factory. It was quiet and in the dark, late winter afternoon, the ancient street lights were the only illumination.

I walked without hesitation to the back of the factory and nudged the charred piles of metal with the toe of my boot, waiting, listening. Luke wasn't here. I knew that, but somebody was. I walked in close to the building, leaning against the old bricks, invisible against the wall.

A small, dark figure scurried past. Good. Not the police. Not Luke either, though. Maybe Higgins. Judas Higgins. The one who had ratted on Luke. I went out to the metal pile, once again stirring the empty tubes with my foot to make enough noise so whoever was there would listen.

"Give Luke a message," I said to the darkness. "Tell him to be at the doughnut place at ten tomorrow morning." Not a sound. Not good enough. Think of something more. Ah! "Tell him I will give him two dollars to give to the person who brings him the message."

I went back to the side of the building and waited.
There he goes! The same small figure scurried even faster
across the back of the lot, this time not stopping by the
piles of tubes.

9

I was parked outside Dunkin' Donuts by 9:45.

March had turned lamblike and April continued soft
and warm, with white woolly clouds tumbling across the
blue sky. I rolled the car window down and waited.

I had surprised myself the night before. We had finished
dinner before I mentioned the fire or Luke to Cal. I had
even thought, for a little while, that I might not tell him at
all. Cal, of course, knew nothing of what had occurred and
attributed my silence to weariness or exams or the flu.

I didn't understand yet what had happened myself. I
wanted to talk to Luke before I tried to explain it to someone else. In the end, I told Cal, briefly, almost abruptly.
He listened, asking only for facts, not interpretations. He
didn't even remind me of what I knew, that it had been
foolish to wander alone in the back yard of a factory after
dark.

Unexpectedly, I slept soundly, deep in a dream that I
could not remember. When I woke, the last residue of the
flu was gone and I was ravenous and wide awake.

Now every inch of my body was alert. Where was Luke?
Ten o'clock. He should be here.

A small dark head appeared in the open window.

"Luke say gimme the two dollars."

"Who are you?"

"Wendell Higgins."

"You're the one who said Luke lit the fire, is that right?"

"No. I never said nuthin'."

"Listen, Wendell. If you know where Luke is, you go tell him to get himself down here right away. No money till Luke shows up."

"I dunno if I kin find Luke," Wendell Higgins whined.

"Well, you just try, Wendell. I'll wait till twelve."

Wendell was instantly gone. He moved so fast I hadn't seen him arrive or disappear; with Wendell he was either there or not there.

At eleven-thirty he was back. Alone.

"Luke's skeered to come here."

"No two dollars then. Sorry."

"You know the park? Luke'll come there."

"Okay. Get in. You can show me the park."

We drove for about a mile with Wendell Higgins crouched, wary and intent beside me. "Cops don't come near here in the A.M. Stop here. I'll get him."

Within five minutes Wendell was back. Luke walked behind him, his face expressionless.

He was so small. Seven and a half. My own son at almost that age was tying knots for a cub scout badge, and Luke was dodging the police.

"Hello, Luke," I said, trying to keep my face as expressionless as his. I took out my wallet. "Here's the two dollars I said you could give to Wendell."

Luke passed the bills to Wendell and once again Wendell Higgins was instantly out of sight. Luke looked nervously around him.

"Will you get in, Luke?" I asked.

Luke quickly stepped into the car and closed the door behind him, obviously glad to be out of view.

I started the car and drove without any particular

thought as to direction. Because it was the route I took most often, I headed back toward college. Luke huddled close to the door on his side of the car, but at least he had come to meet me. That was a beginning.

I had no plan of what I would do or what I would say to Luke. I concentrated my entire energy on trying to feel what he was feeling, trying to listen with the "third ear." I let the car drive itself.

Suddenly Luke sat up straight, leaning forward, peering intently out the front window.

I, too, strained forward trying to see what he saw, but there was nothing. Only the road cutting through the hills on the way to State. Even the trees were bare, except for the pines.

I could feel Luke looking at me. I kept driving, looking straight ahead. Give him time. He's almost ready. Don't look at him now; that will make it harder.

"How'd you know about the mountain?" Luke whispered the question.

What did he mean? What mountain? The hills? These hills must seem very big when you're as small as Luke. And then I knew. This is where he had been. This was his hiding place. Was this also where he had set that large fire last fall?

I drove until I found a flat place where I could pull off the road. After I'd parked I turned toward Luke.

"Are you okay?" I asked. "I'm sorry about this week. I was sick and couldn't drive down. I called school and explained, but somehow the secretary got mixed up —"

Luke nodded, barely listening, intent on something beyond the car.

"Let's walk awhile," I said. There were evidently no answers to be found inside my old convertible.

Luke was instantly out of the car, running down the way we had just come. I followed as fast as I could.

About a quarter mile back he jogged off the road onto a small path, turning once to look back at me.

The ground began to rise almost immediately. Within ten minutes we were on steep rocky ground. Another ten and I was panting. I pulled off my sweater and tied it around my waist. Luke obviously had a destination in mind. This was no casual stroll.

We were almost to the top when the water tower came in sight. I remembered now seeing it from a distance, a large blue-gray metal tank ballooning against the sky, supported by thin splayed legs. Strange that it had been out of sight as we walked toward it.

Luke climbed in underneath the water tower and sat down. I hesitated and then sat next to him, feeling the chill dampness of the earth seep into my jeans almost immediately. There was no board or blanket. Luke would have been very cold if he had stayed here any length of time; there must be some other type of shelter. I looked upward. The metal legs that supported the water tank had small cross bars, not visible from a distance, but up close you could see they formed a ladderlike structure.

Luke had brought me only partway. I stood and began to climb up the water tank. Three quarters of the way up the four legs were joined by a kind of platform; someone had put a piece of plywood over the metal grids. I crawled out on the board and caught my breath at the sight of Falls City spreading out beneath me.

The great falls that had once provided power for the silk mills tumbled and spat foam high against the sky; old, intricate, elegant church spires pierced the smoke puffs of the factories. From here the decay and squalor were not visible, and the city glowed with a luminous dreamy beauty. It was also possible to see beyond Falls City; the highways leading in and out were clearly visible. How had Luke found this place?

It was obvious that Luke was not going to climb up and join me, so I climbed back down and sat beside him on the cold ground beneath the water tower.

"It's nice," I said. "And a good lookout. You can see when anyone's coming."

Luke sat expressionless beside me. How had he learned to keep his face so still? There was nothing in his eyes at all. Was that because he felt nothing, or because he'd learned to cover it so well? I rubbed my thumb across the moss that grew under the water tower and tried to feel what Luke was feeling. What would it be like to be seven years old and have only a water tower for comfort?

Luke spoke suddenly, interrupting my thoughts. "My father brought me here. My real father," he added quickly.

"I don't know about your father."

Luke shrugged. "I don't see him much anymore. Mom and him are divorced and he's got a new wife now. She's got three kids."

We sat without talking again. What was there to say? I watched Luke's small, handsome face for some opening, but it remained closed and immutable. His round brown eyes stared straight ahead, never flickering; his arms were wrapped tight around his knees.

After a long time he turned to me and said, as if he couldn't bear to keep it inside any longer. "This is where he used to shoot up."

"Shoot up?" Why couldn't I do better than echo his words?

But Luke barely noticed. Now that he'd begun, the rest tumbled out in a torrent. "He'd stay here, underneath, see, and I'd go up there to the seat and watch out. I'd call back and tell him if there were copper cars or anything and when it was okay I'd call down and he'd get out his stuff and make a little fire and get it all ready — and then he'd do it."

For the first time, Luke's face changed, crumpled more than changed, and his teeth began to chatter. "I stayed up there on top watching out — and anyway, I didn't like to watch the needle."

I nodded. My own body was trembling. What a way to live. How old would Luke have been then? Five? Six?

"We'd stay till it was almost morning, till it got light; then he'd take me back to the project so I'd be there before Mom and Alice and Frank woke up."

Well, at least I understood one thing. My face had no expression now, either. It's a lot easier not to cry that way.

"Your mom didn't know you stayed out here?" I asked. Somehow we could talk under the water tank. There was a feeling of safety and it took less effort to find the words. I didn't feel as if I was intruding when I asked the question.

"Mom's sick a lot," Luke said. "She doesn't shoot up." He sat up straight and looked me in the eye. "Honest," he said. "She never does. She drinks some and smokes stuff and she gets sick. She throws up a lot, but she doesn't ever shoot up."

"Who cooks? Who takes care of your little brother and sister?" Wrong. Luke turned away, defenses back in place.

"She does," he said. "Most of the time."

I stood up, or partway up, and crawled out from under the water tower. I stretched, my body cramped from sitting and emotion. I looked at my watch. Four o'clock.

Inadequacy and urgency churned inside my stomach. There were less than two hours of daylight left and I had just begun to understand a little of Luke's problems; I wasn't even close to any solutions, but he couldn't stay out here alone much longer, and his home, what there was of it, was far away.

I walked around the water tower trying to think. How was I going to help Luke? I climbed up to the platform, searching for clues, but the enormity of the problem was even greater there. Down in Falls City, in its schools, there were hundreds, maybe thousands of children like Luke and behind them was a society of poverty, ignorance, and neglect spawning new Lukes nightly.

I climbed back down and was glad to see that Luke had come out from under the tower and was sitting on a ledge of rock to one side of it. I sat beside him, feeling the warmth the rock had accumulated from the sun, remembering the fire at the factory. This is what we had come to talk about. I couldn't think of a subtle way to begin, but I knew I had to ask.

"Did you start the fire at the factory, Luke?"

He shook his head. I waited, but that was all.

"Were you there?" I was insisting. I knew it. I also knew it was a risk, but I had to do it.

This time Luke nodded.

"Why? What were you doing in a shed behind the lipstick factory?"

"I wasn't in it. I was just by it."

"All right. Beside it. Why, Luke? What happened?"

"I don't know." Luke scratched at the flat rock where we were sitting with a smaller stone. He hunched his shoulders. "I didn't feel like goin' back to school. You didn't even come like you said and anyway, 'member I told you I had a secret place?"

"Yes," I nodded. "You told me that when you gave me the lipstick tube. I was sick, Luke. I'm sorry." I took the tube out of my pocket and held it in my hand. Maybe it would bring us luck.

"That was the place. I had a little dugout place beside that shed and I kept things there. Some of the tubes I found, a ring my dad gave me . . . special things."

I nodded. There was probably no place in the project apartment that was safe from the explorations of his small brother and sister. I remembered a little cedar chest complete with brass hinges, a lock, and key that my grandmother had given me, a place for secret things.

"Now they're all gone," Luke said. "I sent Wendell back to look, but he says they musta gotten burned up."

"What's Wendell got to do with this?"

"He came there while I was looking at my things. Wendell's always following everybody. Then he —"

Luke stopped abruptly.

"Luke," I said. "It's important that you tell me what really happened. Wendell told the police you set the fire."

Luke looked at me, his face still without expression.

"I never did. Wendell done it his own self. I just went there 'cause I wanted to look at my things. The men all started work again at one o'clock, so no one was out by the shed. But then Wendell came and said he had something to show me, something that would make me feel real good. And he got out matches and a spoon and then he made a fire . . ." Luke's voice cracked, but he kept on, "and then he got out a needle, sorta like the one my dad used to have, and I yelled at him.

"I couldn't help it and then I ran and I guess I made too much noise 'cause Wendell ran, too. And then the fire kept burning — and it got bigger and it got up into that ole wood and next thing I knew, the whole shed was burning."

I nodded silently, seeing it clearly — the small fire feeding on the grass, licking the dry wood of the shed.

Luke chattered on. "We got out of there fast. Me and Wendell. I just kept runnin' till I got here. Nobody ever caught my dad here and I knew they wouldn't catch me. I lost ole Wendell on the way, but it doesn't matter. Wendell's not scared of nuthin'!"

"Luke," I said, "there are papers in your file at school that say you've set a lot of fires. Is that true?"

Luke scratched with the stone. "Maybe some little ones. Leaves in the street."

"Why?" I asked, still pushing, still risking, needing to know.

Luke tossed the stone over toward the water tower and it clanked against one of the metal legs. "Don't know. I just like to watch 'em. They're pretty, all red and blue and orange, dancin' around."

"How about the big fire on the mountain last fall? Did you set that?"

Luke smiled — and I hated the smile.

"That one was real pretty. Red, yellow, orange, lickin' away, eating up the ole grass, runnin' all by its own self."

Luke paused. There was no guilt or repentance in his voice, only admiration for the fire. "It kept on gettin' bigger and bigger and then began going down into town and the pines all started too — and it was taller than me."

Luke stopped and laughed out loud.

He had forgotten about me in his excitement of remembering the fire and was just talking out loud, not to anyone in particular.

"Then the cops began to come, blowin' their sirens and then the fire truck, but they couldn't put it out — they couldn't catch that ole fire, it just kept goin'."

His voice sounded hard and cruel, not like Luke's at all.

"Were you alone?" I asked.

"Why?" Instantly alert. "Why do you want to know?" Luke was aware of me again. The outsider.

"Nothing," I said. "Never mind." Why had I thought that I could reach through seven years of fires and drugs and neglect and touch a child? But Luke wasn't done.

"I got away," he said with pride. "The cops were all stretched out and lined up searching for us — me," he corrected himself. "But I just started running and took an ole belly whopper right through the middle and came out on the other side. My shirt was burning like anything and I knew I couldn't get those little buttons undone. So know what I did? I just layed down in the dirt and rolled and rolled and it went out."

I put Luke's lipstick tube back in my pocket. Now it was my turn to sit staring out at the sky without talking. I could see why there were waiting lists at schools, why clinics couldn't get through, why teachers gave up. It was too much. These delinquents, or whatever label you used, weren't born out of an acute crisis, but out of a chronic, unending sickness in cities.

Urgency departed, replaced by sorrow. I decided to attribute the churning in my stomach to hunger. Neither Luke nor I had eaten for a long while.

"Listen, Luke," I said. "I'm going to go get us something to eat. Want to come?"

He shook his head as I had known he would. He had already made the trip off the mountain once today.

"Okay. I won't be long," I promised.

Down the hill, back to my car, but not back to Falls City. If Luke was watching from his water tower, as I was sure he was, I didn't want him worrying about what I was doing in Falls City. Instead, I drove on toward the college and stopped at a roadside stand and bought sandwiches and soda.

On the drive back, textbook phrases echoed in my head. "Socially maladjusted . . . character disorder . . . sociopathic behavior; destructive, immature, impulsive, manipulative — with a disregard for the needs and feelings of others. A deficit of conscience and judgment; inability to feel guilt and shame." I knew the words; I'd read all the descriptive phrases at night school years before.

Luke would be considered a classic case, who, as he grew older, would continue to steal, destroy and even perhaps sometime to kill. He was a product of his society, and even I knew I couldn't change a society.

I forced my thoughts away from Luke, back to the road.

Where was the place I'd parked? Everything looked different from this direction. There was the water tower. I strained to see if I could see a figure beneath the tank, but none was visible.

Panic never arrives slowly for me. Now it hit — wham! Suppose I couldn't find the place, the path. Suppose Luke waited and then decided that I wasn't coming back, that I had let him down again?

I'd gone too far. I was sure of it. I was getting much too close to Falls City now. Damn, damn! Turn the car around. You'll recognize the spot from this side.

I drove back up the hill slowly, slowly, searching the side of the road for the same place I'd pulled off with Luke. If I could find that spot, I thought I could cut back to the path. Things are easier to remember on foot.

Luke! I'd almost missed him. I slammed on the brakes and backed up. Luke stood up and came out from behind a small bush. I jammed the car into some low evergreens and took the paper bag of sandwiches and soda back to where Luke waited. Luke cared! He'd even come to help. Remember the days in school, the doughnuts, the lipstick tube. Don't sell him short.

"The path's hard to see when you don't know it," Luke said, forgiving me.

"Yes," I said. "Thank you."

Four-thirty now. Time was running out. The sun turned molten red and began to descend into the city. The sky above the sunset changed from blue to gray.

Luke ate two sandwiches without speaking, washing down mouthfuls with gulps of soda. Then unexpectedly, he said, "Sometimes, after my dad was finished . . . underneath, he'd put out the fire and then come up on the platform and sit with me. And sometimes he would stay awake awhile and when the stars came out, he'd tell me their names." Luke had his arms wrapped around his knees so he had to turn his whole body to look at me. "He knew all the names. Big Dipper. Little Dipper. Orion. Cassy Pee's Chair." There was pride in Luke's small voice.

I concentrated on the sky, trying to remain objective, to remember the textbook, to realize what a small percentage of success socially maladjusted kids had, but my heart was thump-thumping for some undefined reason. I watched a small cloud form above the sun, an odd shape, reminiscent of something.

"Luke, look," I said. "See that cloud? It looks like an amoeba."

"What's an amoeba?"

"It's the simplest of all animals. It's really very, very small — only about a hundredth of an inch around. I saw one first when I was in college. I saw it through a microscope and it looked sort of like a starfish made out of gray jelly."

"Where's it come from?" Luke asked, leaning toward me.

"They said in college that you could find them, amoebas, in mud or in weeds in ponds. But I don't think we could see them. Not with just our eyes."

Luke's own eyes were close to mine. He was on his

knees, listening hard. I realized suddenly that our eyes were almost identical in color — brown, almost black, so that unless you looked closely, the pupil was indistinguishable from the rest. I studied his whole face now, searching for answers. Where was cruelty? Not in his eyes or short, straight nose. Where was destructiveness? Not in his wide mouth or small chin.

All of a sudden I knew what to do to help Luke. It was so simple. I would *teach* him. He wasn't, after all, a segment of society. We'd leave society to someone else and just be what we were. I would teach him about amoebas and plants and animals — and numbers and how words could be used to communicate thoughts and feelings. I felt such a rush of energy that it almost propelled me off the ledge. I forgot the college textbook predictions, even the mountain, the day, Luke and myself, totally immersed in my idea.

Luke nudged my arm and pulled me back to earth.

"Hey, look, Mary. Your meba's gone."

I stood up. The sky was hardly any color at all now. It was time to go home, but Luke didn't seem to know it. He had become inordinately cheerful and was hopping about on the rock. Now he tugged at my hand as I bent over to pick up our empty soda cans.

"It's turned into a kite," Luke said. "The meba's turned into a kite."

Luke was right. The shape that had hung amorphously amoebalike above the sun had shifted, somehow changed itself into the pattern of a kite so that now it sailed across the sky, a beribboned tail bobbing just above the dark horizon.

There was the evidence that change could and did occur.

"Okay," I said, recognizing confirmation. No matter

what the textbooks said, Luke and I were going to have to give it a try. "You're right. It does look like a kite. But right now, Luke Brauer, I'm going to take you back to Falls City and then I'm going home and tomorrow we're going down to the police station and you're going to tell them about the fire at the factory." I couldn't go back too far. Forget the mountain fire. Concentrate on now.

"I'm not gonna tell on Wendell," Luke muttered.

"Okay. But you are going to tell about your special place and how you left before the fire started."

Luke stalled.

"Can't go to the police tomorrow," he said. "I gotta go to school."

"Tomorrow's Saturday," I reminded him. "We can go."

Luke inspected me. "You comin'?"

"Looks that way," I replied.

We walked down the hill together carrying the paper bag and soda cans.

10

It was raining when I picked Luke up in the park the next morning. It looked to me as though he had been home. His pants were dry and he had on a clean shirt. But I didn't ask. He had wanted to be dropped off at the park last night and I'd agreed. We had been through a lot yesterday — it was enough that he had been willing to come down off his mountain. Now we needed our strength for the police.

I was worried. The only time I'd been in a police station in the last ten years was to renew a dog's license and I was far from sure of procedure. Cal's advice had been to find a top officer and state who we were and why we were there. Why were we there? Because the police had been hunting for Luke. What would they do to him? Probably not much. The jails weren't set up for seven-year-old kids who set fires and ran away. Nonetheless, I was perspiring slightly as Luke and I walked into the police station.

A wooden rail and gate divided the space in the front office. Behind it two men in dark blue pants and lighter blue shirts sat in front of a switchboard.

The larger of the two looked at us without getting up. "Help you?" he said, although it didn't sound as though help was what he had in mind.

"Yes," I answered. "I'm Mary MacCracken. This is Luke Brauer."

"Luke Brauer? Oh, yeah. The truant kid at Twenty-three who's always setting fires. That you, kid?"

Luke nodded silently.

"All right. Come on over here."

The big man opened the wooden gate and motioned Luke inside. I started to follow.

"Who're you, lady? His mother?"

"No. I'm Mary MacCracken. I'm —"

"Mary MacCracken," he mimicked me. "Come on, lady. Don't play games. I asked who you are."

Anger snapped inside my head like a rubber band. I wanted to stand up close to this fat bully and answer. Who am I? I am a teacher and a lover of children.

But I had learned from Luke. In Falls City the less said the better. "I work with Luke over at School Twenty-three. I'm associated with the Mental Health Clinic."

"Oh," he said. "A social worker."

"Sort of," I said under my breath, nodding. Then, "What is your name, officer?" I'd be quiet, but I wouldn't be pushed around.

"Snow," he answered, obviously annoyed. "All right, come in here, the both of youse."

He pointed to two metal chairs and Luke and I sat down.

Officer Snow stood over us, clipboard in hand.

"All right. How do you spell your name, kid?"

"L-u-k-e." Luke's voice was so quiet you could hardly hear him.

Officer Snow slammed the clipboard against the metal chair next to Luke. I sucked in my breath quickly and then immediately hated myself for reacting. Luke never moved a muscle.

"What're you? A wise guy? Acting like I wouldn't know how to spell a little word like Luke. Just watch it, kid. Now spell your last name."

"B-r-a-u-e-r."

Officer Snow wrote the letters on his clipboard.

Luke sat silently. I forced myself to keep still.

"Now what about these fires? Why'd you try to burn up the lipstick factory?"

Still Luke said nothing.

Officer Snow kicked the legs of the metal chair. This time neither Luke or I stirred. "All right now, Brauer, you better start cooperating or you're gonna be sorry. Did you set that fire up at the factory?"

Luke sat without moving.

"Damn it. Were you there?"

Luke nodded.

"Speak up! Answer yes or no."

"Yes," Luke said.

"That's better. Who was with you?"

Silence.

"All right. I've had it. Get up. Stand over here." He pushed Luke into the middle of the room under the overhead light. "I said who was with you?"

72

"Nobody."

"Nobody, huh? You just run around setting fires all by yourself, is that it?"

Luke shrugged.

Officer Snow walked back and forth, back and forth. He turned suddenly and snapped, "Where's your father?"

Luke shrugged again. "New York, I guess."

"You got an address for him?"

Luke shook his head.

"I told you. Speak up."

"No," Luke replied.

"How about your mother? Where's she?"

Luke studied his sneakers. "She doesn't feel too good."

Now Officer Snow left Luke in the center of the room and descended upon me. "What the hell is going on? How can we put any pressure on him, let alone get any fine, if he doesn't even know where his father is and his mother's sick? What's he doing here, anyway?"

I stood up. "I told him to come."

"You did. How come you did that?"

"Because it was his responsibility."

He stared at me. "Responsibility. Re-spon-si-bil-i-tee! You hear that, Bill? Responsibility. You ever hear a big word like that in this here little station before?"

The policeman at the switchboard shrugged. "Let 'em go. What's the use giving them a hard time? At least we don't have to look for the kid anymore."

Officer Snow walked to the files. He leafed through a folder and then came back. "All right. I'm gonna let youse go. But you better be at School Twenty-three every day, kid, when I come looking for you. Because if you're not, when I find you, you're gonna think those fires you set are cool as ice water compared to what I'm gonna do. Now wait outside."

The station house door clanked shut behind Luke and

Officer Snow said, "What's the matter with the kid's father? Where is he, anyway?"

"All I know is that Luke's parents are divorced."

"All right. All right. A lotta men leave a lotta women and the other way around. But you don't never let a kid not know how to find you. I got six of my own. I oughta know. Now you tell that kid to come down here and ask for me if he's got some kind of problem."

I knew Luke would never do it. Still, in spite of Officer Snow's lack of sensitivity, he was one more person on Luke's team. "I'll tell him," I said. "Thank you."

When I got outside it was still raining and Luke was huddled against the side of the building trying to keep dry. "Let's go," I shouted and Luke and I raced across the street to the car.

We drove in silence for a while and then I said, "You were strong, Luke." I wasn't going to quibble about leaving out Wendell. "I can see it doesn't pay to argue. Officer Snow was impressed too. He said to tell you from now on to come down and ask for him if you need help."

All the time things were becoming clearer to me. By actually being in Luke's world, I could see why he didn't talk in school or at the clinic, why he couldn't express either his anger or his feeling in words.

Luke lived in a world where words were used against him. No wonder he belly-flopped through fire, ran from cops, refused to answer questions from Miss Eckhardt. When you live in the city and live mostly alone at seven years of age, you have to devise ways of coping.

Luke's way was to escape — evasion rather than confrontation. Who could blame him? The faster you ran, the less chance life had to catch you.

"Luke," I said. "I'm going over to the clinic now. Do you want to come?"

"Nope." Luke was clear.

"Okay, then. I'm going to take you home."

"You gonna tell?" he asked.

"Your mother? No. That's up to you. I want to meet her and talk to her sometime soon. But not today. I hope you'll stay home, though, and not hang around the park or mountain."

Luke nodded agreement, evidently relieved that another showdown was not coming up.

Was he telling the truth? I couldn't tell. I could also see now why he had much less respect for the truth than I did. I must remember to give him time to answer, to give second chances, never to force a lie.

I stopped the car in front of the project, a rundown conglomeration of two-story square apartment buildings.

Luke hopped out, then stood by the door waiting. Waiting for what? I couldn't think how to say good-bye. I searched for good advice. "Stay away from Wendell Higgins now, hear?"

Still Luke lingered. What? What was it? Suddenly I knew. A promise. That was all.

I leaned as far as I could across the car and called through the open window. "I'll see you Monday. I'll be there Monday, Wednesday, and Friday next week."

Luke nodded and trotted toward the project. He stopped partway and raised his hand. "See you," he called, sealing the promise.

11

On my way home from dropping Luke off, I stopped at the Mental Health Clinic. Jerry Cotter was in the middle of his sandwich, but he nodded encouragingly between bites as I talked. I apologized for not calling him sooner and asking his advice. The truth was I hadn't even thought of it, and now I was aware of how wrong this had been.

"Yes," Jerry agreed. "You should have called sooner. But no harm done. Everything you did was all right, positive in effect. What are you going to do now?"

I sat without saying anything. That was what I was going to ask him.

★

I called Professor Foster's home late that afternoon, expecting a roar of disapproval. Instead, he was benign and I found myself telling him about the mountain and Officer Snow and my visit to the Mental Health Clinic.

"What'd Jerry say?"

"He asked me what I was going to do now."

Norm Foster let out a bark of laughter. "Sounds like he's laying it right on you, baby. Well, they are busy as hell over at the clinic right now. Incidentally, now that you mention it, what *are* you planning to do?"

"First of all, do you have some kind of reading and math tests that I can give Luke so I can see just how much he knows and what grade level he's on? Jerry says the intelligence test shows he's smart but he's been out of school so much, I think we should find out if he's learned all the first-grade and beginning second-grade material and just refuses to use it, or whether he's missed some basic stuff because of all his absences."

"Stop by my office Monday before you go over to the school. I'll dig up something for you. A space, a rat, or something."

Maybe he drinks too much, I thought. It was only four o'clock, but when I asked about reading and math tests he responded with rats and spaces.

76

I stopped by his office rather cautiously on Monday, not at all certain he would remember our conversation.

"Okay, Mary, here you go," he called to me through his office door. "Here's the rat." He handed me a gray manual and a couple of white test blanks.

I couldn't help it. I had to ask, "Why do you call it a rat?"

Norm tilted back in his chair. "Ho! The Wide Range Achievement Test. W-R-A-T. Get it? That's a good one. Didn't they use the WRAT over at Doris's school? Well, maybe she's one of those that think testing emotionally disturbed kids is a waste of time. Can't say I can altogether blame her.

"Anyway, the WRAT is a quickie. Won't take you more than fifteen minutes and will give you a pretty good idea of Luke's word recognition and spelling. You'll have to add an informal test of your own to round out the math. And natch, there's nothing on reading comprehension or phonetic skills. Try the Spache for that." Another manual — more test blanks. I looked at the cover. *Spache Diagnostic Test.* Not space, Spache. Well, I'd keep that one to myself. I had something a lot more important on my mind.

"I need to talk to you," I said, urgency underlining my voice. "You've been out to Doris's school. You know where I'm coming from — the kind of child I'm used to working with.

"I can't understand why we're losing kids like Luke. It keeps going around in my head — they just don't seem that bad. In spite of the fire, I still feel the same way."

Foster locked his hands behind his neck and then stretched them above his head. "You're right, Mary, Luke's not as disturbed as the children you've known, but in some ways that makes it more difficult. Some people

77

figure that if kids aren't sick, they gotta be 'bad' — and who wants to bother with troublemakers?"

"Sure, there are agencies set up to help, but even when these kids get off the waiting list and finally see a human face, it's usually a different face every few weeks or months. There's a lot of turnover in most social agencies.

"Besides, most people want to do their job, but they don't want to get too involved. And the only thing that's going to help these kids is a hell of a lot of involvement. Once they believe you're not a nosy do-gooder or putting them on, they'll trust you. That's what this program is based on."

I nodded. "I've been thinking about it ever since Luke told me about his father and the fires. It doesn't seem as though I can do much about his world or the facts of his life or even make up for his father. But maybe I can help him learn to use some tools, skills like reading, so that he can handle school better. That's one thing. The other is — I'm going to try to show him that I can't do the work for him — but he won't be alone. I'll be there to help."

Professor Foster stood up and smiled. "Not bad for starters."

Through the open door I could see four pairs of blue-jeaned legs beneath the hall bench.

"Well, look," I said, "I know you're busy. Thanks for the tests. I'll get them back as soon as possible."

★

Luke was standing in the principal's office with two other boys when I arrived. Now what? I hung my jacket in the music room and walked down toward second grade, not acknowledging Luke's presence across the hall. I wanted to hear from Lisa what had happened.

Luke's class was sitting in a circle on the floor. They had

pushed the desks against the wall and the children were quiet for once as Lisa put three magnets and plates of paper clips, hairpins, and nails in the middle of the circle.

Lisa obviously couldn't talk now. She had captured the children's attention, not an easy trick. It would be unfair to interrupt her. I stopped in the doorway and turned around to leave.

Lisa called, "Luke's down in Mrs. Karras's office. You can get him from there."

"Did you send him there?"

"I had to."

"Then I'm not taking him out. Tell him I'll see him Wednesday."

But I couldn't leave. It was two-fifteen. I really should study those tests Foster gave me, I told myself.

At two-fifty-five Mrs. Karras's voice carried across the hall. "All right, boys. Get back to your class. And don't let this happen again."

I heard them pass the music room, but I kept my head bent over the test manuals.

At three o'clock the bell rang. At 3:05 Luke appeared. It had been worth waiting. "How come you didn't get me?"

"How come you weren't in your room?" I countered.

Luke shrugged.

"Listen, Luke," I said. "I can't take you out of the principal's office. If Miss Eckhardt sends you down there, you have to stay there. But it's dumb. First, you can't learn anything standing in the office. You missed a good experiment with magnets, and second, I miss seeing you."

Luke stood silently.

I was beginning to sound like Officer Snow. Come on, Mary. What else can you do? Don't just lecture. Get up. Move around. Think.

I went over to the board and began to doodle with the colored chalk. I think better when I move around.

Circles. Moons. Faces. Yellow stars. Blue stars.

Luke came over. "Will you show me how to do that?"

"What? Oh, the stars. Sure. Up, down, halfway back up, across. Then back to the beginning. Here. I'll do each part in different colors. The top is blue. The halfway up in yellow. Across in pink. Then back to the beginning in white. Here. Try."

Luke said, "I'm gonna do mine all yellow."

He took the yellow chalk. "It's like you make a triangle without a bottom," he said, drawing the beginning part. "And then you start to make an upside down triangle." He drew up and across. "And then you just sorta finish it up."

"Perfect," I said. "Yours is better than mine." And it was.

Luke's yellow stars made me think of the boxes of stars in the materials drawer that I had never touched. Unknowingly, I began my first behavior modification chart. I, who had once said Skinner's pigeons denied the soul of man, got out a piece of oaktag and drew lines for Tuesday, Wednesday, Thursday, and Friday. Forget Monday. That was done. Then I got out the boxes of stars, gold stars, silver stars, red stars, blue stars, large silver stars, large gold stars. I took the top off every box.

"Listen, Luke," I said. "Every day you stay out of the office, we'll put a star under that day." Already my head was teeming. We could add stars for work done, days in school, fires not set. Slowly. Move slowly. One thing at a time.

Luke stirred the stars with his finger. He examined each box. "Just one color?" he asked.

"Pick your favorite," I answered.

"Big gold," he decided.

"Okay. Good. On Wednesday when I come you can stick big gold stars in the days you weren't in the office."

The janitor put his head in the door. "Sorry, Miss. I have to close up in here now."

I glanced at the clock. Ten of four.

"Oh, sure. I didn't realize the time. We're through anyway.

I turned to Luke. "Good-bye," I said. "See you Wednesday."

"Can I help put them back?" Luke asked nodding at the stars.

"Sure." It was so easy to forget how little he had. An empty lipstick tube had been a treasure. Now he didn't have treasures or a place to keep them. The hole in the ground by the lipstick factory was off limits now. I searched for something that could substitute. An empty carton on the closet shelf. I lifted it down, pausing for a second in the dim light of the closet. Luke was talking, not only talking but using words to ask for something he needed. In our bare music room, Luke was using more words than in all his other days in School 23 put together.

"Here, Luke," I said as I handed him the carton. "Put the gold stars in here. They'll be just for you. And your book. And these two pencils. We'll keep your things in this box."

Luke nodded. "Can I put my name on it?"

"Yes." A used carton. A small beginning for a safe place.

12

When I arrived at school on the first Wednesday in April, Shirley, Hud, and Jerry were already in the music room.

"Hello, Mary. I'm glad I was able to get you all together. Sorry to interrupt your sessions with the kids," Jerry said, "but I wanted you all here so we could review where we are right now and where we're going. Norm Foster's sorry he couldn't get down."

For an hour and a half Shirley, Hud, and I went over our work with Milt, Vernon, and Luke. Milt and Vernon had both made good progress. Luke was the only one who had been in trouble with the police since we'd started.

When we finished, Jerry said, "You've done a good job, Shirley. Milt's teacher says he is attending better in class and the bizarre behavior is decreasing. John" — Jerry never could bring himself to say Hud — "Vernon's time in the office has decreased by one third and truancy by one half. Congratulations. Mary, I know things have been rough with Luke the last week, but remember, Mrs. Karras said right in the beginning that Luke was what she called 'hard core,' meaning he would probably be the hardest to reach."

I nodded. Our record, Luke's and mine, was certainly unimpressive compared with the others'.

Jerry looked at me carefully. "There is one thing. Please don't misinterpret this, Mary, but if you don't feel comfortable working with Luke, I want you to say so. We can make some other arrangements. . . ."

"What do you mean?" I interrupted, as my heart lurched slightly.

"Well, the rapport between the therapeutic teacher and the child is vital."

Oh, no, I thought. You can't take him away. I made my voice level. "I'm comfortable. We just need a little more time." Please, God, let me sound competent.

"Fine," Jerry replied. "As I said, I didn't want my meaning misconstrued. I just want to emphasize the importance of the relationship. In fact, I'd like to review again that part of the written project that defines who you, 'the therapeutic tutors,' are. I know we went over this at our first meeting, but just let me read this out loud again.

" 'The development of the therapeutic tutor is predicated on the belief that in the vast majority of school referrals, emotional and learning disorders are inextricably intertwined and that both aspects of the problem should receive attention. Educational therapy as defined in this project would require developing the tutor's capacity for creative listening — an alertness, sensitivity to, and an ability to reflect and clarify the child's underlying feelings and a strong empathy, honesty, and positive regard for the child, coupled with some knowledge of reinforcement techniques.' "

Jerry put down the paper and looked at all of us. "Do you understand what that means?"

We all nodded silently — Luke's small face clearer to me than any in the room.

"There is just one more point." Jerry resumed reading. " 'In contrast to traditional psychotherapy, there would be no direct attempt to evoke unconscious material, offer analytic interpretation or attempt to reconstruct a personality. Stress will be on developing self-confidence, ego skills, and developing means of coping.'

"Agreed?"

Again we nodded silently. Luke knew how to cope. He coped with his environment better than I did. He "coped" by not letting it get to him, by shutting it out or running if it got too close, by covering his feelings, turning off his tears.

Jerry put the paper back in his briefcase. "The main reason I called you all together this morning is to go over the program for the rest of the year. I'm sorry I haven't been able to be here more. I've been talking to Norm Foster and we've decided that there is just no way to add more children now. We're at the beginning of April and we'll be through the semester in another two months. John and Shirley, as seniors, will be finished even before that. In order to get reports, grades and records completed, we have to formally close this project by the fourteenth of May."

"May fourteenth?" I said. "That's only about a month away and we didn't start till February."

"I know," Jerry continued. "You notice I said 'formally.' Certainly you're welcome to continue as long as you want to. Falls City schools don't close till the end of June."

I could come in June. Another month. Eleven weeks in all. Would that be enough? Could Luke and I recoup in eleven weeks?

I would have to plan carefully. The luxury of doing what came into my head was over, at least for now. I had to sit down and prepare for each meeting with Luke. I had to give him the tests I had got from Norm Foster and find out where he was academically, what he knew and didn't know, and what I must help him learn.

After everyone had left the music room, I went over to the files and got out a copy of the experimental elementary school mental health project that Jerry had been reading from and reviewed the points he had made once again.

Creative listening. We did that; Luke and I listened to each other. Alertness, sensitivity to underlying feelings. Yes. Strong empathy, honesty, positive regard for the child. Yes. I felt all those. Where was I going wrong? Why had Luke not made more progress?

Even as I asked myself the question, I knew that I must remember his strengths and what he had accomplished. In spite of the trouble with the police, he had made progress. He who never talked, who never got involved, had talked to me. And he trusted me. I must remember that and trust myself as well. Luke had grown. I knew it. I felt it deep in my bones. Just because he hadn't shown it to anyone yet didn't mean it hadn't happened.

I turned back to the printed sheet and read beyond Jerry's quotes. "Therapeutic tutoring includes the academic skills, positive regard for the child, coupled with reinforcement techniques, but is primarily concerned with increasing self-esteem and motivation." Luke was just beginning to use stars. I knew very little about behavior reinforcement techniques. Could I learn enough in eleven weeks?

"Includes the academic skills . . ." I had not done enough of this. I must set up more academics for Luke. But first, I must find out how much he actually knew.

★

"Listen," I said to Luke. "We've got to find out what you know and how you learn best. Okay?"

Luke stared at me silently and hunched his shoulders.

"There are two tests here."

"I hate tests," Luke said flatly.

"I know. But it's no good calling them games when they're not. Right? Each of them takes about fifteen minutes. The Spache and the WRAT. You can pick which one you want to do first."

"A rat test? What's that? You trying to find out if I'm a rat or something?"

"It's just a funny name," I said. "It's really spelling, reading, math. A little of each. Here. Write your name here and then I'm going to say some words for you to spell."

Luke wrote the letters of his first name carefully on the line I indicated. "Do you want my last name, too?" he asked.

I smiled at Luke. How could anyone say there hadn't been progress when he volunteered to do more than he was asked?

"Sure," I answered. "That's good. Now, these words start out easy and then get hard. I'm supposed to say the word, read a sentence that has the word in it, and then say the word again. Okay?"

"Okay." Luke picked up his pencil and looked at me hard.

"*Go,*" I read. "Children go to school. *Go.*"

Luke sat without moving.

"Write it on the line by number one. See? Here." I pointed to his page.

"Write what?" Luke's eyes searched my face.

"*Go,*" I repeated. "Just write the letters that make *go* right here." I pointed again, letting my hand touch his shoulder, just a little.

"Oh. I get it. I thought you were just saying *go* like ready, set, go." Luke carefully lettered *g-o* on the first line.

"Word number two, *cat.* The cat has fur. *Cat,*" thinking as I said it that if this had been a group test, Luke would probably have failed. He wouldn't have written the first word because he didn't understand what he was expected

86

to do and he would never have asked. He would have sat silently, getting farther behind and more bewildered, figuring that the best way out of trouble, since he couldn't run, was just not to do anything.

Luke wrote *cat* and looked at me. "Is that right?" he asked.

"I'm not supposed to say till the end. You just keep going until you think you've missed about ten and then I'll check it."

"Ten's a lot," Luke said.

"It is," I agreed. "Number three. *In.* We are in the room. *In,*" thinking all the time, there's a lot to learn about this testing business. One thing's for sure. I'm not going to trust anybody else's testing. It's as important to know what the child is doing and saying as to know what his score is.

Luke worked hard, saying the words to himself.

"Number twenty-four. *Surprise.* He may surprise you. *Surprise.*"

Luke hesitated. "I think maybe I've missed ten."

I had, of course, been watching carefully, but I took his paper and inspected it.

"Not quite. One more."

"Jeez," said Luke. "I got some of those? They're hard."

"Yup. They are. Now this one — *surprise.*"

Luke wrote *sprize* and I said, "Okay. We'll give you, mmm, five points for each word you wrote and let's say you get a star for each one hundred points. Okay? Can you count by fives?"

"Easy. Listen. Five, ten, fifteen, twenty, twenty-five, thirty, thirty-five, forty, forty-five, fifty, fifty-five, sixty, sixty-five, seventy, seventy-five, eighty, eighty-five, ninety, ninety-five, one hundred." He hesitated. "Uh — one hundred and five . . . one hundred and ten." Picked up speed again. "One hundred fifteen, one hundred twenty. One hundred and twenty points. Right?"

"Right."

"Jeez," said Luke, pleased with himself. "What do I gotta do now?"

"Now you just read these words." I was as pleased with myself as Luke was with himself. We had got through the first section of the test and Luke hadn't become discouraged. Testing was not the easiest thing in the world. It seemed to me that I wouldn't get a true picture of how much Luke knew if he got discouraged, and yet the test was set up so that he had to fail in order to finish the test. Tricky. I was glad we had thought about the stars.

As Luke read the words on the reading section, I wrote what he actually said in order to understand how he figured out words. If he read *saw* for *was* it would be an entirely different kind of error from *walk* for *was*.

Luke read through the first two lines of words quickly. The ones he knew he knew cold, and he read them without hesitation; the ones he didn't know he read just as quickly with no attempt to figure them out or admit he didn't know. He just guessed from the first letter and the approximate length of the word.

I glanced at my watch. Twenty to three. Oh, boy. And this test was supposed to take fifteen minutes. "Listen, Luke, we're poking along here. We won't even have time to do the Spache today. We'll be lucky to finish this one. Wait till we're done to count your points, okay? Finish the arithmetic section first. Okay. Now read these numbers . . ."

Luke did his arithmetic problems carefully. Addition and subtraction facts up to ten were both automatic for him; there was no counting on his fingers. He was also more confident. Instead of guessing, he looked at the problem and said easily, "I haven't had that yet."

"Just skip it. See if there are any others you know how to do. A lot of this you don't learn till fourth or fifth grade."

He found one more problem about how many minutes were in an hour, did it, and then pushed the paper toward me. "That's it."

"Good. Thank you, Luke."

"Are you going to pay?" he asked. Those points were more important to him than I'd realized.

"Of course. How much do you think the words should be worth and how much for the arithmetic problems?" I asked.

Luke considered. "Five. I think five is fair. They're as hard as spelling. Five for each word I read and five for each 'rithmetic problem I did."

"Okay. Count up."

Luke counted everything twice, careful to be fair. Would that be in a report? I will remember to put it in mine.

"Two hundred and twenty plus ninety more for the 'rithmetic — three hundred and ten altogether." Luke was grinning at me. "That's three stars and a piece of another."

"Right. Get the box and pick your stars. You earned them."

Luke dragged a chair to the closet and carefully lifted down the box and looked through the contents: the box of gold stars and some colored chalk, two pencils, his book, and some red and silver stars that I had added. Without hesitation, he took out the red stars. "Three red ones. I'll put them right here under the gold for today. Red for tests and gold for not getting sent to the office. Right?"

"Sure." What could I say? Luke had this behavior mod stuff figured out better than I did.

He held one more red star flat on the palm of his hand.

Then he put it back in the box. "I don't want to cut it up," he said.

The three o'clock bell clanged. He looked hard at his cardboard chart, ran his fingers across the red and gold stars, and then put everything in the box and handed the box to me.

"I'll save those ten extra points till the other test. You write it down, though, so you won't forget."

"I'll write it on the box so we can see it. And I'll get a book, a notebook, so we can keep track in there. Okay?"

"Yup." Luke was already out the door, but he put his head back around the corner. "See you."

I leaned back in my chair and closed my eyes. Tired. Happy.

"See you," I whispered to myself. "See you, Luke."

13

Professor Foster looked over Luke's tests carefully. I had corrected and scored them as well as I could and then written up an anecdotal report of Luke's actions. What he did, when, where he seemed confident, and what seemed to me to be his strengths.

"This is nice, Mary. Too damn many of us forget to look for the things that are working. We test and then say 'he's a year behind in reading' or 'on grade level in math.' What the hell good does that do? Everybody who knows him, including the teacher, could tell that before he was tested. What they wanted to know is why?"

I nodded. "I know," I said. "And yet what they ask is 'What's wrong with him?' I wish once in a while they'd ask, 'What's right with him?' It just seems to me we're never going to help anybody catch up until we see what he's good at, and if he's survived, he's got to be good at something. With Luke it seems to me that he remembers what he sees, but not what people tell him. He knows his math facts; he can spell *light* — and there's no way you can spell that if you haven't memorized what you've seen."

"Hey, wait a minute," Norm said. "You're beginning to talk like a learning disabilities specialist and that's a whole other department, a graduate department at that. You're supposed to be a therapeutic tutor. Remember?"

"And a junior in college," I completed the thought. "What's a learning disabilities specialist?"

Norm feigned annoyance. "Who knows? Another crappy title. For Christ's sake, Mary, you got picked for this program because of your background in work with seriously emotionally disturbed kids. You're supposed to be interested in how they feel — and how to make them feel better, and now you start giving me this stuff about visual memory."

"Visual what?"

"Never mind. You can read about that somewhere else."

"Okay," I said. "I know what you mean. But you can't feel good about yourself if you're at the bottom of the pile every day." I sighed. "I really don't know what to do. I believe, like you do, in being close to Luke, letting him know I believe in him, building his confidence, giving him support. But I've been doing that and —"

"Professor Foster?" Long blond hair swung around the door, followed by a pretty face. "Oh, sorry. Didn't know you were busy."

Foster handed Luke's tests back to me. "Just finishing. Be with you in a minute," he said to the blond hair and braless T-shirt.

He put his arm around my shoulders and walked me to the door. "Motivation, Mary. That's the key. You gotta motivate him. Remember that."

Foster was probably right. It sure seemed to work for him with his students, anyway. But how was I going to motivate Luke? No, that's not right, I thought as I drove toward Falls City. We started working with points and red stars on the tests, and earning gold stars for staying out of the office, and Luke loves this. I just haven't carried it over to academics — maybe it will work there, too.

I stopped at the corner store on the edge of town and picked up a couple of black and white marbleized notebooks. I could keep track of Luke's points in here. I could also make a plan for each day. Not a long plan, just a list of things to do — both therapeutic and academic. Maybe if I kept track of what we actually did each time, I'd get a better idea of how to help Luke.

Lunch period was just ending when I arrived. The usual chaos was going on in the yard, but suddenly it organized itself. Like gulls swarming to a sandbar, the children converged on an old blue van that was pulling into the parking section of the asphalt play yard.

"Beep. Beep. Beepidy-beep-beep." I stopped to watch. There was a huge map of the United States painted on one side of the van, and across and up and down the map went a trail of red dashes, evidently marking the journeys of the van.

The kids responded by shouting, "Be-be-beepidy Lisa," and crowded around as Miss Eckhardt opened the door, grinned at them all for a second, and then raised her arm and hurled something above their heads. A paper airplane. The wind caught it and the children cheered again as the little plane whirled over their heads and they raced toward the plane as it crashed on the asphalt.

Lisa caught sight of me on the stone steps and waved. I

was impressed. I had never seen a teacher so at ease with children.

I smiled as we walked toward her classroom together. "That's quite a car."

"I've had it ten years now. It was a high school graduation present. My dad was never very good about remembering birthdays or holidays, so when I graduated he just lumped all the presents he'd forgotten into one and gave me the van. I think maybe he was sorry later, because I took off the next day for New Mexico. At least that's where I ended up. And every summer since then, the day after school ends, I just get into the bus and go. Doesn't matter where. I just go."

"Alone?"

"Sometimes. Mostly with a friend." I itched to ask more about the friend, but decided on discretion.

"Who painted the map?"

"Me. That's right, you don't know. I was an art major, thought I'd be a painter. Took me awhile to realize nobody was going to buy my paintings, and I needed to earn some money. Anyway, Mrs. Karras hired me last year as an art teacher. Only when it came time for school, it turned out they'd cut the budget — no art or music. Fortunately, or unfortunately, I haven't decided yet, the second-grade teacher moved, the one who was going to be the second-grade teacher, I mean, and Mrs. Karras offered me the job."

Lisa unlocked the classroom door and straightened the paper sign on the glass window that read:

Room 112
Grade 2
Miss Eckhardt

"Come on in, if you've got a minute."

"Thank you. I really did want to talk to you about Luke, but I can do it after school —"

"Now's fine. In class, he's a little better. He's finishing some of his math, he's showing up every day, which is something new. He still won't read a word and never touches his workbook."

"What does he do to get sent to the office?"

Lisa finished watering the last plant and put the can by the sink. She sat down on one of the desks and looked at me.

"If you were the superintendent or even one of the other teachers here, I'd make up some story. Since you're not, I'll tell you the truth. Whenever it gets to be over a hundred decibels in here, I just point to the part of the room where there's the most noise and yell, 'You three — or four or whatever — get down to the office. Right now!!' It may not be fair, and probably isn't when it comes to Luke, he doesn't usually make much noise, but it works. Gets rid of part of the class and scares the rest into being quiet for two minutes. Sorry, but that's the way it is. Otherwise, I'd lose my cotton-pickin' mind."

"Listen, Lisa. Do you have any books I could use with Luke? Borrow, I mean. The clinic — uh, nobody seems to have any kind of reading material."

The kids were coming into the classroom now. One had picked up Lisa's airplane; four others were in hot pursuit. Lisa took her keys from the top desk drawer. "Go on down to the storeroom. Help yourself. Most of the stuff is ninety years old, but maybe you'll find something. The brass key on the end." She tossed the keys to me over the heads of the children and then shouted at the kids racing up and down the room. "Hey, you guys! What's going on?"

I signaled my thanks, waved to Luke outside the door and went off in search of the storeroom.

★

Lisa was right. The books did look ninety years old. The covers were faded and the pictures were all of sweet little children with golden curls, rosy cheeks, and frilly clothes. How could the kids at School 23 relate to them? Who bought the books? Why?

At least they were organized. The lower shelves were for first and second grades, the higher shelves for the upper grades. I sat on the floor and picked out a book from each section of the first and second halves of first grade — spelling book, reader, handwriting manual, math book, teacher's editions of science and social studies. Then the same from the second grade. I'd get to know what you were expected to learn in first and second grade. They hadn't got around to that yet at college, and in the school for seriously emotionally disturbed children where I had taught, there had been little emphasis on and less expenditure for academic materials.

I carried the books to the music room and put them on top of the file cabinet, and then went back to Lisa's room to return her keys and pick up Luke.

"Any luck?" she called over the heads of the kids, who were taping cardboard boxes together. "We're making totem poles," she explained. "Social Studies says you learn about Indians in second grade. I figured this was as good a way as any.

"Could you try to have Luke back by two-fifteen today? The second grades are going to get together for baseball." I nodded. It was so hard to get anything done in forty minutes, but I would have to learn.

Luke was quiet as we walked toward the music room and he shut the door quickly as soon as we were inside.

He sat down at the long table and stared at me. "Wendell says you lied."

"Wendell Higgins? I thought you were going to stay away from him."

Luke was not to be diverted. "I told him you were gonna tell me how I did on those tests and he says teachers never tell, and I told him you weren't a teacher and he says you're the same as one."

I added another notch to my dislike for Wendell Higgins and went over to the file cabinet where we kept our own records on each child and took out Luke's folder.

I went back and sat down beside Luke. "Whatever I do, I won't lie to you," I promised. "Not now. Not yesterday. Not tomorrow, and I hope you won't lie to me."

Luke's soft, stubborn little voice asked, "Are you gonna tell me how I did?"

"Of course." He had a right to know about himself. Facts I found out in testing belonged to him more than to me. He should know as much as he could understand.

I spread Luke's test papers out in front of him. "In Mrs. Karras's office they have another file for you where they keep the pink slips for the times you're absent, times you got in trouble, things like that. They have a file for everybody in the school."

Luke looked at me disbelievingly. "Not everybody. Not the good kids. That'd be hundreds and hundreds of files. That'd take up the whole office."

"Well, they've got them," I said. "Anyway, they also have a test for you and the other kids that are in our program, like Vernon and Milt, that's supposed to tell how smart you are. I can't show you that because I didn't give it to you and it's not mine, but I've seen it and I know what it says."

Luke's black-brown eyes never left my face. "And it says," I continued, "that you have average intelligence."

Luke squirmed beside me.

"And are in the fiftieth percentile." The squirming increased. "Luke, listen now. I know some of this is hard to understand, but it's important." I pulled a blank piece of paper in front of us and drew a line from the bottom to the top. I wrote 0 by the bottom and a 100 at the top.

"You're good at counting," I said, as I made a fat black dot halfway up the line. "If this is zero here at the bottom and you were going to count up this line to one hundred by ones, what do you think this dot would be?"

"Can I count by tens?"

"Sure. Why not?"

"It's quicker," Luke said.

"Yes."

Luke pointed to the line. "Zero, ten, twenty, thirty, forty, fifty, sixty, seventy, eighty, ninety, one hundred. That dot would have to be fifty. It's like right halfway up."

"Yes. That's right. And that's where the test says you are. That's what fiftieth percentile means. You're smarter than half the kids."

"Nooo." Luke couldn't help himself. "You're kidding me. I am not smarter than half the kids."

"Yes. Half the kids your age."

"Like in second grade? Smarter than half of them?"

"Yes. Smarter than half of all the kids in all second grades."

"Mrs. Jacobson's, too?" Luke stared at me in disbelief.

Again I nodded.

Then Luke said, "What test was it?"

"It's called a WISC, the Wechsler Intelligence Scale for Children. The psychologist gave it to you a few months ago. He asked you a lot of questions and gave you some puzzles and things to do."

"Yeah, yeah. I remember him." Luke was kneeling on

the chair now. "He had a stopwatch just like you!" Suddenly, Luke was quiet, thinking hard. Then he turned so he could look at me full in the face. "Listen, Mary. How do you know how smart he, that sico, whatever he's called, is? Maybe he didn't get it right?"

I laughed out loud, thinking, by God, Luke, I think you're smarter than the fiftieth percentile, maybe smarter than most of my professors. To Luke, I said, "He got it right. I checked it. Besides he's been to lots of colleges and is even a special kind of doctor."

Luke was impressed. He thought hard for a while and turned around again full face. "Well, if I'm supposed to be so smart, how come I'm dumb?"

"What makes you think you're dumb?"

"Jesus," Luke sneered, forgetting his usual detachment. "Look at all the zeroes I get. And F's." He got out his lipstick tube just like the one he'd given me, and spun it on the table. "You don't get F's if you're smart."

"I know," I said. "That's what we have to try to figure out. It doesn't make sense to me either. Anyway, let me quickly tell you about these other tests before you have to go back. Our time's almost up."

Never enough time. Now I realized how lucky I had been when I taught emotionally disturbed children and had them five hours a day, five days a week. How could I teach anything in thirty or forty minutes? Never mind. Don't waste time now.

"See, Luke? Here on the math — you're in the fiftieth percentile too, grade score two point six. That's right where you should be. But spelling and reading are in the sixteen to twenty percentiles. Not so good."

"Maybe that's why I get F's."

"Maybe. But I don't think so. It doesn't make sense if you're smarter than half the kids."

We looked at each other. Neither of us mentioned the undone work, the unfinished pages, the fact that he didn't read in reading group. I figured he could bring it up if he wanted to, but it was too late today for me to start on something that big. Maybe Luke felt the same way.

"We're five minutes late already, Luke. Can you get your box?"

Silently, Luke got the box and put the gold stars by his name and then started to put the box away.

"Wait. Put on another red one."

"Why? I didn't do nuthin' today."

"Sure you did. You did a lot. You listened hard and you thought a lot and that's hard work. At least one hundred points' worth."

Luke's face lit up at least a one hundred watts' worth as he licked the star. Soon I would have to give the stars some value, so that Luke could "cash in." But for now it was enough just to earn five or ten points for doing a problem or spelling a word — and when there were a hundred points, Luke traded them for a red star.

"Jeez," Luke said, as he pasted the star on the page. "One hundred points just for thinking."

14

I stopped by the office on my way out to make sure it was all right to take the pile of books I had gathered from the storeroom.

Mrs. Karras was alone in her office and motioned me to sit down. I realized how seldom I ever saw her by herself. She was either in the classrooms or in conference with teachers or board members or out in the halls talking to the children. I mentioned this to her now.

"Well," she said, "I've been in this business over twenty years now and one thing I've learned. If the principal doesn't work, nobody else does either. You can't wander in at nine and expect everybody else to be here at eight. And these teachers have a hard job, these are tough kids — and if they say that Bobby Ferraro, say, is disrupting the whole class, I'm not much help if I don't know who Bobby Ferraro is. Besides" — Mrs. Karras smiled at me — "I love these kids. I always have. They have so little and yet they survive. They're not quitters. I suppose that's what gets to me the most. They keep on when other kids, even adults, would go under. Yet these kids just keep on living on inadequate food, rags for clothes, no toys, absentee parents, and they never complain.

"I asked to be transferred here. I was vice-principal in a posh school on the other side of town. The principal was retiring in a year and, as everybody kept pointing out to me, 'I had it made!' But then this opening at Twenty-three came up and I applied and got it. That was six years ago and I've loved every day of it. Of course, everybody else thinks I'm out of my mind. But, you know, like the kids, we're surviving. And unlike a lot of the schools around here, we haven't had fires or broken windows or looting here. Plenty in the surrounding neighborhood, but not here at the school. I like to think it's because the kids feel like the school is theirs.

"Well, speaking of loot," Mrs. Karras continued, "what are all the books?"

"I got them from the storeroom to use with Luke. I also got a couple of reading and math tests from Norm Foster and gave them to Luke. It turns out his math isn't too bad, but he's almost a year behind in reading and spelling. But

100

neither the clinic nor the college have any books I can use to teach Luke."

Mrs. Karras glanced through the books. "Well, you're certainly welcome to these, if you want them. We haven't used those editions in five years. One of the first things I did was get a new series in here. But if Luke is turned off now, Mary, do you really think these books will turn him on?"

"I don't know. But it's a place to start. As long as you don't mind what I do with them."

"I don't care if I never see them again." Mrs. Karras waved at the secretary, who was signaling from the door. "And thank you again for coming down here. It's going to mean a lot to Luke and the others. I'm sure of it."

I stood up. "We thank you. I know a lot of other principals turned the program down, didn't want 'college kids' fooling around in their schools."

Mrs. Karras's upright bearing suddenly became limber and loose and she surprised me with a slide step from an old soft-shoe routine. As we neared the office door, she whacked me softly on the arm. "Be my guest, kiddo. Fool around all you want."

I drove back to college smiling all the way.

★

That night after dinner, I got out the books from School 23 and spread them on the floor in front of me. There was no doubt they were unappealing. But that was mainly because of the pictures. The words in the first-grade books were first-grade words, the same words as in the newer, more attractive texts. I knew because I was always searching for and reviewing "high interest, low content" books for the children I had taught before. Their academic skills had often been even lower than Luke's. The language experience stories, such as Luke was writing for his book, worked well with all kinds of kids and I planned to keep on doing them with Luke, but books using a phonetic or linguistic approach, which needed good auditory abilities, didn't seem right for Luke right now.

Foster had teased me when I told him I thought Luke remembered what he saw better than what he heard, but I still felt this way, even though I didn't understand why it was so.

If Mrs. Karras had learned that a principal had to be a working principal, I had learned that the only way to teach a child who is in trouble is to give him success. I didn't want to drill where Luke was weak. I needed to use his strong points. Just telling Luke he was smart wouldn't mean anything. He had to be able to do something he hadn't been able to do before.

I sighed and Cal looked up from the yellow pad where he was sketching a design for the return header on an ice mat, one of his many patents in the field of heat exchange.

"Trouble?" he asked.

I leaned back against the couch. "It doesn't come. The right way to teach Luke, I mean. I know it's there. I can almost touch it, and then it's gone."

Cal nodded. "I know. Strange how the solution to a problem can be so elusive." He put his pad in his briefcase. "Maybe if you sleep on it."

By ten o'clock the next morning, I had it, or at least the beginning. I knew what to do with those books. I'd begin with the first half of first grade, words I was sure Luke knew, and that were in large type. I'd glue each page on a piece of heavy cardboard and then cut them up and Luke could use the words in his stories. That way, there'd be no dippy pictures and no "baby book." And most important, success was sure. Of course, I could only use one side of a page, but that was okay. There were plenty more books in the storeroom if I needed them. But I didn't think I would. First-grade sight vocabulary is pretty well controlled and the same words were used over and over.

★

I had the box of word chips out on the table when Luke came in, but if he noticed, he gave no sign. In the little black and white notebook I had our "lesson plan" for the day. Six lines long. The date at the top of the page. Then, 1. Best Thing, Worst Thing. (We always started with this. It was an old and loved routine for me and Luke liked it, too. Luke's telling me the best thing and the worst thing that had happened to him since I last saw him gave me a quick check on where he was and what he needed. It also encouraged his use of language.)

        2. Dictate Story
        3. Word Bank
        4. Addition Problems
        5. Flash Cards
        6. Mystery Box

At the bottom of the day's page in the notebook was the number 75 — Luke's leftover points from the day before.

We read the list together. Luke knew most of the words from other times. He pointed to number 6. "What's that say?"

"Mystery Box."

"What's that?"

I pointed to the box that held the word chips. I'd quickly slapped some red contact paper on it and put a big yellow question mark on the top.

"Can we do it first?"

"Not today. Let's get through this other stuff first. Best thing?"

"I got a hit in baseball. A good one. Whacko. Ole Bobby Ferraro couldn't even hold onto it and I got to second."

"A double. Good, Luke. Give yourself ten points. You know, I never got a hit ever when I was in school."

"How come?" Luke asked, interested.

"I don't know. I just couldn't get the bat to connect with the ball. They both seemed so little. I just struck out every time. I hated spring to come because of that."

Luke nodded, understanding. "Yeah. Well, a baseball is pretty little, a lot littler than a basketball. But it's not too hard." He looked up at me. "Maybe we could play some, sometime."

"Maybe. Maybe you could show me. Do you have a worst thing?"

Luke thought for a minute and then shook his head.

"Nothing?" I asked, pushing a little, but needing to know. "No bad dreams — not in any trouble —?"

"Nope." Luke's voice was sure. "Well, only thing — I burned my arm a little." He turned over his right arm and there was a large red welt halfway to his elbow.

"Ugh! How did you do that?"

"Cookin'. I was frying the hamburgers for Alice and Frank and Alice began throwing her shoe around in the kitchen. I told her not to, but she just did it anyway, like a dumb ole girl, and then it landed right on the stove and hit the pan and, plop, the ole fat popped up on my arm."

"What did you do?"

Luke looked at me. "What do you think? I put her shoe up high where she couldn't get it till after supper."

I nodded, thinking a hundred things at once. Where was his mother? Why couldn't I ever get her on the phone? I'd have to see her somehow. Had anybody put anything on his arm? Was it bad enough to send him to the nurse? Would he see that as a betrayal?

Out loud I said, "I didn't know you could cook hamburgers."

Luke laughed. "That's nuthin'. I can cook thousands of things. Hot dogs. Beans. Hamburgers. Jelly sandwiches. Chocolate milk. Lots of things. I cook for Alice and Frank and me all the time."

I kept the sigh inside, remembering his defensive silence on the mountain when he thought I'd criticized his mother. "You better pay yourself twenty," I said. "Ten for the burn, worst thing, and another ten for the cooking."

"All right," Luke said, keeping score on a piece of paper.

Forget the burn. It doesn't look that bad. He'd hate to go to the nurse. I checked off 1. "Okay. Two: Dictate story. What's the story today?"

Luke settled back. This was old hat to him now. We had at least twenty stories in his book, some long, some short. "Once upon a time," he said, "there was this baseball team and it was the Bust um up team."

"Bust um up? How do you spell that?"

"Just write it any way," Luke said impatiently. "Like bust um up. Anyway, they were playing a game against another team called the Killers . . ."

Luke's story was one of blood and violence. Everybody got hit on the head, blood drenched the ballpark. His stories were much more related to his world now. Instead of writing about lions in Africa, he was moving away from fantasy and was beginning to write about the guts of his existence.

I was always moved by his stories, and now as he finished, I had to clear my throat before I said, "Okay. Let me read it back to you." Luke made a few small corrections and then read the story to himself. "I'll get it typed and bring it next time," I promised. "Now pick your word. Anything but Bust um up."

We kept a word bank of special words Luke wanted to learn.

"Baseball," he said without hesitation.

"Okay." I was pretty sure he already knew it. He'd used it several times in his story, but his word was *his* word, and we used the one he chose. "That's called a compound word." I printed it onto an index card with a Magic Marker. "A compound word has two real words in it. See? *Base* and *ball.*" I handed Luke the card. *"Baseball."*

Luke looked at it carefully and then put it in with the other words in an old wooden recipe box I'd brought in.

"Baseball, blackboard, sidewalk. All compound words," I said.

"And Bust um up," Luke said, teasing me.

"Bust you up," I said. "Here. Two addition problems. They're hard. Ones, tens, and hundreds."

Luke bent his head over the paper, adding out loud, "Four and three are seven."

I watched him as he worked. He made it all worthwhile, all the dumb, dreary courses. All the wasted time memorizing useless facts. It didn't matter. I could do it because of Luke.

"There." Luke pushed the paper back to me. "How's that?"

I checked the problems. "Add the ones, add the tens, add the hundreds. Perfect. Give yourself ten points for each. And an extra five for this one. Look. See how neat it is? All your answers are exactly under the right columns. That's good. It's important to keep them straight. Okay. Check off addition. What's next? Ah, flash cards. They're over on the file cabinet."

106

Luke was already on his way. Good. He needed to stretch his body a little. He had been sitting so still, concentrating so hard.

He brought the box back, put it on the table, and stood beside me.

"Thank you, Luke," I said. "What'll it be today? Easy or hard?" We had divided up the addition facts from one to twenty into two piles, one easy, one hard, and were gradually moving more to the easy pile as Luke became certain of them. Now he answered.

"Both. First the easy. Then the hard."

I grinned at him. "Pretty sure of yourself."

"Gimme the easy ones fast, Mary. I know 'em so good."

He was right. He did. He had at least thirty of the cards down cold. Automatic for him now.

"Thirty more points," I said. "You're going to break the bank today."

Luke marked the score sheet. "Boy, those 'dition cards are easy. You know what?" Luke put his hand on my arm to get my attention. "Those easy 'dition cards are so easy, I know 'em outside in."

Outside in? Maybe that's the way to get to know a child. Outside in or inside out. What did it matter? We both knew what he meant.

"And now," I said, "for the Mystery Box."

Luke jumped up on the chair eagerly and my heart clunked downward. What a letdown this was going to be. Why hadn't I let him open it in the beginning and use the words in his story as I'd planned? Now he would be bored by this and what I had thought was such a good idea wouldn't work at all. I shook my head at myself. Dumb. What was I going to do now? Luke sure wasn't going to want to make sentences out of those words now. I knew it.

Luke was still waiting, looking at me.

"What is it?" he asked pleasantly. "What's a mystery box?"

I looked at him. "To tell the truth, Luke, I don't really know. I just called it that because I didn't know a better name. Here. Look." No use trying to fake it. I pushed the box toward him and waited. He took off the lid and silently stirred the word chips with his finger. "What are we gonna do with them?"

I shrugged. "Well, I had a plan, but now it doesn't seem so great. I'm trying to get a new idea." I piled a few words in front of me, trying to think, but Luke was way ahead of me.

"Look," he said. "We can make it like a TV show. I'll close my eyes and pick a word and then see if I can read it."

"Yes," I said, warming to Luke's idea. "Listen. We can get the tape recorder and pretend it's like a microphone." I was already up, lifting my tape recorder down from the closet shelf.

"Good morning, ladies and gentlemen. Welcome to the —" I snapped the recorder off and turned to Luke. "What are we going to call the show?"

Luke knew. "The Mystery Show. Today it will be words. Other times we can make it other things."

I nodded. "Welcome to the Mystery Show. Our first contestant is Luke Brauer. He will pick words absolutely unknown and never before seen by him, from this box right before your eyes and attempt to read them."

Luke tugged at my sleeve. "Pretend I win money for them," he said. "That's the way they do it on TV."

"How much?" I asked.

"A dollar for every word I get right," Luke said seriously and then whispered to me, whispered because the audience was getting so real to us. "That's just pretend, Mary. Not real money, okay?"

I nodded and turned on the tape again. "We have a fortune waiting here to be won by some lucky someone. A dollar for every correct word. Are you ready, Mr. Brauer?"

Luke nodded, closed his eyes tight, and reached for a word chip. He held it in the center of his hand, opened his eyes and said triumphantly, "*Play*. The word is *play*."

"Correct. Absolutely correct. That is one dollar." I tore off a small piece of paper and handed it to him.

I picked up my stopwatch and grinned at Luke. "You now have three minutes in which to earn as many dollars as you can. Ready. Go."

Luke grabbed a handful of chips. "*Ball. Said. Ran. It. Blue. One,*" shouting out the words, piling them in front of him as the stopwatch ticked away.

When the three minutes were up, Luke had emptied the box and won eighty-seven dollars, and I knew he knew all the words. Our next show would have the words from the second half of first grade. Maybe they should be worth two dollars.

One thing was sure. I didn't have to worry about how to teach as long as I had Luke around. If I couldn't figure it out, he'd show me how.

15

I tried to call Luke's house once more from the office, but again there was no answer. Was his mother home and just not answering? Perhaps she was sleeping. According to Luke, she was now working as a waitress at Joe's, a roadhouse at the edge of town, and left for work at five o'clock each afternoon.

The idea of the therapeutic tutorial program at School 23 was good, but there sure were a lot of loose ends. Less than four official weeks left and I hadn't even met Luke's mother yet. When I complained about this to Shirley and Hud, I found they were having the same trouble, although Hud had finally met Vernon's mother one afternoon when she came to pick him up at school.

I told both Jerry and Norm Foster and they were sympathetic, but we barely saw Jerry now and Foster really did have difficulty finding time to get down to School 23, between classes and the long rows of students waiting to be advised.

I went back to the music room and took out a pad of lined paper. "Dear Mrs. Brauer," I wrote. "I am Mary MacCracken, Luke's tutor here at School 23. I am enjoying working with Luke and would like very much to meet you. When and where would be good for you? Mary Mac-Cracken."

I wrote the note five times without getting it much better. I didn't want it to sound threatening or superior or condescending. Finally, I just folded it up and put it in an envelope and wrote "Mrs. Brauer" on the outside.

But then I had to figure out how to get it to her. I didn't want to mail it. Luke could take it, but then he would wonder why I was sending a note to his mother.

I glanced at my watch. Two-thirty. I would wait for Luke and give it to him after school so I could explain.

I took out my notes on the reading practicum course, to go over while I waited for three o'clock. We were supposed to be teaching a retarded child to read, only it turned out that we just simulated the child and talked about what we would do if we were teaching an "educable" child. "Educable" was supposed to mean an IQ of fifty to seventy-five;

"trainable" was twenty-five to fifty; "custodial," zero to twenty-five; seventy-five to ninety, "slow learner"; ninety to one hundred and ten, "average"; one hundred and ten to one twenty, "bright"; and on up the scale. Somehow it seemed very artificial when Mrs. Riley lectured about it during reading practicum. Maybe it was because I had the feeling I wouldn't want to answer her questions if she were testing me, and if I didn't answer, what label would I get? Slow learner? Educable?

More and more I was coming to believe that testing was an art, that no group IQ test should ever be given, and that somehow I was going to have to take enough courses so that I would have the training to do my own testing.

The three-o'clock bell rang and chaos was instant. It was spring and the kids couldn't wait to get outside and the teachers couldn't wait to get them there.

I stuffed my notebook back into my canvas bag and caught up with Luke as he was going down the stone steps. I should have known he'd be the first one out.

"Hey, Luke. Wait a minute."

He turned, pausing only for a second.

"Will you take this to your mom?" I took the note out of the envelope so he could see for himself. "I can't get her on the phone so I wrote to ask her when we could meet. Okay?"

"Okay. I'll tell her." I put the note back in the envelope and handed it to him. "See ya," Luke called back, already on the sidewalk with Wendell Higgins close beside him, and then gone around the corner in a second. Where did they go? What did they do? How little I knew of Luke's life.

★

At ten o'clock on Friday morning I sat alone in the music room. Strange how different a room can seem at varying hours of the day. Luke and I were usually here in the early afternoon; then the room was full of sunlight and I had come to think of it as a cheerful, pleasant place. Now, as I waited for Mrs. Brauer, the sun had not yet reached these windows and the long white overhead tubes gave off a thin cold light. I shivered and took the paper from my pocket and spread it on the table. On the bottom of my note, Mrs. Brauer had written, "I will come to school Friday at ten."

The clock over the door clicked loudly. It had never made noise before. Impatiently I walked around the room, wondering what Luke's mother would be like, how much she knew about the program, what she thought of it.

Click. Click. Click. Ten-fifteen. I would wait until eleven, I decided. I had cut my nine-thirty class. No great loss, but I had to be back by eleven-thirty. We were having a quiz in Current Methods of Teaching Mentally Retarded Adolescents.

"Mrs. MacCracken?"

"Mrs. Brauer?" I moved quickly to the doorway and held out my hand. "Good morning. I'm glad to meet you." How young she was. And small. Her hair was like Luke's, short, brown, wavy, cut the same way.

"Would you like some coffee? I can get us some from the office."

"No. No, thank you. I can't stay long." Mrs. Brauer looked back over her shoulder nervously. Was someone else with her? Or waiting?

"May I take your coat?"

"No, thank you." She pulled it closer around her.

"All right. Let's sit down over here. I laid out some of Luke's things."

We moved to the long table where Luke and I worked and I showed her some of Luke's pictures and stories, the lesson plan book, his pages of arithmetic.

112

She looked at each carefully and then put them neatly in front of me. "Is he doing good?" she asked. "Is he behaving?"

"Oh, yes." How could I tell her what fun he was? How I loved working with him? I searched for words that she could take home. "Luke's smart, Mrs. Brauer. And he's hardly sent to the office anymore."

She nodded and we again sat silently, until I said, "How are things going at home?"

"Fine."

We were getting nowhere. This wasn't helping Luke.

"Mrs. Brauer," I said as gently as I could. "I've read Luke's file. I know he's been in trouble for setting fires. In fact, I went down to the police station with him once. Do you know why he does it?"

"No. He didn't do it. Luke's a good boy. He didn't do nuthin' wrong." She gagged slightly and took a tissue from her pocketbook and wiped her mouth. She couldn't have been more than thirty-two, but there were dark circles under her eyes. Still, it was clear that she had once been a very pretty woman.

I half stood, remembering how Luke had said his mother wasn't well. "Would you like some water?"

Mrs. Brauer shook her head. "No. I'm fine. Fine. Luke's a good boy."

"Yes," I agreed.

"Helps around the house. Helps with Alice and Frank."

"Yes."

"The only thing" — the tissue turned back and forth between her fingers — "is some of those other kids in the project. I try to keep him away from them, but Luke doesn't talk much so I don't know . . ." her voice trailed off and she wiped the corners of her mouth again.

"It must be very hard." Hard? It must be hell. Somehow she made it seem so real. Not by what she said, just by her existence. The poverty, the sickness, the constant struggle — for what? So you can stay alive to struggle one more day?

"Listen," I said, silently shaking myself. Feeling sorry for her wasn't going to do anybody any good. "Luke is doing better. But he has a way to go. He's behind in both reading and spelling and he can't afford any more absences, whatever the reason. It's important that he do his homework and get to bed early. I agree he shouldn't hang around with kids who'll get him in trouble."

Mrs. Brauer smiled slightly. This was better. Tough talk was more reassuring than sweetness and light.

She nodded her head. She looked happier for a minute, the expression around her mouth almost like Luke's. "Maybe if you speak to him. Maybe he'll listen." She pushed her chair back and stood up. "I have to get back," she said.

"All right. But I'd like to see you again soon."

"It's hard to get away — so much to do." She was fading away, going out the door, almost not there. Running silently, just like Luke, dealing with life by running away.

"Yes. We'll see — I'll let you know . . ."

She was out the door and down the stone steps, her small thin shoulders hunched together, both arms wrapped around her pocketbook. I watched her until she was out of sight.

Then I walked back to the music room and closed the door. What could I do about Mrs. Brauer? Not much. Not much. All she wanted was to be left alone. And who could blame her?

Alice and Frank. Where were they? All I knew was that they were younger than Luke. I asked in the office. The secretary checked the file. Yes, Alice Brauer in kindergarten, Frank in first. Both classes in the basement.

114

I walked down the stairs slowly. I had never been in this part of the building before. There was one large, dark, damp room with tables set up in the corners. One of the teachers came toward me. "Yes?" Her voice was cold. It was apparent visitors were not welcome.

"I'm one of the tutors from the college," I explained. "Working with Luke Brauer. Could you point out his brother and sister?"

"Those two at the paint table," she said. "Don't be long. Disturbs the children. Besides, there's nothing to see."

Two blond heads bent close together. Blond hair, not brown like Luke's and his mother's, but wavy, cut the same. What were they doing at the same table if they were in different classes? Open classroom? Ha!

I walked back upstairs even more slowly, fighting the urge to go get Luke. Go get him and set him free somehow. How could he survive under all that weight? The responsibilities, poverty, illness. I walked through the office without looking at the secretary and sat down opposite Mrs. Karras. She was on the phone, but I waited, needing to talk to her.

"What happens to these kids?" I asked her as soon as she was done. "I mean when they're twelve or twenty or thirty. Does anybody ever have a decent life? Or do they all end up like Mrs. Brauer?"

Mrs. Karras stood up. "Not all. Most maybe, but not all. A few get out, but they don't usually come back. Why should they?

"You know something, my husband's a principal here in Falls City, too. We live here. We work here. But you know where we spend our time? Down at the shore. As soon as we had enough money, we bought a house just a block from the ocean — and that's where we go whenever we can.

That's how we survive, and in another five or six years, that's where we'll retire."

She walked over to the small window that faced the street. "Come here a minute, Mary." She put one arm around my shoulders and pointed with the other hand. "See over there? The house with the wire fence."

"Yes." I knew the house. That was where the white dog hurled himself against the fence at each passerby.

"I was born in a house like that, just two blocks down."

If Mrs. Karras could get out, maybe Luke could too.

16

I drove slowly through the streets surrounding the school. Where was Luke? What did he do after school each day? Where did he race with Wendell Higgins close beside him?

There was no point in admonishing Luke to stay away from Wendell. If Luke didn't find Wendell, Wendell found Luke. But what did they do?

There was no one Luke's size on the streets or sidewalks near the school, only a few adults walking slowly. Over by the project, girls were jumping rope. "Teddy Bear, Teddy Bear, turn around, Teddy Bear, Teddy Bear, touch the ground." One little girl ran out from under the rope, another one in. The chant continued. "Teddy Bear, Teddy Bear, climb the stairs, Teddy Bear, Teddy Bear, say your prayers." Luke would not be here.

I turned out of the narrow streets back onto the main road, down toward the park. High school kids standing or sitting around on the grass, smoking. I left the car and walked through the park, past the fountain. Conversation stopped as I neared. Obviously, I was not welcome. Luke and Wendell would not be here either.

I went back to the car and drove through the small business district, past the movies to Dunkin' Donuts. Kids covered Dunkin' Donuts like flies — inside, outside, leaning on the glass window, sitting on the sidewalk in front, lounging on the cars parked in the street. These kids were all ages, but still no Luke or Wendell.

The mountain? Would Luke have taken Wendell there? I wasn't sure. The mountain meant a lot to Luke. Memories of his father were strong there, and yet Wendell must know about it. He was the one who had taken my message to Luke when he was hiding out.

Should I hunt for them there? Could I even find the place? Wherever Luke was, he wouldn't be there much longer. His mother went to work at five and she said he was good about being there to take care of his brother and sister. Maybe the best thing was to go back to the project and wait and see which direction he arrived from.

I parked my car a block away and waited. "Teddy Bear, Teddy Bear, touch your shoe, Teddy Bear, Teddy Bear, twenty-three skiddoo." Why didn't they jump to a different tune? I smiled to myself. Or march to a different drummer? Who can lead anyone else's life? Or even understand it. Prime example, me.

There's Luke. Wendell, too. Coming from the direction of town. But not walking now. They sat down on the curbs as I watched. Luke was dirty, face and hands black with grime or soot. From fires? As I watched, Wendell took out a pack of cigarettes, lit one, and passed it to Luke. Luke took a deep drag and handed it back to Wendell. Two little kids sitting on a street corner, smoking.

★

"Why can't we?" I said to Hud and Shirley. "Nobody knows what we're doing now, anyway. When's the last time you were supervised?"

Shirley said, "I haven't seen Jerry in weeks. I don't know what's happened, but he's not around much. I hear you, Mary. I hear what you're saying, but I can't help you out. I'm having enough trouble getting down here for my regular sessions with Milt. I'm working forty hours a week now at the store, trying to get enough money to cover the first semester's tuition at graduate school. I sure can't take any time off to play baseball."

I turned to John Hudson. "How about it, Hud? You're the one we really need. You and Vernon. What's one afternoon a week? You can work out after we finish. Look, all we have to do is organize the teams. Get them started and then they can play by themselves. Once a week isn't going to kill you."

"Jeez. I don't know. I agree those kids need something to do besides hang out. Maybe they will play baseball. Who knows? All right. There are only a few weeks left anyway. But it has to be Thursday. That's the only free afternoon I've got."

"Okay. That's good." I'd miss part of Statistics and Orientation to Psychological Testing, but that was no big loss. I'd get the notes from somebody. "How should we start? We've got Vernon and Luke. They're both nuts about baseball. What about Milt, Shirley — will he play?"

We needn't have worried about kids. Thirty showed up the first afternoon and Hud was better than terrific with them. We divided them into two teams by lining them up and counting off by fours. Ones and threes on one team, twos and fours on the other. We named the teams the Yankees and the Red Sox.

They were scheduled to play only on Thursdays, but by

the second Thursday, it was clear they were playing on their own almost every afternoon. They had captains, they had their own team names, the Shirts and the Skins, and they had a batting order.

Vernon was the captain of the Red Sox (alias Skins) and a big blond kid named Willie was the captain of the Yankees (alias Shirts). By now, of course, they had rearranged the teams the way they wanted them; each captain had taken turns picking players. Luke was on Vernon's team.

I loved to watch them play. Racing around the blacktop, stealing bases, banging the ball with all their might. Thirty kids having fun and also keeping themselves in order. On Thursdays Hud had permission to use the school's equipment — bases, bats, balls, gloves, masks. I don't know what they used on other days, but somehow most of the kids had got caps of some shade of red or blue, so everybody could tell who was on which team. Of course, on every day but Thursday, half the kids took off their shirts and identification was easy. On Thursdays Hud umpired; who knows who made the rules the other days?

I was late getting to the game the third Thursday because I'd stopped to talk to Lisa. I ran down the steps and out onto the blacktop side yard. Hud shouted to me, "Second half of the fourth inning. Five to two, Yankees." I walked out on the field next to him and he added in a quiet voice, "Keep an eye on Vernon, will you? He's not the world's best loser anyway and something's buggin' him today."

I went back to the sidelines thinking about Vernon and how far he'd come. He had even signed up for a paper route this coming summer, but some of the anger that had been behind the previous knife fights was still there.

I was so busy thinking about Vernon that I walked straight into Officer Snow.

"Hey," I said. "What are you doing here? Is Luke okay?"

Officer Snow shrugged his beefy shoulders. "How should I know? I just stopped by for the game. One of my kids is playing. Our youngest. See him up there? He's right behind the batter."

The Red Sox got two runs in the last of the fourth and Officer Snow bellowed approval. "Aw right, team. Way to go. Keep 'em down now. Don't let them Yankees score. You can tie it up next time."

I moved down the line away from the cheers of Officer Snow and crouched down on my heels looking for Luke. I finally spotted him in the outfield. He caught my eye but gave no sign. Nor did I.

But Officer Snow's shouts seemed to be having an effect, and at the middle of the fifth inning the Yankees were only one run ahead of our team.

Vernon led off with a double and then Luke was up. He looked so little opposite Willie, the pitcher. I got up and walked back and forth, unable to sit still.

Officer Snow was pounding the fence. "Come on, youse Brauer kid. Knock him in! Knock him in! Tie it up!"

My mouth was dry and I whispered under my breath, "It's okay, Luke. Whatever happens, it's okay. Good luck." I turned the lipstick tube inside the pocket of my jeans.

"Ball one," Hud yelled.

Luke struck at the next ball and tipped it off the side. "Foul ball. Strike one. Ball one."

The next pitch was straight across the middle of the plate and Luke swung and connected and the ball sailed out beyond second base. Luke headed for first and Vernon was already halfway to third.

One of the Yankees pegged the ball back to Willie and he hesitated for one second as Vernon touched third and started home before he threw to first and Hud called Luke out. Willie threw to home and Vernon retreated and made it back, just in time, to third.

Inwardly, I raged at Hud. How could he do that to Luke! It was so close, how could he tell for sure. Poor Luke.

Poor Luke, nothing. Luke was out in the middle of the field, hat in hand, yelling at Hud. I couldn't hear what he was saying, but then I couldn't believe what I was seeing either. Luke wasn't running away. He was standing up there, yelling, protesting, telling it his way.

If I couldn't hear Luke, I could hear Officer Snow loud and clear. "Thataway, kid. You tell him. That ump's blind as a bat."

Luke was sure telling him, his cap on the ground now, hands on his hips, words pouring out.

Suddenly Vernon raced out from third and swung at Hud. Hud hammerlocked Vernon and yelled out loud and clear.

"You guys have ten seconds to quiet down or this game's over. Luke, you're out, get off the field. Vernon, you're safe, get back on third. The score is four to five with one man out. Now let's play ball."

Nobody moved, and then Luke picked up his cap, swatted it against his rear, retrieved his bat from the side-lines, and went to wait with the rest of the Red Sox. Vernon grumbled something but went on back to third.

Luke had won. He'd made his protest, he'd used words, and even though he hadn't changed Hud's mind, Hud had listened to him and Luke had abided by the rules. He hadn't run away, and no matter how the score came out, Luke was a winner.

Above the hubbub of the game, Officer Snow resumed his cheering. "Never mind, kid. You'll get on next time. That ump should have his eyes examined."

I moved back down by Officer Snow and shouted with him.

"All right now, Red Sox. Let's tie 'er up."

17

I could not believe I had gotten so far behind. Two papers and ten abstracts due for Professor Drobuy's course in Current Methods of Teaching Mentally Retarded Adolescents. Two book reports for Practicum in Reading for the Mentally Retarded, plus two months' lesson plans for teaching reading to a simulated mentally retarded child. Piles of notes to copy over for Orientation to Psychological Testing from the times I had come in late from baseball, plus a page each on the description of twenty different psychological tests. Describe what they test. What is the validity? The reliability? What is standardization? How much do they cost? Where can they be purchased? Who is considered qualified to use them? I spent hours in the library searching for information, taking notes, then writing reports, typing them up.

At least there was no backlog in Background of Mathematics II. We had to hand in homework daily. Our silent, dark professor corrected, graded, gave it back to be redone the next day. Quizzes twice a week. I thought I understood it a little better this semester. Probability. "Two dice are thrown. Find the probability that the sum is nine and at least one of the two faces is even." $\frac{4}{6} \times \frac{1}{6} = \frac{1}{9}$. Easy. Ian Michaels slouched beside me nodding approval. Each night I prayed that probability would etch itself into my brain so that I could retrieve it on the exam three weeks away.

Where had the days gone? I, who had thought they had dragged endlessly, now raced to catch up. In and out of School 23 in an hour three times a week. No baseball for me now, either, but the kids kept on playing. Lisa reported that Luke was reading a line or two at his reading group. "Hang in, Luke," I told him. "Exams will be over in a week and then college will be closed until June twenty-eighth, when we start summer school."

"Summer school? What are you going to go to summer school for?" Luke looked at me unbelievingly.

"A good question," I said. But I knew it was the only way I could finish in two years.

Shirley and Hud had said their good-byes, written their anecdotal reports on Vernon and Milt, and left the state college behind. Hud already had a job teaching a neurologically impaired class at a junior high, and Shirley had accumulated most of the tuition she needed to begin graduate school.

"How come they left?" Luke wanted to know.

"They graduated," I explained.

"You gonna graduate?" Luke asked.

"I hope so, Luke," I said. "But not this year. That's why I can still come in June and they can't. I won't graduate till next year. I don't think that they are going to have the same kind of program next year, but I can still come down sometimes if you want. You'll be in third grade by then."

Luke was working well in class and was high scorer on his baseball team. Mrs. Brauer came back to school twice, unexpectedly, without appointments (I suspected Mrs. Karras was somewhere behind those visits), but at least she came and I felt that she was beginning to trust me a little.

I forced my head back to Statistics and Orientation to Psychological Testing. The Wechsler Primary Preschool Scale of Intelligence, the Wechsler Intelligence Scale for

Children, the Wechsler Adult Intelligence Scale. WPPSI, WISC, WAIS. Mr. Wechsler would certainly feel at home in the world of acronyms in Washington, D.C.

★

The last week of May was hot and muggy. Clothes clung, tempers frayed. I was lucky in exam scheduling — one a day, Monday through Thursday, and then the anecdotal report on the School 23 project. Monday: Practicum in Reading for the Mentally Retarded. Tuesday: Current Methods of Teaching Mentally Retarded Adolescents. Wednesday: Statistics and Orientation to Psychological Testing. Thursday: Background of Mathematics II. Friday: Report on School 23 project.

Done. Done. Done. I'd done it. I'd finished one year of college. Now three weeks off, then summer school and one more year and I'd be through.

★

The phone rang in the middle of the night and I heard Cal's voice answering as I swam up from sleep. "Yes. She's right here." He turned on the light and handed me the phone. "It's your dad. Your mother has had a stroke."

The northbound parkway was almost empty in the early morning, and I was at the retirement community in less than two hours. My father was waiting by the glass doors as I came in. He looked the same, strong and clean, although he must have been up most of the night.

"Are you okay?" I asked as I kissed him, loving the familiar smell of Aqua Velva.

"Fine. You're good to come. Have you had breakfast?"

I nodded. I'd had a thermos of coffee in the car. "How's Mother? Can I see her?"

"Not till nine. And that's an exception because you're

from out of town. Regular visiting hours at the nursing home are two to four in the afternoon."

"Nursing home?"

"That's what they call the little hospital we have here."

I nodded, but it was hard to think of my mother in a nursing home. She had always been the first one up in the morning, sitting at the table in the breakfast room, planning the meals with Maud, who lived with us, pouring my father's coffee as he walked in. In the evenings before it was time to meet my father's train, she would play the piano and sing softly. I loved coming home after school and so did my friends.

Because of my mother, our house was always full of clean, good smells and soft, friendly sounds. In the summers at the river, she cooked breakfast herself. (Maud went back to the West Indies each summer.) She gave us large bowls of steaming oatmeal, topped with brown sugar and fresh cream. My grandmother stayed with us in the summer and I loved to watch them together — my mother and her mother. They were gentle and quiet with each other, sitting on the porch looking over the water, writing letters, sewing, talking, having tea in the afternoon. They touched each other often, straightening a sweater, picking up a ball of yarn that had fallen, tucking back a strand of hair. It was through watching them that I first understood the strong bond of love between women.

The nursing home smelled like any other hospital. There were cheerful nurses on duty and wheelchairs in the hall. And then my mother's room, her bed by the window.

I knelt on the floor beside her bed and kissed her face. Still lovely. Chiseled bones. Fine skin. She raised her hand and gestured toward her mouth. Good. She can move. I looked up toward my father.

"She can't speak," he said. "The stroke's affected her speech."

I put my hand over hers. "It will come back. There's no need to talk now, anyway. Just rest. I'll be here awhile and I'll tell you all the news a little later."

I stood up and looked at my father. "You must be very tired. Why don't you go back to your apartment and rest while I'm here?"

My father rubbed the back of his hand across his eyes. "All right. This wasn't the first time, but she never wanted me to say anything. And she always came back fast." He kissed my mother. "You always were a plucky girl, sweetheart." Her brown eyes searched his face. "I'll be back this afternoon," he promised before he turned to me. "You'll come over for lunch?"

"Yes."

"All right, then. I'll meet you in the lobby at twelve-thirty."

I pulled a small chair up near the bed and sat beside my mother throughout the morning, except when the nurses came asking me politely, but firmly, to move to the hall.

"She's mine," I protested inwardly. "My mother. Let me do that." But outwardly, I obeyed and stood among the wheelchairs in the hall.

At eleven-thirty they served lunch in the nursing home. A nurse rolled a cart into the room, cranked up the hospital bed, lifted a tray onto the bed table, tied a bib around my mother's neck, and began to spoon a thin clear soup into her mouth.

A bib! How she must hate it. She had headed our table so graciously, with a silver bell beside her glass and a damask napkin in her lap.

"I'll do that." This time my own voice was firm. "You have so much to do."

As soon as the nurse was out the door, I untied the bib. "No need for that." I smiled and thought I could see an answering smile somewhere near her eyes.

She couldn't swallow much, but I made the spoonfuls small, wishing I had one of the demitasse spoons that she had given me to feed my babies, showing me how the slender shape of the demitasse fit small mouths so much better than the usual fat baby spoon. She had taught me so much, cared for me so tenderly. I touched the napkin to her mouth after each small sip. It was my turn now.

Then when the nurse had taken the cart away and I had washed her face and hands, then finally, she slept.

In the parking lot with my father, I said once more, "Please think more about moving down with us. There is enough room; you could have your own bedroom and both Cal and I would like to have you there."

"Thank you, dear. We're fine here. One reason we moved down from the country was in case anything like this happened. I can have all my meals in the dining room and see your mother every day."

I knew he meant it, knew he would hate being cooped up in a city apartment. Here he had his garden and his golf, and they both had many friends.

He patted my arm. "We'll be fine. The doctor wouldn't let your mother be moved yet, anyway. Now don't go worrying about us. You know she wouldn't want that. She's so proud of you, going back to college, all the work you're doing with the children."

Tears stood in my eyes. I cried too easily these days. "How long? How long will she have to be there?" I wished I could tell him about the bib, but that wouldn't be fair. He wasn't allowed to visit until two o'clock, anyway.

He shook his head. "Nobody knows. We'll just have to take each day as it comes."

I nodded at the familiar words.

"Okay." I climbed into the car. "I'll see you tomorrow."

"Not tomorrow. That's too long a drive."

"I have three weeks off now. Let me come as often as I can."

I was down at School 23 the next morning before it opened, waiting for Luke. As soon as he arrived, I signaled to Lisa, and Luke and I headed for the music room.

"How come you're here so early?" Luke wanted to know.

I shook my head. "Luke, I have bad news. My mother is very sick and I need to be with her as much as I can, so I can't come down here these last weeks of school like I had planned. I'm sorry. I really am."

Luke picked at the edge of the table. "What's the matter with her? What's she got?"

"She had a stroke —" hesitating, not sure how to describe it. "She can't talk now, she's in a hospital. I'm going up to see her when I leave here."

Luke sat, head down, picking at the table. How could I leave him like that?

I went over to the closet and got down his box. "Why don't you keep this, Luke? Will you keep this for us over the summer?"

Luke looked at me. "The whole thing? The chalk, crayons, notebook, pencils — everything?"

I nodded. "Everything but one notebook. I need the one that we wrote our 'lesson plans' in."

"Even the stars?" he asked.

"Sure. Of course. Especially the stars. You know how to do them now."

"Yup. Red for work. Gold for bein' good. I did a whole page in my reading workbook yesterday."

"That's terrific, Luke. Hey, what do you say we celebrate? One last doughnut for the year?"

"Allll right."

My mother would understand. She would know that it was necessary to end it properly. I would miss lunch at the nursing home, but maybe I could stay through supper.

It was wonderful outside. Later in the day, the heat would hang heavy in the city streets, but now the air was still cool, and in almost every yard someone was watering or weeding, trying to make something grow on the tiny patch of land in the coolness of the morning.

"Yrrr. Yrrr. Yrrr." The white dog threw himself at the fence as we walked by on the opposite side.

"Yrrr. Yrrr," Luke replied, baring his teeth and hunching his shoulders. I smiled at them both. Mrs. Karras had got out. It was possible.

As we hit Main Street, I said, "You know what? It's pretty hot for doughnuts. How about an ice cream cone instead?"

Luke knew where to go — Dave's corner store.

"You got a holiday today, Luke?" Dave asked from behind the counter. Luke shook his head. "Uh-oh! Playing hooky then, huh? Well, I won't tell." Dave winked in my direction. "Looks like you got a nice friend." He added another little scoop to each chocolate cone.

We stood outside the corner store licking our cones.

"Do we have to go right back?" Luke asked.

I glanced at my watch. "Not right away. We could stay a half hour."

Luke was quiet, thinking. Then he said very quickly, "Wanna see my shortcut?"

"Shortcut?"

"Yeah. The quick way from school back to my house. Nobody knows but me and Wendell."

Back to the school. Down past the lipstick factory. "That's where I got the cases," Luke said. I nodded, remembering the last time I had been there after the fire without him. And now he was here. "Race you to the corner," I said. Running. Running hard. I will not be sad this last day with you, Luke. It is wonderful to be here with you. That's all I'll think about right now.

We ended at the corner together. "Now we gotta cut across the field," Luke instructed me. A choppy field filled with rocks and beer cans, but Luke knew more. He leaned down to point out a small hole. "There's where the mole lives," he said. "No kidding. A live one."

I picked up a small stick and wiggled it around in the hole. "That won't make him come out," Luke said scornfully. "I done that lots of times. He's too smart. You just gotta wait til he's ready."

Maybe this was where Luke came after school — maybe he just sat waiting for the mole to come out.

Luke scampered ahead, then back. This was his territory. He knew it cold and I was glad to be included. "We're coming to it now. The river. You gotta walk across it." Luke looked at my feet and I was glad I had my sneakers on — skirt and sandals were in the car.

Sure enough, there was a stream, small and dirty brown, but moving steadily through the field.

Luke walked along the side until he came to a large rock. "See," he said. "This is where you cross. Wendell and me made the bridge, kind of."

I mellowed a little toward Wendell. He couldn't be all

130

bad if he came out here in the field and helped Luke build a bridge across his river. And sure enough, there were three large flat stones forming a path to the other side, water gushing around and sometimes over them.

"You gotta go pretty fast," Luke said, demonstrating. He was nimble as a mountain goat, hopping from one rock to the other, across and back in less than a minute.

I shook my head at him. "I'm not sure I can go that fast. Are they slippery?"

"Kind of. Specially that big ole middle one. But just step right in the middle of it. See." Luke hopped across again — happy, happy as I'd ever seen him. Showing me how to do something. The teacher now himself. I stood a minute, savoring him, wanting to remember him this way.

"Come on, Mary. Just hop across real fast. Don't think about it."

"Okay. All right. Wish me luck." I stood on the flat stone by the side, stepped over to the next stone with my right foot, then to the middle one. Water splashed onto my sneakers. Luke was yelling something unintelligible. I tried to concentrate. One more to go.

The last stone rocked under my weight, teetered back and forth in the muddy water. Oh, no. I didn't want to sit down in that water. I moved quickly, missed the far side, and stepped in water and mud, halfway to my knees.

"Hey, Luke. Give me a hand."

Luke reached across the side and holding his hand, I scrambled out.

"What happened?" I asked. "What did I do wrong?"

"You didn't step on the mid —" Luke couldn't finish the word. Giggles flooded up out of his throat. He tried again. "In the mid —" Again laughter took over and he sat down rocking back and forth.

"Terrific," I said with mock anger. "Here I am with

131

both feet soaked and you're laughing." But all the time I was thinking, Luke's actually laughing. I'd never heard him laugh before.

Luke looked at me contritely. "I'm sorry. But you just looked so funny . . ." Laughter threatened to take over again, but Luke controlled it. "Did you get hurt?"

"No. A little soggy, but fine. Where now?"

"We're almost there. See, you can see the project over there."

"Okay. Let's go."

We were so near we might as well go the whole way, finish it. I squished across the field beside Luke, water oozing out of my sneakers with every step.

When we came to the street, Luke said, "Wanta see my room? Nobody's home."

We walked up to the project and Luke pulled a key out from under his shirt and slipped the string over his head.

"Luke, wait. Let's not go in. I'll come back sometime when your mother is here."

"She wouldn't care," he said. "I'm not allowed to bring kids in, but she knows about you."

I couldn't explain to Luke, but somehow it seemed like spying, and Mrs. Brauer's trust of me was so tentative that I didn't want to do anything that would weaken it.

"Are you on the first floor? Which is your room? Maybe we could just look in the window."

"Here. This one. See. Gimme a boost up." I lifted Luke so his head cleared the sill, thinking, you trust me, anyway. How naturally you let me hold you now.

"Yup. This is it. This is where Alice, Frank, and me sleep. Mom and Uncle Chuck sleep on the pull-out in the living room. You look now. See that big ole snake skin on the wall? That's mine. I found it on the mountain."

Luke was chattering in his excitement. I put him down and looked in. Three stained mattresses on the floor, three cotton blankets folded neatly at the end of each mattress. Uncle Chuck? Was he new? Don't think about it now.

"See the snake skin?"

"Not yet."

"There, over the table."

I shaded my eyes. Now against one wall I could make out a narrow table covered with blue jeans, underwear, and T-shirts. That must be where they kept their clothes. Above the table, almost the same color as the wall, I saw the snake skin.

"I see it. It is big."

I turned back to Luke. "I'm glad you found the skin and not the snake. It's good you have sharp eyes."

Time to go. Time to go. I started walking back toward the field. Luke walked beside me. How to leave him? How to say good-bye? Not good-bye. What did they say? *Auf wiedersehen?* Till we meet again. Whatever you say, don't cry.

We were back at the field. When we got to the stream I said to Luke, "Okay. Watch this. This time I'm going to do it right." I held my arms out like a tightrope walker and never missed a step.

"Allll right, way to go," Luke rewarded me. We were almost to the mole hole. Do it here. If you're going to say good-bye, do it here. Not in front of the whole school.

I knelt and looked down the mole hole, more to get myself on Luke's level than for any other reason.

"What are you going to do this summer, Luke?"

"Visit my father," he answered without hesitation. "Maybe we're going to go to Florida, even."

I nodded, missing him already. "You deserve it, Luke. You've worked hard, your reading is really coming along, and your math's terrific. How many days were you absent this month?"

"None," Luke said.

"Great. And I know you haven't been in the office or the police station. You can feel real proud of yourself, Luke. Now, listen, I'll write to you," I said. "I'll send you a postcard with my address and maybe you'll write back."

Now it was Luke's turn to nod.

I stirred the mole hole a little. If I couldn't find the mole, maybe I could find the words to say good-bye.

"Will you be all right till school ends? Do your work? Keep out of trouble? Call me if you need me?"

Again Luke nodded.

"Okay, then, Give me a hug good-bye and I'll see you in the fall."

Luke's arms went tight around my neck. I could feel his breath against the side of my face, but he didn't say anything. Not "good-bye." Not even "see ya." He just held on tight. We stayed like that for a couple of seconds and then Luke dropped his arms and started to run, turned and ran backward, and said, "I'll race you. All the way back."

"Okay." I ran just behind Luke, down the narrow streets, past the lipstick factory, leaving wet footprints on the hot sidewalk. Neither of us raced. We ran together, Luke leading.

There was the school, my car parked on the opposite side of the street. Both of us knew Luke wouldn't stop, wouldn't even look back. We ran down the street in front of the school, and then when we reached the steps, I stopped and Luke ran on alone. Up the stone steps, not turning his head, through the door, into the school.

I unlocked the door to my car, sat down and took off my wet sneakers and put on my sandals. I put the wet shoes on the floor in back, then changed my mind and put them on the front seat. I drove to the hospital with the smell of Luke's river beside me all the way.

19

My mother improved a little every day. Her speech was still sparse and slurred; she could not feed herself or walk alone. But she was better, and when we found Mrs. Hubbard, a retired nurse, who agreed to come and help care for her during the day, the doctors agreed that she could move back to the apartment.

Summer school began on June 28. I had classes five days a week, four hours a day. I could visit my mother and father only on weekends now, so I was glad that she was back home, surrounded by familiar things, near my father.

I was taking three courses, the maximum allowed, but they added up to only six measly credits. Three for Speech Correction, two for Teaching Social Studies, one for Elementary Swimming. It was the swimming that nearly did me in.

"Gym" was a required course. No gym, no graduation. I didn't believe it at first, but it was true. My forty-five-year-old body was going to have to go to gym.

Fortunately, at least I had thought it was fortunate in the beginning, there were many choices — archery, golf, tennis, swimming. I didn't hesitate. During the first eighteen years of my life, I had spent two and a half months each year at the Thousand Islands. We lived on the St. Lawrence River all day long, changing only from a wet bathing suit to a dry one, adding a sweatshirt if it was cool. All our waking hours were spent fishing, sailing, swimming. Elementary Swimming would be a snap, I thought as I registered. Thank God I didn't sign up for intermediate.

Because the summer session was only six weeks long, classes met every day. Swimming was from 8:00 to 9:15, Speech Correction from 9:20 to 10:45 and Teaching Social Studies from 10:50 to 12:00. Plus an hour or so at the library digging out material for the abstracts and papers.

★

It was raining the first day of the summer session. College was an hour away, so it was 7:00 A.M. when I pulled out of the underground garage with my bathing suit on the seat beside me, and I felt the first misgivings about Elementary Swimming.

At least there was no traffic or trouble finding a parking spot. I walked through the misty rain to the gym. Inside the girls' locker room, a dozen young girls in tank suits were clustered together chatting. I nodded to them, dreading the thought of donning my three-year-old flowered, two-piece suit. Misgivings multiplied.

I stripped quickly, pulled on my suit and hung my jeans and shirt in the locker, put my books on the floor and closed the locker door. I had forgotten a towel. How could I have forgotten? Maybe there were some by the showers. I felt naked in my outdated suit as I walked by the waiting girls, thankful at least for the cover of my tan. No towels anywhere. I hovered beside the shower curtains for a few minutes and then went back and sat on a bench and waited for the instructor to appear.

One of the girls was demonstrating what looked like the belly dance. "See, just lock your hands here, behind your head, and rotate. This is the center of gravity." She nodded downward. "And you just moo-oo-oove around it." Her slim young hips undulated faster. "It drives Frankie absolutely wild," she said. Her feet picked up the rhythm and she began to dance down the aisles.

136

The outer door slammed shut and a whistle blast interrupted the belly dance. "All right. Line up over here. Bring your class cards with you. Hand them in as I call your name." It was Mrs. Hogan. The same Mrs. Hogan from Adapted Phys Ed, the one who had made us demonstrate in front of the class. What was she doing here? The catalog had listed the instructor as Fuller.

"Avigammo, Bishop, Barrati — thank you — stand over there now alphabetically," Mrs. Hogan called out. "Coggan, Gentula, Grossman, Gruber, Hall. No card? Wait there." She pointed behind her.

"Let's see. Where was I? Mmm. Hall. Okay. I've got Hall — now, all right . . . Kenny, Lanzana, MacCracken. MacCracken?" The surprise in her voice made the others turn in my direction. I handed in my card without speaking.

"Ritter, Schwarzenbach. Is that right? Schwarzenbach." A tall blond handed in her card. "Well, is it?" Mrs. Hogan demanded. "Yes," the blond muttered. A small giggle went round the locker room. I eyed Schwarzenbach. Maybe she would help me plan the demise of Mrs. Hogan.

"Thirteen. Right?" She counted our bodies. "Including Hall." She turned to the plump girl behind her. "Where's your card, Hall?" The girl shrugged her shoulders. "I can't find it," she said.

"Well, get another one today or don't bother to come tomorrow. Get in line now." Hall scurried over behind Schwarzenbach. "Not there," Mrs. Hogan bellowed, consulting her list. "Behind Gruber, for heaven's sake. Stay alphabetical."

Mrs. Hogan advanced to the head of the line. She was wearing green camp shorts, a gray T-shirt, green socks, sneakers, and a whistle on a silver chain. Evidently, she was not planning to swim.

"Ms. Fuller is unable to teach this course as planned, so I am taking it over. Now there are thirteen of you. There are also seven boys. Men. They're at the pool now. I already have their cards. There will be no homework for this course; there will also be no exceptions. Go through the door to the pool now and I'll go over the requirements."

She blew a blast on her whistle. I couldn't believe it. It was like the one week I'd spent at scout camp when I was ten. "All right, Avigammo, go ahead. Single file. Be sure to step through the disinfectant."

The pool itself was large and well lighted. Seven assorted male shapes stood by the shallow end. Mrs. Hogan now read the total list, inserting the men in their alphabetical slot. "Fisher. Step in before Gruber. Raise your hand, Gruber. Michaels. Down there between MacCracken and Ritter. Raise your hands, MacCracken and Ritter." It was Ian. I hadn't recognized him without his hat. He slouched his way into line.

"Good morning," I said under my breath.

"You're nuts, MacCracken. You gotta be nuts," he replied.

Mrs. Hogan blasted her whistle. "There will be no talking during class. None. Save your breath. You'll need it." Her mouth curled in what was evidently intended to be a smile. "Here are the requirements. We will be working on four strokes — breaststroke, sidestroke, backstroke, and freestyle. Freestyle does not mean you do what you want. It means you do what some of you refer to as the crawl.

"This is an elementary class, so I do not expect perfect strokes. I do expect mastery of each stroke, plus a few simple dives. Mainly, I expect you to build stamina. No one will pass until they complete fifty laps of alternating strokes."

"I told you," Ian whispered.

I stared straight ahead.

"All right. Everyone in the water. Line up at the shallow end and take your alphabetical positions."

The water felt warm and wonderful. I crouched down under it.

"You will swim the length of the pool, four people at a time, alternating strokes, so I can get an idea of your ability. All right. Let's go. Avigammo, Bish —"

"Excuse me — uh — Professor Hogan." Beside me, Ritter, a tall black girl, was waving her hand. "I can't swim."

Hall called out, "Me neither."

Blood was rising in Mrs. Hogan's face, staining it a reddish purple.

"Can't swim? What are you doing in here, then?"

"Thought I'd learn," Ritter said coolly. "Elementary, it said in the catalog. Didn't have no prerequirements like knowing how to swim."

She was absolutely right. I silently cheered her on. Schwarzenbach, Ritter, and I could form a conspiracy and do in Mrs. Hogan.

Mrs. Hogan paced back and forth, chewing on her whistle. Finally she made her decision. "All right, Ritter and Hall. Get out of the water. I'll talk to you later. What about the rest of you? Is there anyone else here who can't swim to the end of the pool?" Her gaze lingered on me, but neither of us said anything.

"Regroup then. Swim down four at a time. Don't worry about changing strokes. Just see if you can get there, for heaven's sake."

Ian was in my alphabetical group and he swam the way he did math problems, lazily, elegantly. My style was far from elegant, but I made it to the other end.

Mrs. Hogan spent the rest of the hour dividing us into groups according to ability. Ritter and Hall were in the bottom group, unable to swim, relegated to imitating strokes at the side of the pool. My group was next. I could see that Mrs. Hogan expected me to sink any minute. We were each assigned a "buddy," who was supposed to send up a warning if we had any difficulty.

I was busy thinking about trying to transfer to another course. Surely there must be something else I could take for one credit. But when? I was taking the maximum load for both fall and spring next year. I would not be allowed to add another credit there. It would have to be this summer and that would be a problem. There were no afternoon courses and my other morning hours were full. What else, I wondered, was offered at 8:00 A.M. that would fill the gym requirement? The familiar feeling of despair crept into the swimming pool. What was I doing here, anyway?

At last we were dismissed. I'd been down and back three times and I was exhausted. Fifty? I'd never make it fifty times. I dragged myself to the locker room. No towel. I'd forgotten. No hair dryer, either. The young crew were wrapped in towels and blowing their long manes — practicing the belly dance at the same time. Only Hall, plump and dismal, sat alone in a corner. I would not ask any of them for a towel or dryer.

I carried my jeans and shirt to the shower room. Rinsed briefly under the warm water, dried myself on the shower curtain, combed my wet hair, and walked out of Elementary Swimming straight into Ian Michaels, who was sitting on the floor in front of the door.

I was not glad to see him.

He walked beside me out into the rain. If he made one wisecrack, I would kill him. I would use the karate chop I'd seen on TV and then carve his heart out with my ignition key.

140

We walked in silence, rain running down my face, dripping off my nose.

Ian touched my arm. "Want my hat?"

I shook my head, not looking at him, but deciding not to kill him, after all.

"You can still drop it, you know," Ian said. "Substitute something else. There's probably still room in archery."

I stopped and looked at Ian silently. I had been heading for the registrar's office. For the last hour I had been planning to drop swimming. Now suddenly I changed my mind.

"Why," I asked coolly, "would I want to do that?"

★

Speech Correction was taught by Andrew York, a tall, handsome black man in his late thirties. His voice was gentle as he introduced himself and told us what text to buy. Then he asked us each to introduce ourselves and designate our major. Again, there were twenty of us, only two males this time. Most were special ed majors, a few were in nursing, one other was like me, with a dual major in elementary and special ed.

"What is defective speech?" Andrew York asked and then when we replied with silence, he continued, "Speech is defective if it deviates so far that it calls attention to itself, interferes with communication, or causes its possessor to be maladjusted. In other words, if it is conspicuous, unintelligible, or unpleasant. It is always important to remember the degree of the defect. When the defect is slight, speech improvement is needed rather than speech correction."

I listened intently, taking notes. For the first time I felt I was listening to someone who knew and cared about the course he was teaching. I smiled. This more than made up for swimming.

Not so Teaching Social Studies. I had no high expectations for TSS, as the students called the course. This would be my first exposure to what were known as "method courses" and were required for elementary certification. I had teaching math, science, language, and music coming up in the fall and I had been warned that they were "all a crock."

The methods courses were taught in a small brick building that had once housed an experimental nursery school. It was situated across the street from the rest of the campus, a ten-minute walk, or a five-minute run, away so I was out of breath and the class had already started when I arrived.

Stevie Wonder's version of "The Star-Spangled Banner" rolled through the room, and at the front of the classroom, Professor Figerito waved his arms in front of the portable record player as though conducting an invisible orchestra. His pink shirt was wet with perspiration. The record ended and he grabbed a pile of yellow paper and passed it down the rows.

"Write how you feel about that record. Were you affronted? Shocked? Should the national anthem be treated as a sacred hymn? Do you object to difference?"

We sat looking at him.

"Well, write. Write. Don't just look at me. Unless you'd rather tell us. Uh. You, little lady, there in the back row —"

He couldn't mean me. I was five feet seven. "You. The one who arrived late. Yes. You, dear. Do you want to tell us what you thought of the record?"

He did mean me. He had come to the back of the room and was standing right beside me. I could feel the blood rising in my own cheeks as chairs squeaked and the class turned to look at me.

142

I shook my head. I was blushing. I couldn't believe it. I hadn't blushed in twenty years and here in this idiot class before this idiot man, I was blushing. I looked down at my piece of yellow paper.

"No. Well, all right, dear. Maybe tomorrow you won't feel so shy. How about you, blondie?"

The class shifted its attention to a new victim and I put my hands together in my lap to stop their trembling.

At the end of an hour, Figerito said, "You can all keep your piece of paper as a memento. I hate to correct papers, anyway."

I hurried out the door and back to the parking lot. Every spot was taken now and the roofs of the cars were steaming in the sudden sunshine. I put down the old canvas top and ate my apple and cheese. In some ways my car seemed more like home than any other place — it was ten years old now and more familiar to me than the apartment or the house in the country.

I thought about Figerito and Teaching Social Studies. It was going to be a problem. The only way I could get there before class started was to leave Speech Correction early, and it made no sense to cut short the one good course I'd found. But walking in late was going to call Figerito's attention to me every day, and that meant trouble.

★

Three weeks later, after exactly twelve sessions, we had midterms. In swimming we would be required to do twenty laps and a demonstration of a racing dive and two of the four strokes. Of the original twenty, six students, including Hall, had dropped out. Ritter had stuck it through and was now paddling back and forth at the shallow end. She was given permission to do thirty abstracts on the benefits of exercise for her midterm.

Ian and Amy Schwarzenbach were the stars of our class.

They had speed as well as style and raced each other playfully up and down the pool, diving and surfacing like two young porpoises. I did not play. I worked every minute of that class. I had got a tank suit and towels and a hair dryer, so I was less conspicuous. But fifty laps was still a lot of laps. At least for me. I could do a passable freestyle and sidestroke, the backstroke was easy, but I could not master the breaststroke. My head was always up when it should be down and I could not snap my legs together frog-style. I had made myself do two more laps each day so I was pretty sure I could pass the midterm.

Swimming had become much more than a one-credit course to me. It had become a symbol. If I could pass swimming this summer, I would be able to make it through the next year to graduation and certification. I apologized to Cal during dinner every evening, then fell asleep before nine o'clock, and was up and gone again by seven the next morning. Cal checked off the days till the end of swimming on the kitchen calendar.

All midterms came on the Thursday of the third week. I wished they would stagger them, put some on Tuesday or Wednesday, but they didn't.

★

The third Thursday of summer school dawned hot and humid. I stood on our terrace drinking my orange juice, watching the sun rise over the Manhattan skyline. Hot and red, burnishing the tops of the New York buildings across the river, gilding the bridges. My spirits rose with the sun. I could do it — swim and pass Speech and Social Studies. I went back into the kitchen and poured a thermos of coffee to keep me awake after swimming.

Mrs. Hogan lined us up at the edge of the pool. She had an assistant with her this morning, dressed in identical

144

green camp shorts. They each had two stopwatches and somehow or other would keep each student's time for twenty laps. Mrs. Hogan lectured us sternly: we must start with a racing dive, demonstrate one stroke up, a different one back. After that we could use any stroke we wished, but we must go for eighteen more laps. *"There will be no stopping at either end. Swimming will be continuous."* A blast on the whistle and the first swimmer, Ian, was off. Three minutes later she started Amy Schwarzenbach in the second lane. I would be next to last. I sat down and pondered Mrs. Hogan while I did my breathing exercises. What could the rest of her life be like? How could she care so much? I winced. Look who's talking.

"MacCracken! Go!"

I dove in. At least I went in head first and she didn't call me back as she had some of the others. Ian said we'd have to go off the board for the finals — I couldn't do that. Don't think about the board now. Freestyle first. Flutter kick. Pull right. Pull left. Breathe. I was at the end before I knew it and almost cracked my head against the cement. I recovered just in time and turned underwater and came up to do the sidestroke back. Easy. Stretch. Pull. Scissors kick. If anything would get me through the finals it would be the sidestroke. It had become as easy or easier for me than the backstroke and I could tell where I was going. "An old lady's stroke," Ian teased. "So, who do you think I am, anyway?" I'd answered.

Lap sixteen. Only four more. I can do it. I know I can. I did twenty-two yesterday. Just don't panic or cramp. Stretch. Pull. Stay relaxed. Pretend you're lying on your own bed . . . Luke. All of a sudden an image of Luke's small body appeared above the pool. What are you doing here, Luke? I thought you were in Florida. I've called you seven times now and sent four postcards and you haven't answered once. How come?

"Hey. Watch it." I had veered off my lane and kicked the body in the next lane.

"Oh, sorry. Sorry." Pay attention. Keep in line. Luke? Where are you? Are you okay? But Luke was gone. There was nothing above the pool now but lights, shimmering like rainbows because my eyes were full of water.

Eighteen. Turn. Pull. Glide. My shoulders ached and my pulls grew shorter. Tension. The ache must be tension. Twenty-two. Remember, you did twenty-two yesterday.

Nineteen. Turn. This is it. Come on. Don't let your legs sink.

Ian was waving from the side of the pool. "Hey, Mac. This is it. Go out in style." Ian had been keeping track.

I pulled long and strong — and glided like a fish until my fingers touched the wall at the shallow end. I stood up and smiled at Ian.

★

Luke appeared again halfway through the Speech exam. I had outlined the four types of speech problems. I. Disorders of Articulation. II. Defects of voice. III. Language. IV. Rhythm.

I knew articulation disorders. They spelled soda: substitutions, omissions, distortions, additions. Voice disorders were easy, too: pitch, pitch breaks, quality, volume.

Language was more difficult. Delayed speech and aphasia, which was a breakdown in language. There are four areas of language. But what are they? My mind wandered. Did my mother have aphasia? Her language had certainly broken down. Broken down.

There had been something strange about Luke as he hung over the swimming pool. What was it? Something different — I shook my head. Not now.

The four areas of language are — ah — I remember. Two major areas: "receptive" and "expressive." Under "receptive" come "understandability and readability" and under "expressive" come "speakability and writeability." A miniature image of Luke superimposed itself on my exam book. I strained to see him more clearly. Were those tears on his face? Luke never cried. Was that what was different? The image faded and I forced myself to finish the exam as quickly as possible. Just this and then Social Studies and then I would drive to Luke's house.

As I handed in my exam I asked Andrew York if my mother's stroke could have caused something like aphasia.

He nodded. "I'll bring you a book, two books, in fact, one of exercises on Monday. I know what you're feeling. My mother had a stroke when I was twelve. That's how I got interested in the field." I was lucky to have Andrew York. A professor who is caring and knowledgeable is one of the most important elements in a teacher's training.

★

Figerito pranced around the front of the room like a peacock. Lime green was the color of the day. Matching shirt and socks, set off by white bucks and cream-colored Dacron slacks. The effect spoiled only by the patches of perspiration beneath his arms.

Amy Schwarzenbach lifted her books from the chair beside her so that I could sit down. Amy had saved me from Figerito's ridicule by coming early (she had another class in this same building after swimming) and staking out two seats in the rear of the class by the outside door. I would wait just outside the door until Figerito's back was turned and then slip silently into the seat Amy had saved. So far he'd never noticed.

Now I poured coffee from the thermos and offered it to

Amy. She shook her head. "Good going today," meaning swimming. I smiled my thanks and leaned back, grateful for Amy, the hot coffee, and Andrew York.

"Only one question today." Figerito smiled at us. "I'll write it on the board."

DISCUSS THE SIX THEORIES OF RACE PREJUDICE.

Everyone began talking at once to everyone else. What six theories? What did he mean? What was this?

Figerito raised his hand for quiet. "What's the problem?" he smiled.

Bedlam. Everyone shouted at once.

Figerito raised his arm again. "What do you mean you haven't had it? It's right in the text."

Double bedlam. People were standing up now. We had never had a text.

"You never had a text?" Figerito mocked us. "It's listed right here on the course description I handed out the first day. Did you think because I didn't mention it you didn't have to read it?"

Groans. Figerito took two turns around the classroom, then stopped and smiled at us.

"Well, don't worry. Just in case you forgot to buy the text, I've had the page run off for you." He displayed a large pile of typed pages. "Just rewrite it in your own words in the examination book, add your opinion, and leave it on the desk."

Games. He'd been playing games. This was no way to teach teachers to teach children. I scribbed an essay and left it on the desk and got my car and drove to Falls City.

School 23 was empty, the black macadam side lot without cars or people. A school without children is a desolate place. I left my car on the street opposite the school, wanting to walk, to get in touch with Falls City again.

The city was different in the summer. Maybe it was because it was lunchtime, but shades were pulled and there were no children anywhere.

No one was outside at Luke's project, either. I walked past three times before I gathered the courage to ring the bell at Luke's apartment, but there was no one home.

I walked back to my car. What was the matter with me? School was over for Luke. He'd said he was going to Florida — that's probably where he was. With his dad, fishing, swimming. I was just tired, imagining things. Well, only three more weeks for me, too, and then in August we'd go up to the country and spend time with our own children, home from college or on vacation. Just get through the next three weeks — and trust Luke.

The July days were uneventful, one so like the other I never knew what day it was. Swim, study, sleep. Then weekends in the country, stopping at my parents' on the way up and back, guiding my mother through the beginning exercises in the aphasia manual. It was both painful and a joy to see her working hard to pick up seven raisins one by one and put them in her mouth. She was better, or so the doctor said, but she still dropped more raisins than she ate.

She had all her meals at the small dining table in the apartment, refusing to be wheeled to the dining room because she could not handle her knife and fork, was unable to find the exact location of her mouth. Unintentionally, she spilled and knocked things over and she would not do this in front of others.

My father was patient and gentle. He wheeled my mother's chair into the garden so she could sit beside him while he weeded or tended the roses. It was a difficult time for them both, though neither complained.

Most of all, Cal and I tried to bring them a little laugh-

149

ter. We saved each small story that might interest or amuse them. My mother loved hearing stories of the children. She knew each small step forward that Luke had made. She still had the rare, wonderful ability of making my small accomplishments seem special. And I loved her for it. Often, though, she could not say good-bye because tears clogged her throat. Would Luke have understood? Somehow I was sure he would.

★

My father always walked with us to the parking lot. "Melancholy often accompanies strokes, the doctor says. It's not always lasting."

"Come visit," I urged. "We could put the wheelchair on the ski rack."

"Not yet. The doctor says not yet." He smiled at me. "We're fine, you know. She knows you care and that's what's important."

I nodded and waved as we pulled out, remembering how my mother always ran up and down our stairs, my father cautioning her to be careful, to go more slowly. He'd never need to do that again.

★

It was the last week. No exam in Speech, only a take-home project that involved taping young children's speech and a paper discussing the quality and quantity of their language.

Figerito had handed out the final exam the week before. Amy Schwarzenbach said he did it to make himself look good. I didn't know or care. I only wished to get through TSS and away from the likes of Figerito.

The last day. I saluted the sun with my orange juice, feeling strong, good. An hour later, I plopped my body off the low diving board at the pool in an almost dive that Amy and Ian had drilled me in and were sure would pass. Not the first time or the second — but finally on the third try, Mrs. Hogan did not call me back and I stroked the first of my fifty laps. Amy Schwarzenbach and Ian were finished when I was only half through, but they stationed themselves at either end and counted off the laps for me so I didn't have to try to keep track. I had come to like swimming itself, the feeling of moving through another environment. Some primal instinct in my body was roused, and I wished that there were rocks and sand and weeds and other living organisms beneath me instead of painted blue cement.

"Forty-two," Amy shouted, kneeling at the edge of the shallow end. I was breathing hard now and I rolled onto my back, almost floating, knowing it was not allowed, moving my arms and legs just enough not to inspire the wrath of Mrs. Hogan.

And there once again was Luke, floating in the air above me, his arms stretched wide as if he were flying — dipping, gliding like a gull against the river sky. At least I thought it was the river sky. I was back at the Thousand Islands. I rolled over and began a slow Australian crawl, pretending I was up, flying with Luke, moving with him across the sky, out of the gym, out of the state college, out of Falls City.

I felt my head touch something and my feet sank. It was Ian's hand, cushioning my head from cement.

"Don't stop!" he said. "Kick. Kick. Keep going. Only two more. You can do it. Just count the strokes. Count to a hundred. You can do a hundred strokes."

Can I? Onto my side. One. Two. Three. Four . . . I tried to look up at the skylight to see if Luke was still there, but my head would not turn that far.

At the shallow end, Amy said, "You're almost done. You've got it now, only one more lap."

I looked around the pool as I turned. I was the only one left. I swam the last lap alone. But not quite. Amy walked beside me, counting off the strokes — and I was sure I could see a little of Luke's blue jeans against the skylight.

"Seven and eight and — kick your feet — ten and —"

Her voice faded and I swam in a dream, moving through ghosts and voices from far away. And then Ian grabbed my hands and held them against the end of the pool.

"Okay. Okay. You did it, Mac. You swam the whole goddam fifty laps. Way to go! Breathe easy, now."

★

A half hour later, Amy, Ian, and I sprawled on the grass behind the gym. They had bought a bottle of white wine to give to me. "For celebration if you passed, for consolation if you didn't."

There was, of course, nothing to do but open it. I toasted Amy and Ian, they toasted me and each other. State was a long way from Wellesley, but as far as I knew, nobody there had ever bought anybody a present for passing a course, or for failing it.

There was time to spare. There was no Speech class today, since there was no exam. All we had to do was drop off our tapes of children's speech and typed comments and I had done that on my way to swimming as I passed the Speech building.

Figerito wanted us there, though.

"Gotta go," Amy said.

Ian tipped his head back and drained the last of the wine from the bottle and then buried it in the soft dirt under a maple tree.

"You should have put a note in it," Amy said. "So when

they dig it up in a thousand years, they'll know it was us."

"Jeez," Ian said. "This isn't the Atlantic Ocean. I'm just cleaning up."

But I noticed he touched her hand before we left and mumbled, "Pick you up at eight o'clock."

He did not touch me. He stood with his hands in his pockets, body bent like a question mark, his head forward as he peered out at me from under his hat.

"See ya around, Mac."

And all of a sudden he reminded me of Luke, and I answered him, promised him.

"See you, Ian."

★

"He's nice," Amy said as we walked across the campus.

"Yes. He is." My head and stomach felt slightly unstable, as though they were not connected to my arms and legs. Maybe drinking that wine at ten in the morning had not been such a great idea after all. I put my hand on Amy's shoulder to steady myself as we crossed the street.

"You two should build a pool," I said, remembering their lean, graceful bodies swimming, diving, rolling, turning in the water.

"Watch the curb," Amy said.

A mistake. We'd lingered too long. Class had already started. Figerito was in canary yellow today and he swirled upon us as we lingered by the doorway. "Come in. Come in, little ladies. Don't be shy."

I slouched toward a seat in the back, imitating Ian, trying not to be visible. I wished I had a hat.

"No need to sit way back there. We're a small group today. Come on down here, dears. Join us."

I followed Amy to the middle of the room. The room

153

was half empty; obviously a good percentage of the class had not come. Wiser than I. I put my hand on top of my head to adjust it. It seemed to be sloping to the right.

Canary yellow passed back and forth before my eyes as Figerito paced across the classroom lecturing animatedly about something. Big Bird. He looked rather like Big Bird. Unexpectedly he lighted beside me.

"Is it always evil?" he shouted at me.

"Pardon?" It was difficult to focus on him when he was so close.

"Evil? Wrong? Malodorous? . . . Well, is it?" His arms worked up and down. Big Bird flapping.

"I don't know," I said. I didn't have a glimmer of what he was talking about.

"Well, think. Think. You must have some opinion. Is violence always evil?"

His voice seemed far away, loud but far away as though he was shouting through a muted mike. Perspiration rolled down the side of his face and gathered in little pools at the end of each sideburn. Had I really been frightened of this man?

"Is violence always evil?" I repeated.

"Well, is it? Is it?"

I shook my head watching the perspiration patches darken on his shirt.

"No? Are you saying 'no'?" He took a handkerchief, unbelievably bordered in yellow, out of his back pocket and mopped his face. "How can you say that? Give us an example."

And from somewhere to the right, just beyond my head, I heard my voice telling Big Bird coolly, "Love-making can be violent without being evil."

Silence. No one spoke. Only the squeak of chairs as a dozen or so twenty-year-old bodies turned to stare at me.

I could feel the blood rising in my own face, but my head was suddenly clear and firmly back in place.

Big Bird flapped to the front of the silent room.

"Love-making!" he squawked. "Love-making, whatever that may be, can be violent? Amazing! You learn a little something every day."

Blessedly, the bell rang and I was up and out before it had stopped ringing.

★

The last I ever heard from Figerito was in a note fastened to my exam that he sent back to me by mail. "Excellent paper. I'd like to discuss it further. Call me next week to arrange lunch."

I dropped both the exam and the note in the wastebasket. Enough of TSS. And wine at ten in the morning. But even so, I don't think I'd take it back.

I had completed a day and a half of fall classes when I decided I couldn't wait any longer to see how Luke was doing. There was no official program at the school this year and my days were crammed with six different courses that I needed in order to graduate in June. But I had an hour's break at one o'clock and on impulse I drove down to School 23.

Mrs. Karras's door was closed, but I stopped at the secretary's desk to find out which room Luke was in.

She checked the records. "Room one twelve."

"One twelve?" I repeated. "Are you sure?" None of the third grades was on the first floor.

The secretary turned the printed sheet around so that I could see for myself. Her finger pointed to the line. "Brauer, Lucas. Room 112. Miss Eckhardt."

"Thank you." I forced myself to walk out of the office, but I began running as soon as I hit the hall. Something was terribly wrong. I slowed when I got to Lisa's room and stood to one side and studied the sign on her door. It was exactly the same as last year.

Room 112
Grade 2
Miss Eckhardt

How could that be? I edged up to the glass window and peeked in just for an instant, careful not to be noticed. The instant was as long as an hour.

Luke was there. He was sitting in the same seat as last year.

I took another look. I couldn't see his face. His head was down on his arms and only the back of his head was visible, but his body was limp and dejected. I went back to the office.

"How soon can I see Mrs. Karras?" I asked the secretary.

"Well, a group of room mothers just left, planning the first PTA meeting, you know. She might be able to see you now, though she's terribly busy. Want me to find out?"

"Please."

I paced the tiny waiting room. No wonder I'd worried about Luke over the summer. But what had actually happened? Why wouldn't someone have called me?

"Mary! I'm so glad to see you. I've thought of you so often."

Mrs. Karras looked tan and healthy and I was glad, but there was no time to talk about that now.

156

"What happened to Luke?" I asked. "I just saw him in Lisa's classroom. What's going on?"

"Come on in the office. There. Sit down. I tried to call you in June when it happened, but I never seemed able to reach you."

I nodded. That was the time of my mother's stroke.

"When what happened?" Impatience edged my voice.

"Well, it was decided that Luke should be retained."

"Retained?" I couldn't believe it. "You mean he's still in second grade? What happened?" I repeated again.

"Nothing specific happened," Mrs. Karras said. "I mean he didn't suddenly set the school on fire or anything. In fact, Lisa said he was reading out loud a little more every day. True, it wasn't the regular class reading text, but he was reading and working more than he ever had before."

I shook my head. "Then I don't understand —"

"Well, Mary, to put it as simply as I can, the Child Study Team decided that Luke wasn't ready for third-grade work."

"The Child who?"

"Study Team."

"Who are they? I never even heard of them before."

"Yes. Well, they weren't connected with the Mental Health Clinic project — except, of course, the psychologist did give the IQ tests, but that has to be done for referral anyway." Mrs. Karras sighed. "It's too involved to go into in detail, but just between you and me, there was some resentment of the mental health project, some feeling of 'outside interference.' Now whether that had anything to do with Luke or not, I can't say for sure."

I got up and walked around the room. "How could they retain him? None of them had even worked with Luke." I shook my head. "He had come such a long way. He had. He was coming to school every day, even beginning to like it a little. He was doing his work, reading out loud, not in trouble with the police."

"I know. If it had been up to me . . ." Mrs. Karras stopped for a minute before she continued. "The worst part was nobody told him. We each thought someone else had. He didn't know until he came back this fall."

"Can I see him?" I asked abruptly.

"Of course. He's in the same room. You remember?"

I nodded and walked back down the halls to Lisa's classroom once again.

I stood to the left of the door and looked at Luke through the window.

There he was, still in the same seat as before, head on his arms, looking out the window. What must it have been like for him the first day of school? Thinking he'd be in third grade along with Wendell and the others, and then being told to go to second. His brother must be in second grade this year, for God's sake! How could this happen? And I wasn't there. I was at the hospital with my mother and didn't even know. Not that I could have made them change their minds, but at least I could have told Luke, warned him.

I walked away, back down the halls, anger, sorrow, defeat tumbling through my head. I wasn't ready to see Luke yet, after all. I wouldn't be any help to him feeling like this.

I left a note with the secretary in the office asking Lisa to meet me for lunch the next day.

★

Lisa looked pretty and clean and young as she climbed out of the van and walked into the restaurant. She was just back from Mexico. She'd met a terrific guy in Arizona, she said, and he'd gone with her the rest of the way and back as far as Mississippi, but the relationship had ended there by mutual agreement.

"What about Luke?" I asked, not able to wait any longer.

"He's terrible," she said flatly. "Worse than the beginning of last year, if that's possible. He won't talk at all. Not even to Wendell. I even tried to get Wendell and Luke together at lunch one day, but it didn't work."

"Why did they do it?" I felt like throwing my water glass across the room. Instead I set it down more softly than usual.

"Because they don't care," Lisa said, leaning back in her chair, her long legs stretching out beyond her short skirt. "What the shit does it mean to them! They look at the scores, see he's reading at one point eight or whatever, and is in a one point two reader. Check his absences, see he's been absent thirty-eight days during the year . . ."

"But not in May or June."

"You don't get it, Mary. It's the system. The system looks at the total — the absences, the fires, the grade scores. Add the numbers, count the slips. Luke loses."

"Well, so does the system," I said. "Where does the system think Luke will be in ten years? How much money will it cost 'the system' then?"

"Don't shout at me. I couldn't agree more. Besides, who's worried about ten years? How about this year? How about me? To be honest, I don't relish being stuck with Luke again. Much as I like him, he's a difficult kid. And I gather that that project you were in last year is kaput. Fini. So that means no help at all."

"Lisa, listen. Don't say that. You're good with Luke. Look what you did in his reading group last year. He wouldn't have a chance with Mrs. Tenton. You know that, she's way too old. I don't know anything about the other second-grade teacher, except every time I've seen her in the halls she's fishing for her bra strap. Not a good sign. Besides, I'll be down. When's the best time for me to see Luke?"

Lisa took another sip of coffee. "Anytime. What difference does it make? I'm telling you, Mary, he does not do one thing all day long. Not even draw. He doesn't even show up until around ten." She put her cup back on the saucer and looked at me. "Maybe I shouldn't say this, but does it ever occur to you that maybe you, unlike the system, care too much? There are a lot of kids in this world who just aren't going to make it no matter what you or anybody else does. That's just the way the cookie crumbles. And you aren't going to do anybody any good if you go around breaking your heart over each one you run into."

Lisa glanced at her watch and stood up, shaking out her skirt. "Me and my big mouth. Listen, thanks for lunch. I'll see you over at school."

I sat at the table after she had left, thinking about what she'd said. In some ways it made sense. Survival of the fittest. Darwin had been around a long time.

But what about the not so fit? Kids like Luke didn't just die or disappear. Instead, they moved further and further outside society, traveling alone. No longer caring or even really knowing what was right or wrong. Surviving. Getting even. Finally convincing themselves that they were the ones who were right, everyone else wrong. The "I'm okay — you're not okay" syndrome of the criminal that makes sociologists believe he's the hardest to reach.

Maybe it was because my first work had been with seriously emotionally disturbed kids. Psychotic children. Children labeled autistic and schizophrenic, children that not only shut out the world, but replaced it with another of their own making, so that you had to move through barriers and strange lands of other worlds to reach them. And yet, some of those kids made progress, some of them grew. A few even made it to public school. If they could do it, Luke could. He almost had. We'd just have to start over.

Luke left the classroom grudgingly. He walked at least three feet behind me down the hall and if I slowed, trying to be closer to him, he slowed his own steps so that he kept the same distance between us.

In the music room he did not sit down. Instead, he stood just inside the door, looking down at his feet.

I shut the door and he glanced at me briefly. I thought he might bolt, but he stood silently, head down.

I went over to the long table where we had always worked and slouched in one of the metal chairs. I wasn't expecting anything to happen. I just wanted to get a feel of Luke, be in the same room with him so I could absorb his vibrations and begin to understand where he was.

We stayed just like that for fifteen or twenty minutes. I had the feeling Luke could have stood there for hours. He had always had control, too much control. No tears, few words, at least in the beginning. Now no movement. Now his running away was even more complete.

I looked at the clock. I wouldn't keep him over thirty minutes. Not fair to make him stand so still so long. I got up and moved toward him, but his head snapped to one side almost as if I'd hit him and I couldn't bear that. I walked away to the other side of the room and stood there next to the blackboard, looking at Luke. We'd known each other so well. He must feel let down by me, as well as by everybody else. How can I tell him? What can I do?

He won't listen to me, won't let me near him. Maybe I can write to him. I picked up the chalk and printed large clear letters on the blackboard.

> LUKE,
> I AM SORRY. I WANT TO HELP.
> LOVE, MARY

I turned around slowly, not wanting to startle him. His head was up! He was looking at the board. Was he reading it? Don't ask. Don't push too hard. It was enough that he had raised his head.

★

I walked into Professor Foster's office without knocking, not caring about the kids on the bench.

"I need to talk to you."

He swirled in his chair, among the piles of books and papers.

"I might have been in a conference, you know. Would you please the hell knock next time?"

I sat on the pile of books by his desk.

"What happened to your wonderful program? Where were you and Jerry and the Mental Health Clinic and the head of special services and this whole state college when they left Luke back?"

"They left him back? What are you talking about? I didn't know anything about it. How come?"

"Not ready for third-grade work. At least that's what they say," I sighed, some of the anger gone. "And maybe he wasn't. But he was moving. He was doing better. And if he'd just had some kind of extra help in reading this year he could have caught up by the end of the third grade. I'm sure of it. Now they've got him in second, the same grade, although at least not the same class, as his little brother.

"Mrs. Karras says the Child Study somebody reviewed Luke's records and saw he was a year behind. I realize that makes sense on paper, but he isn't paper."

"I know the Falls City Child Study Team," Foster said. "They do a pretty fair job on the whole. The trouble is numbers. They have thousands of kids in that system. There's no way the team could see each child individually. When did this happen?"

"The end of June."

"I see. I was in Maine. Probably why they didn't contact me. How about yourself?"

"I was away a lot, too."

"So the kid arrived at school thinking he'd passed, ready for third grade, and finds himself shuffled back into second?"

I nodded.

"What's Luke say?" Foster asked.

"He doesn't say anything. Or do anything. I don't know why he shows up at school at all."

Foster stood up and shook his head. "It's a shame. It's things like this that made us get the clinic program started. Well, I'm sorry, Mary. We did have high hopes for the program. Just didn't work out. There was a lot of political stuff going on at the clinic. I think I mentioned it once. Reorganization. Personnel changes."

I stood without speaking. None of what he said helped Luke.

Foster sat back down again. "I honestly don't know what else to say. I will call Bernie and get Luke on the waiting list for the clinic." He paused, studying the papers on his desk. Then he cleared his throat and continued. "While you're here, Mary, I might as well give you the other bad news and get it over with. Trouble never travels alone, they say." He shuffled the papers on his desk and finally found what he wanted. He handed me a white sheet of paper with a pink slip attached to the back.

I recognized the white sheet. It was the waiver form I had filled out the year before at Foster's suggestion.

All students were required to student teach for six weeks in their senior year. My only quarrel with this was that it was too little and too late. In my view, students should be out in actual classrooms during some part of each of their four years.

As my adviser, Foster had suggested that since I had taught full time for six years, I should apply for a waiver that would allow me to substitute other courses for student teaching. Although he didn't mention it, I was quite sure that my age and the growing scarcity of student teacher positions contributed to his feeling that more would be lost than gained by my student teaching. Besides, it would give me a chance to catch up on the required courses I'd missed while working in Falls City.

I turned the sheet over and read the pink slip. "Waiver denied. Teaching was not supervised so unable to determine if it was good or bad." The slip was signed by the head of the department.

I turned the paper in my hand. "What does this mean?"

Foster shrugged. "That you have to student teach this spring. I'll try to find you a good spot."

I took the pink slip and walked out of the office, across the campus, to the parking lot. I climbed into my car and drove out the gates, not heading anywhere in particular, just needing to be in a familiar place so I could think.

I knew I was angry, but I wasn't quite sure why. Luke had been given a bad deal — that was a legitimate thing to be angry about. I knew I also felt some guilt about not being there to help him, but I'd have to forgive myself for that. It had been right to spend that time with my mother. I wished I'd reached him over the summer. Where had he been? I still didn't know. Would I ever? Was he ever going to talk to me again?

As I drove I thought about this and also about the rejection of the waiver for student teaching. How could they say they had no way of knowing whether my teaching was "good or bad"? They could have asked the director, Doris Fleming. Whatever else had gone on between us, she would have said I was a good teacher.

But that's not how "the system" works. Not neat enough. You need a living, breathing supervisor to observe and write reports.

Okay. It's the system. I guess that's why I'm angry. "The system screws everything up." I'd heard the kids in my classes and teachers at the school use the phrase a hundred times and I'd always felt that it was a cop-out. Shifting the blame. Well, fair's fair. Now you're a victim of the system yourself, Mary. You and Luke both. Wait. A glimmer of an idea. Be still. Wait. Let it grow.

I felt a surge of happiness and I tooted my horn at no one in particular. I had it! I knew what I was going to do! Student teach in School 23. I'd spend the required time, six weeks of it, student teaching in Luke's school. I wasn't sure how, but that's what I was going to do. One way or another Luke and I were going to beat the system and get out from under.

22

The lights on the bridge came on just as Lisa and Mrs. Karras arrived at our apartment for dinner. We stood together on the terrace for a minute, looking out across the river at the Manhattan skyline. The swag of lights I loved so outlined the arch of the George Washington Bridge, forming a necklace across the dark hollow of the Hudson River.

When we walked back inside, Lisa surveyed the room — the thick white carpet, my grandmother's cherry chest, the old dining table with leaves almost touching the floor, contrasting with the low, nubby white furniture and slate coffee table that Cal had made.

"Nice," she declared, and flopped full length on the couch. "I love it." Then she sat up and stared at me. "What the hell are you doing in a dump like School Twenty-three?"

I shrugged. "I don't know. All I know is that I want to be there more and I need help. From both of you."

I explained my idea of student teaching at School 23 to them during dinner. Mrs. Karras was immediately enthusiastic; Lisa was not. She felt that if there was any way for anyone to stay out of the grubby world of Falls City, he or she should do it.

We took our coffee back to the living room. Lisa sat cross-legged on the floor.

Mrs. Karras urged me once again to call her Jo, and I did, but in my head she was always Mrs. Karras. She stirred her coffee and said, "I have a good eye. I know who can teach my children and who can't and it has nothing to do with race, color, or creed, or age or education. It's a gift. Pure and simple. The art of communication is just that, an art, as much as painting or music or literature, and it's especially important when you're working with children. You either have it or you don't. You, Mary, have it. And if you have it, you have to use it."

The front door opened and closed and Cal came in, back from a long day in Washington.

I got up and hugged him and introduced him to Lisa Eckhardt and Mrs. Karras. They chatted for a moment and then Cal excused himself and went to change his clothes.

Lisa lay back flat on the floor. "Now I know you're crazy. You have the best of everything. Why do you want to leave it?"

"I'm not leaving it. Cal's work is important to him, too. We value that in each other."

"Okay," Lisa said. "Tell you what. You go. I'll stay. We can have a little menage à trois."

Mrs. Karras said sharply, "Hands off, Lisa."

Cal returned in worn blue corduroys and a sweater, carrying a beer. "What can I get for anyone?" Wine for Lisa, a small liqueur for Mrs. Karras and for me.

Together we plotted. Mrs. Karras agreed to call Professor Foster and ask to have me placed in School 23 for student teaching. She herself would supervise, but she did not want me in a classroom. What she wanted was for me to continue the mental health program by myself.

"So it's only three or four kids. It's three or four kids that have some kind of chance instead of none. Say you started at nine and saw one child from nine to nine-forty-five — another till ten-thirty — a third till eleven-fifteen and another till twelve. Then you could set up the other courses you need for graduation in the afternoon."

"What about lunch?" Lisa asked. "Or aren't you going to let her eat?" She turned to Cal. "What do you think about all this?"

Cal was silent. When I first knew him I took his silence for uncertainty or disapproval. Now I knew he was organizing his thoughts, careful with his words. At last he said, "It's a good idea. I'm not sure Mary would make it through another year of courses, if they're like last year's courses, without the children."

"What about your dinner and the wash and the shopping —?"

"Lisa!" Mrs. Karras warned.

Cal smiled at them both. "We manage."

★

A week later Professor Foster caught up to me outside the book store.

"Congratulations. Your student teaching forms for School Twenty-three are filled out, signed by me, the dean, everyone. All you have to do is stop by and pick them up. You start in January."

"Thank you," I answered, not sure how much he knew.

Foster stood staring at me, rocking on his heels a little, chewing on the end of his pipe.

"Isn't it amazing how that student teaching position opened up, just like that? We've never placed a student at School Twenty-three before."

"It's a good school," I said. "Maybe you'll have other students there next year."

"Maybe. Maybe we will. Anyway, Mary, good luck."

He turned to leave and then turned back. "How's Luke doing?"

I shook my head. "Just about the same. I've seen him three times now. He comes with me but it's not like it was before. I think he's so angry about being in second grade that he doesn't care about anything else. It really was a rotten thing, especially not telling him. He'd been working, trying so hard, not running away, or setting fires, beginning to open up. It's as though it proved to him that he's no good and there's no point in trying. It doesn't make any difference.

"I don't know. I just hope we can get through this fall term. Both Luke and myself. I've got a heavier load of meaningless courses than I've ever had before." I hesitated, "And my mother's very ill."

"I'm sorry. Let me know if I can help." He shook my hand, holding it for a minute between his. "I mean that."

"Yes," I said, liking him. "I know you do. Thank you. Just keep thinking about Luke, of some way to get through to him."

★

My mother died on November first — alone. My father found her in her wheelchair, her head slumped down against the table, when he came back up from dinner.

"She had another stroke," my father said. "The doctors say a 'massive hemorrhage' this time." He touched my arm. "They say it happened instantly. That she wouldn't have been in pain."

I nodded, not able to speak, thinking only that I wished I had been there with her when it happened. I somehow couldn't bear that she had been alone. I hardly heard my father.

"You know she wrote letters to you and each of your three children today. I mailed them before I went to supper."

It was true. The letters arrived two days later. She had written to me and each of her grandchildren to tell us she

169

loved us and thank us for the Halloween cards we'd sent. Her writing was tiny and cramped, sloping every which way across the page. It must have taken her hours to write those pages. Had she somehow known?

I stayed at their apartment and my father and I worked together, doing the necessary things — arrangements at the funeral home, notices to the papers, the lawyers, sorting her things from immaculate drawers and closets. The funeral, the memorial service. I could not believe that she was dead. She had been my first teacher and beloved friend for over forty years.

Death was a common visitor in the retirement home and my father said at the end of the week, "It's better this way, Mary. She hated sitting in that wheelchair day after day."

I kissed him, nodding agreement, thinking how he had been the one to help her dress each day and reach the wheelchair. He had been the one that lay beside her as she sang the hymns of her childhood trying to get to sleep each night. He knew better than anyone how difficult it had been. It was not his fault that he had been at dinner when she died. It was just that I could not shake the sadness.

★

The phone was ringing when I walked into our apartment. I let it ring. I did not want to talk to anyone. I went out on the terrace, everything gray in the November afternoon. The sky, the bridge, the city itself.

The phone rang again. One, two, three, four, five. Maybe it was Cal or my father, or one of the children. I pulled the sliding glass door closed behind me and picked up the receiver.

"Mary? This is Jo Karras. I'm sorry to bother you at home. All you all right? They said you'd been absent from classes the last few days. Are you better?" she asked, assuming I'd been sick. "I wouldn't bother you except I've got Luke here in the office. I just picked him up at the police station. His mother's in bed sick and couldn't go down."

"The police station? Why was he there?"

"Same thing. Fires. Could you possibly come over?"

I didn't want to go. I needed time to mourn my mother's death, to work it through. But how could I refuse?

"All right. I'll be there. It will take me an hour from here, though."

"That's all right. We'll wait."

It was almost four o'clock by the time I got to School 23. The door was locked, but through the small side window I could see the janitor mopping the front hall. I tapped on the glass. He recognized me and unlocked the door. I walked directly to Mrs. Karras's office. She was behind her desk working on a pile of papers. Luke sat on a wooden chair in the corner of the room. His head was down so I couldn't see his face. His sneakers and pants were dirty and he held the bottom of the chair seat tightly with both hands.

"Hello, Mary," Mrs. Karras said. "Come in. Thank you for coming down."

I nodded and sat in another wooden chair in front of her desk, my body turned toward Luke.

"Luke?" Mrs. Karras asked. "Do you want to tell Mary what happened?"

Luke didn't even look up.

Mrs. Karras sighed and said, "They say he set twenty-five fires this afternoon. Twenty-five! All by himself. Wendell was in school. We know that. So we can't blame Wendell."

"That's a lot of fires."

"Well, you know we haven't had rain for a week or more. Everybody got their leaves and trash raked out of

171

their yards and piled in the streets over the weekend. We don't have that many trees, thank God in this case, in this part of the city, so the piles weren't terribly large. But from what they say, Luke would light one pile of leaves, then move down the street and light another pile, then run to the next street and begin again. Pretty soon he had fires burning on a dozen different streets. People were calling in to the police about a boy the size of Luke in brown pants and a plaid shirt who was setting the fires. He was starting another one when they picked him up."

Luke's head stayed down while Mrs. Karras was talking.

Now she sighed and continued. "They called Mrs. Brauer, but she's in bed sick, so she called here trying to find you, thinking maybe you could go down. She said something about your being down there once before."

Mrs. Karras paused.

I nodded.

"I don't believe you mentioned that to me," she said. "In any event, I couldn't reach you so I went down."

Mrs. Karras stood up and walked to the window. "They've had it. The police. There was an Officer Snow there, a big man who seemed to know Luke, but even he wanted to send him over to the shelter. Said Luke would be better off there than in a family that didn't care about him."

"The shelter?"

"It's part of the county hospital, a wing where they keep kids while they're trying to decide where to send them, what to do with them."

I looked at Luke. He was holding onto the chair so tightly that his knuckles showed white through the soot and grime.

Mrs. Karras turned back from the window. "I told them they better be damn careful before they sent Luke anywhere. That he had an established home, that his mother was working regularly, that his brother and sister were both doing well in school, that his mother was only temporarily indisposed, that I was representing not only Luke's family, but the Mental Health Clinic, the college, and the school, and that we all had a vested interest in Luke."

I wished I could have heard Mrs. Karras reading the book to Officer Snow.

"Whatever a vested interest is," she said. "Anyway, it worked. And they let Luke out in my custody."

She turned and walked back to her desk. "However, Luke doesn't seem to have any ideas on how to keep this from happening again, or for that matter, any ideas about anything." She glanced at her watch. "The police called at one o'clock. I got him at two. I called you a little before three; it's almost four-thirty now." She sighed and rubbed her temples. "I can't stay here much longer. I've got a board meeting at eight."

I stood up myself. I wasn't feeling anything, not anger or disappointment in Luke, or even pleasure in the Karras-Snow encounter. Not anything at all. My mind and body seemed to work; they just didn't feel anything. It was as if I'd had a massive injection of Novocain. But Mrs. Karras was right. She had a school to run. Hundreds of kids to think about. I could at least go through the motions.

"Do you want me to take Luke home?" I asked.

"Would you? I called his mother and said you were coming down. Maybe," she said, "you and Luke can talk on the way over." Mrs. Karras was putting on the jacket to her suit, taking her pocketbook out of the bottom drawer of her desk, turning out the light.

★

I unlocked the door of my car for Luke and he crawled in and pulled it closed behind him. I went around to the other side to unlock my own door and then stood for a second watching the lights on Mrs. Karras's car as she pulled out of the lot next to the school. With daylight saving gone, night arrived early. I wished they could have known each other — my mother and Mrs. Karras. Sadness enveloped me and I got in quickly and turned the ignition key. Luke had his legs pulled up under his chin, his arms wrapped around his legs. Talk, Mrs. Karras had suggested. What was there to talk about? Luke and I had run out of words.

"Are you ready to go home, Luke?" were the only words I could find.

He nodded and we drove the few blocks to the project in silence.

"I'll wait," I said, "to make sure you get in all right."

He nodded again. At least I thought he did, but he didn't get out right away. Finally, he said, "You want me to get the box?"

"Box?"

"The box with the chalk and stars and stuff. You want me to give it back?"

He must mean the box with his things that I'd given him last June. I'd forgotten all about it and he'd never mentioned it this fall.

"No, Luke. Of course not. Those are yours. They belong to you."

Again we sat in silence for a while. Then Luke opened his door and put one leg out. "Maybe," he said, pausing between words, "maybe I could bring the box to school."

So we are not done. Luke is saying as clearly as he can, in his own words, that he wants to try again. And I want to say to Luke — don't. Not now. I don't have the energy to think about you or anyone else right now.

I put my head against the side window, pressing my forehead against the cold glass, trying to clear my thoughts,

174

and suddenly I realized what I should have known before. Luke knew me as well as I knew him. My added years did not make me more expert at this kind of knowledge. Out of his own sorrow, Luke intuitively recognized mine and he was reaching out not so much for help himself, but to help me.

"All right," I said, straightening up. "Okay, Luke. Maybe you could. Maybe we can. I'll come down to school late tomorrow afternoon. How's that?"

Luke nodded and I said, "Okay. I'll see you then. I'll watch now till you get to your door."

Luke pushed the car door closed and ran to his apartment, opened the door with his key and ducked inside. I backed the car around and started to pull out when Luke was back outside waving, calling something. I slowed and rolled down my window.

"She wants to talk to you. My mother does."

The front door opened directly into the living room and Mrs. Brauer stood in the open doorway, pulling her pink bathrobe together around her throat.

"Thank you," she said. "I got the flu pretty bad. Thanks for getting Luke."

"Mrs. Karras did that. I just brought him home."

Mrs. Brauer coughed and shivered as a gust of wind blew through the open door. I could hear children arguing somewhere behind her and a deeper voice, or was it the TV?

"You should get out of the draft," I said. "You don't want to get chilled."

"Mary — uh. I don't mean to call you that. It's just that it's what Luke says —"

"Mary's fine."

"Could I talk to you? They're not going to send him away or nothing like that, are they?"

"No. I don't think so. Not this time, anyway."

"Could I come over to school? When I'm better, I mean?"

My heart lifted a little. Maybe if she would help — maybe.

"I'd like that," I said. "Just let me know when's good for you. We'll work something out."

★

Cal was home when I got there.

He looked at me carefully. "Tired?"

I nodded, tears so close I couldn't speak.

"Sue and Nan both called to see how you were. You just missed them. They both sent their love."

My daughters. "I'll take a shower. I'll just be a minute."

I leaned against the side of the shower and let the water run hot against my shoulders, my face, my back. Thoughts and tears mixing with the hot water.

I stepped out and rubbed myself dry with a towel, rubbing away rivulets of water and the last remainder of tears.

Luke was already in the music room when I arrived at School 23. He was sitting at the long table, the carton in front of him. He watched as I hung up my coat.

"Miss Eckhardt said I could wait here," he said.

"Okay." I went and sat beside him.

The cardboard box was dirty and cracked. At least he had used it. I touched it tentatively. "Can I look?" Luke nodded and I pulled the box toward me and took off the cover.

There was the box of colored chalk, the stars, the note-book, pencils, Luke's story book, the mystery box. I lined them up in front of me; the accoutrements of our time together were so few.

"There's more," Luke said. "See. I put this in." He put a flattened penny with the other things. "And this." He laid an empty lipstick tube beside the penny. "You know 'bout that?" he said nodding. "You know where that came from?" I nodded in return.

"That's all. Except for this."

"A tooth?"

Luke nodded. "A mole's tooth. I found it in the field." He looked down. "No. It isn't. It's mine own. I put it in there myself." He looked at me straight now, full face. "They told me, some kids did, that there was a tooth fairy and that if you put your tooth under your pillow when it came out, this fairy'd give you money. I didn't have a pillow, so I put it in the box. But nuthin' happened."

Luke was forgetting to sit straight. He was up on his knees looking at me. No more standing in the corner, head down. His eyes were only inches from mine.

"Is there a tooth fairy?" he asked.

I took a breath and then let it out. What a place to start. "That's a hard question, Luke."

"Well, did you ever get any money?" he insisted.

"Yes. A quarter. A quarter for each tooth."

"Under your pillow?"

"Yes."

"Maybe if I'd had a pillow —" Luke's voice trailed off. "Maybe she wouldn't know to look in a box."

He was such a little kid, street-wise, savvy with the po-lice, a budding arsonist, and here we were talking about tooth fairies.

I looked around the room. It was too small for all we

had to say. I wanted to take Luke to the mountain, to walk, to picnic, to feed him. But it was already late. It would be almost dark by the time we reached the mountain. The music room would have to do. I turned so I was facing Luke.

"How was your summer, Luke? Did you get my postcards? I tried to call you, but no one answered."

"Okay, I guess."

"Did you visit your father?"

Luke began putting the things back in the box. "Yeah." The pencils and chalk were back in. Luke took the cover off the gold stars and held one on the tip of his finger. "I didn't stay too long. He hadda go to the hospital so I came back and stayed with my grandma. Alice and Frank went to Florida with Mom and Uncle Chuck. Mom doesn't like Grandma. She says she spoiled my dad rotten."

Things seemed worse than ever to me. Somehow Luke's family was dividing up and because he loved his father, he was being shunted toward his father's mother, while his mother and brother and sister moved in another direction.

"I'm sorry, Luke," I said. "You were the one who was supposed to go to Florida."

Again he hunched his shoulders and put the cover on the box.

"How's your dad now?" I asked, not wanting to end here.

"Better, I guess. I don't know. My mom says he's better, but still in the hospital. She says it's the best place for him."

Luke turned toward me. "Did your mom get better? Did she get out of the hospital?"

I looked at Luke and then got up and walked around the room. How did I answer that? So many ramifications to any answer. What would help Luke? I walked to the blackboard and then back to the table. There was no choice. We couldn't begin again on lies.

"Yes, she got out of the hospital, but she's not better, Luke. She died a couple of weeks ago."

Luke looked at me without saying anything. He took the cover off the box and dug down in and found the lipstick tube and the penny. He balanced the penny on the top of the lipstick tube. I sat down beside him again.

"I knowed it," he said. "I knowed something was wrong when you came to take me home after the fires."

"Yes," I said. "I felt like you knew. I didn't tell many people. It helped me to think you understood. My mother was very old, Luke. Over eighty. Much, much older than your father."

Now Luke turned the penny on edge and tried to spin it on the table, but it was no longer round and it fell back to the table each time.

"Do you believe in the tooth fairy?"

Impatience surged in me. Back to this? Why?

"I don't know, Luke."

"How about Santa Claus? Do you believe in him?"

Okay. I see now! The tooth fairy? Santa Claus? And life? And you? Do I believe in you? That's what you're asking.

Easy now, I told myself. Don't come on too hard.

"Santa Claus? A grown-up like me? How could I believe in Santa Claus?"

But Luke heard behind the words. "Do you hang up your stocking?"

"Well, now that you mention it —"

"Does he come? Does he fill it up?"

I smiled at Luke for the first time that day. "So far. So far he has."

Luke let out his breath and his tense tight body relaxed a little.

Now I could ask, now was the right time.

"What's going on, Luke? You've got to level with me. What's with all these fires and coming to school late, not doing any work and not talking to anybody?"

Luke shrugged. "I don't know." He twisted back in his chair and flicked the lipstick tube with his finger so that it spun round and round on the table. Almost inaudibly he said, "I'm the tallest one."

"The tallest one? In your class, you mean?"

Luke nodded. "The other kids are shrimps. Babies. Same as my brother."

I nodded. What was there to say?

"Frank. My brother. He says I'm mental."

"Mental?"

Luke tapped his head. "Crazy. Re-tard. Frank says it comes from drugs."

"How come Frank thinks he knows so much?" I asked.

Luke hunched his shoulders. "Frank's smart." Then without looking up, Luke said, "Does it come from drugs? Like old Mr. Spencer drinking out of his bottle and telling me it's his birthday. Every day he tells me that. Are drugs like drinking? Is that what's the matter with me?"

"No, Luke. It's not like that at all. Look. The Child Study —"

"Mary," Luke interrupted. "I could of caught it maybe from my dad." He was crouched back on the chair, his small body intent, fierce. "See, I never told nobody but you. About the shots and things. And I didn't even tell you, but sometimes I used to pick up the needle and stuff and throw it away. See. I coulda caught it."

"No, Luke. Frank's wrong. You can't catch it. And besides, there's nothing wrong with you." Even as I said it, I knew it was foolish. Luke would never believe it. How could I get through? The issues were so big, the hurt so

180

deep, the answers so elusive. Better begin with something on the smaller side.

"Let's get back to why you're late for school every day, Luke. Miss Eckhardt says you don't come in till around ten o'clock." That's it. Start with the little things. Leave the fires till later.

Luke shrugged. "I gotta come or Frank will tell on me and Chuck'll, Uncle Chuck'll gimme the strap. But Frank doesn't come lookin' for me till he goes to the bathroom in the middle of the morning."

"Frank and Alice get here on time." I said.

"They leave with Chuck at eight. He says they're too little to walk so he drops them at school on his way to the factory. But he can't make me ride with him. I take the shortcut."

"I remember. But why not till ten? Why don't you get here at nine so you don't start out the day in trouble?"

Luke shrugged. "I just put the milk back in the 'frigerator and then I look at Mom sleeping and then I go lie back down again."

I knew the feeling. When things are really hard sometimes, it just seems safer in bed.

"You could look at the clock. Maybe set the alarm. You could get up when it says eight-forty. You know how to tell time. I remember you knew on one of those tests."

"Don't have a clock," Luke mumbled.

Excuses. He'd never get anywhere till he got through with excuses. "Well, look at the clock in the kitchen."

Luke shook his head. "Don't have one."

Not an excuse. Another way of life. A home without a clock.

"We got a TV, though," Luke said. "They say what time it is sometimes."

181

★

At home I counted our clocks. The grandfather clock in the living room that I often forgot to wind. Two clocks in the kitchen, one on the wall and one on the back of the stove. Another, digital, clock in the bedroom radio, a travel alarm in my bureau. Five clocks, plus Cal's watch and two of mine. An embarrassment of clocks.

I took the travel alarm out of the drawer and wound the little key. It ticked cheerfully all night and its alarm buzzed beneath my pillow the next morning. I wrapped it in tissue paper and took it down to Luke.

He loved the clock. He set it on the table in front of us. "Does it really work? I mean keep going all night?"

"If you wind it," I said. "It's the right time now, but you'll have to remember to wind it every night. I forget sometimes to wind the ones at home."

"I won't forget," Luke promised.

I showed him the alarm and how it worked and how you could slide the case up so it covered the face of the clock altogether. Luke tried to put the clock in his back pocket, but then he couldn't sit down, so he just sat holding it against his stomach. He reminded me of the black Lab puppy we'd had once who huddled tight against the cushion under which we'd put an old alarm clock.

Out loud I said, "Okay. Now what are we going to do about the work?" Not the fires. Not yet.

"I'm too big to be in that class," Luke protested again. "The biggest kid, next to me, only comes to here." Luke put his hand just above his chin. "And she's a girl." Scorn filled his voice.

"Hey," I said. "There's nothing wrong with girls. I hear what you're saying, Luke, but that isn't going to get you out of second grade. The only thing that's going to get you to third is to prove you know all the second-grade work."

"Suppose I don't? Suppose I can't learn it?"

"That's foolish. Of course you can learn it. In fact, you already know a lot of what they're doing now."

"It's dumb anyway. It's dumb stuff."

I looked at Luke. "What do you like to do, anyway? You don't like to get up, you don't like school. What *do* you like?" I challenged him.

"Hunting. That's what I like. Deer hunting. I went with Dad once, I think I did, anyway. And once I went with Mr. Berkus. He lives behind us."

I wanted to cry. Deer hunting. If there was anything I hated, it was deer hunting. Now at our house in the country, the deer came to feed in the meadow, rooting under the apple tree. There was a fawn, tawny, the same color as the last leaves on the trees, quick, graceful, wary, jumping the stone fence, into the woods at the slightest sound. Fast. Faster than a thought could be spoken. How could anyone want to kill that swiftness?

"I'm maybe going to go hunting again this weekend."

Skip the lecture on hunting. "I don't think you ought to go anywhere until you're doing your work and getting to school on time."

Luke said nothing.

"Luke, you can't quit now. You know you can learn that stuff. Even by yourself you could learn it and I'll come down and help you. In fact, in a few weeks I'll be here every day. The only reason they didn't pass you to third grade was that they didn't think you could do third-grade work."

Luke thought about this. "Can you show me some sometime? Some third-grade work?"

"Sure. It's not that hard, you'll see. If you can do second, you can learn third easy." I opened the box and took out the mystery box of word chips. "Just run through these, Luke. Let's see how many first and beginning second-grade words you remember."

And of course, he knew every one.

After Luke and the other children had left, I copied down the names of each of Luke's books and got duplicates from the storeroom. I found out from Lisa what page they were on in reading, math, and spelling. I took the books to the music room so that if there was anything Luke didn't understand in class and didn't want to ask about in front of the other kids, he could show me and I could explain it to him in the music room. I had to be absolutely sure that Luke's first- and second-grade basic skills were solid enough not to crumble under the Child Study Team's testing at the end of the year. I was going to be sure they did test him. His knowledge must be so solidly built by learning and relearning that no amount of anxiety or apprehension could shake him.

★

My courses at college were a joke this semester. Although I was taking the same or more hours than ever before, the courses were almost all "method" courses — teaching this, teaching that — and yet I learned nothing about teaching. I was making a scrapbook for Education of the Mentally Retarded Trainable; I was learning to print in round fat letters in Language Arts, Special Ed; I was making a game to teach the concept of ones, tens, and hundreds in Teaching Elementary School Math; I was making a terrarium in Teaching Elementary School Science; I was listening to other seniors talk about student teaching in the seminar for Special Ed; and I was playing the piano by number in Methods and Materials for Teaching Music.

I practiced on the piano in the music room and Luke, at least, loved this part of my college course. Soon he memorized which keys were C D E F G A B and together we could play "Merrily We Roll Along," "London Bridge," and a snappy rendition of "Jingle Bells." For my final exam I was practicing a solo of "Aura Lee," complete with left-hand chords, followed by a seasonal "It Came upon A Midnight Clear." I was fairly confident about the piano, since the keys obligingly stayed in the same place; it was just like typing once you got everything memorized.

Not so the recorder. A recorder is a wooden instrument that looks like a short flute. By blowing down into it and covering different holes with different fingers, one was supposed to be able to produce a melody. I had taken my first recorder back to the music store, sure that it was defective. Only a shrill squeal came out. In disdainful tones, the clerk informed me it was not the recorder, it was me. My breath was not controlled. Each evening after dinner, I cut out pictures for my scrapbook and practiced my assigned song, "Twinkle, Twinkle, Little Star," on the recorder.

Cal thought I was making it all up. I concentrated on breath control.

★

Luke was up and out of his seat before I could even open the door to Lisa's classroom.

"Come on," he said. "I got something to show you." He almost ran to the music room.

"Mrs. Karras said I could put it in here." He opened the door to the music room and then quickly closed it behind us. He opened the door to the coat closet in the back, pulled a metal chair over to it, stood on the chair, and lifted down a long box from the shelf.

He put it on the table. "Go ahead, Mary. Open it. It's for you."

I stood in front of the table — we hadn't had time to sit down yet — and looked at the box. A florist's box. Long and thin. A memory of long-stemmed red roses stirred somewhere in my mind. Where would Luke have got flowers? I looked at him questioningly.

"Go ahead. Wait'll you see."

I pulled up the top of the box, expecting green waxed paper. Instead, there was aluminum foil.

"Open it, Mary. I got it for you my own self."

I separated the aluminum foil gently, carefully. There was an odd odor, and my fingers were sticky.

Hair. It felt like hair. An animal? I pulled the aluminum foil wide open and almost vomited.

A deer's leg. From the hoof to the first joint. Sticky with blood where it had been severed.

"Oh, Luke." I sat down.

Luke was dancing with excitement. "I killed it myself. Well, almost. Mr. Berkus hit it first, but he let me pull the trigger for the shot that really killed it. And then we put it on the car and brought it home and then we spent all day yesterday out in Mr. Berkus's garage cleaning it and cutting it up and Mrs. Costa's even got a freezer and we put it in there all wrapped up and we're going to eat it on Thanksgiving. Venison. That's what it's called. Not deer meat. Venison. It's very expensive. I'da brought you some, but Mom said it would spoil without 'frigeration, so I brought you the leg instead."

I had never heard Luke say so many words all at one time. I forced myself to rewrap the leg in aluminum foil. It would be better if I couldn't see it. "Thank you, Luke, for thinking about me." I put the top back on the box and swallowed, trying not to think about what was inside.

"Do you like it, Mary? Were you surprised?"

He was so excited. In his culture this was a coming of age. I couldn't take that away from him. "It must have been scary, Luke, shooting that gun all by yourself."

"You shoulda heard it. It was louder than any ole firecracker ever —"

He was off again, talking a mile a minute, describing each detail. I listened hard, because I knew Luke was teaching me something important that I must learn. To see things from his point of view. It would have been easy to misconstrue the deer leg. But Luke hadn't brought it in to scare or horrify me; he had brought it as a gift of friendship, like the clock I had given him. As I listened, another idea was beginning.

I couldn't replace Luke's world of violence, but perhaps I could give him a glimpse of a different kind of world.

"Will you be hunting every weekend now?" I asked.

Luke shook his head. "Not for a while. Mr. Berkus can't take me all the time. He's just like a neighbor, know what I mean?"

I nodded, my own excitement growing. "Would you have time then, some weekend, to come to the country with us, if your mom said it was okay?"

Maybe if he could see the deer in the meadow, maybe if he could see how beautiful they were and if he saw Cal watching them, just watching, without a gun — maybe it would make some difference in his life.

"I guess," Luke said, "if Mom said it was all right, I guess I could." He looked up at me, his small face round and open. "I could probably come this next weekend, if you want."

24

We picked Luke up at ten o'clock on Saturday morning. Cal waited in the car while I rang the doorbell of Luke's apartment.

Mrs. Brauer opened the door herself. She was dressed in a skirt and sweater, her hair curling around her face, and she looked so young that for a minute it seemed impossible that she was old enough to be Luke's mother.

But there was Luke, right beside her in his jeans and shirt and jacket, carrying a suitcase.

I smiled at him. "All set, Luke?"

He nodded without answering.

"Okay. Let's go then."

"Don't forget the present," Mrs. Brauer whispered to Luke. And he picked up a small rectangular box wrapped in flowered paper from the arm of the couch.

Cal was standing beside the car and I introduced him to Luke and Mrs. Brauer. He shook hands with Mrs. Brauer and took Luke's suitcase and box and put them beside ours in the back seat. Luke started to crawl in with the suitcases, but I touched his arm.

"Sit up front with us. There's lots of room."

Mrs. Brauer watched silently as Cal got in behind the wheel and Luke eased through my door to perch in the middle, on the edge of the seat.

I stayed outside next to Luke's mother. We hadn't been able to meet at the school yet, but we'd talked several times on the phone and I felt we knew each other a little better.

"Thank you for letting Luke come. We'll take good care of him."

"He's so excited," she whispered. "He didn't hardly sleep all last night. Was up before dawn packing his suitcase all over again." She shook her head. "I hope he's got everything he needs."

"I'm sure he does. Besides, there are extra sweaters and things at the house." I handed her a slip of paper. "Here's our phone number if you need us for anything, but don't worry if we don't answer right away. We may be outside, but we'll be back by suppertime. Would you like Luke home by any special time tomorrow?"

Mrs. Brauer shrugged. "Doesn't matter." Worry lined her face, making her old again. "I hope he minds his manners and doesn't be too much trouble."

I put my arm around her shoulders for a second. "He'll be fine. You try and catch up on a little rest now. Okay? We'll see you after supper tomorrow night."

I got in next to Luke and we both waved as Cal turned the car around. Mrs. Brauer waved back, calling to Luke, "You be good now, hear." We waved until the project was out of sight.

Luke sat tense and tight between us, his back straight, hands squeezed together in his lap.

Cal talked to me about small, unimportant things and then casually pointed out the barges in the Hudson as we crossed the bridge, then the ice-skating rink by the river, the license plate from Texas, small things that he thought might interest Luke. Gradually Luke's body relaxed. He leaned back against the seat and even let his shoulder brush my arm. I smiled across Luke's head at Cal.

Our house was two hours away. At the halfway mark stood the Red Rooster, a fast-food stand with picnic tables outside — hamburgers, hot dogs, milkshakes inside. It was more than a place to eat. It was a place to shake the city and suburbia off your feet and out of your mind. I had never known anyone to be unhappy at the Red Rooster, at least not driving up. Somehow we never stopped there on the way home.

Cal ordered a hot dog with sauerkraut and mustard; Luke and I had ours with relish. Cal and I shared a black and white milkshake. Luke drank a whole one on his own, down to the last drop.

Back on the road we all felt full and comfortable. Luke leaned against me and I told him stories of trips I had taken when I was little, how my dad made a real bed for us in the back seat, a mattress on top of suitcases, sheets and pillows on top of the mattress. Cal told about going to the world's fair in Chicago with his father. Luke loved every word.

We came to the covered bridge and Luke couldn't believe a bridge made of wood could be strong enough to hold a car. He held his breath until we were across. Just beyond the bridge Cal pointed out the stone painted to look like a frog that had been there for fifty years.

No sign of the city now. Only winding country roads, a few houses, mountains in the distance. And trees. Luke couldn't get over how many trees there were. Not just one mountain full of trees, like his outside of Falls City, but mile after mile of trees, thick and deep along the road. Most of the brilliant color was gone, only a few sturdy brown November leaves still clung to the branches, but the age-old trunks stood weathered and strong.

We turned into our dirt road and Cal said to Luke, "See if you can see the roof of our house. What color do you think it is?"

Luke leaned across me to see out my side window and I could feel quivers of excitement running through him.

190

"I see it!" he shouted. "No, I guess not." His voice sank.
"What color?" Cal asked.

"Green. Light green," Luke said softly. "But it couldn't
of been."

"You're exactly right. It's a copper roof, and it's fifty
years old now and that's the color copper gets when it's
old. Well, here we are."

We parked in the turn-around one hundred feet from
the house. All of a sudden, for no apparent reason, Luke
began to run, down the path toward the house, back out to
the dirt driveway, out to the dirt road, back in again, passing me on the path, not saying anything, just running. He
ran with his arms straight out to the side, stretched wide,
wheeling like a glider turning in the autumn sky. It almost
seemed that in another second Luke would fly.

Cal and I carried in the suitcases and paper bags of food,
doing ritual things, unlocking doors, turning on the water,
putting things in the refrigerator, carrying in wood to pile
beside the big stone fireplace at the end wall of the living
room.

Suddenly I realized Luke was standing absolutely still in
the middle of the living room. He looked so small, the
high rough wood ceiling rising thirty feet above his head.

"You okay, Luke?" I asked, setting down the log,
straightening.

Luke nodded and came over to where I was standing
beside the fireplace. A rush of thoughts. Had Luke ever
seen a fireplace before? Not at the project. At his father's
place in New York? His grandmother's? Well, surely on
television. Did it make him think of fires? The ones he'd
set. Why he did it? We had never really talked about the
fires. I sat down on the low bench in front of the fireplace
and pulled Luke close. "I'm so glad you're here."

Cal appeared suddenly with a last armful of logs. I had

191

told Cal about Luke and the fires and the deer leg. Now he knelt before the fireplace and began to lay the fire and then stopped and turned to Luke.

"Would you like to light some matches before I get the fire going?"

Luke nodded solemnly, his eyes round. Cal handed Luke a box of wooden matches and showed him how to strike a match against the rough side of the box.

Luke lit a match and threw it in the fireplace, and then another and another and another.

I looked at Cal questioningly.

"Good." Cal spoke to Luke, not me. "Light as many as you want. That's the right place for fires."

There were two hundred matches in the box. Luke lit every one, putting each match carefully in the fireplace.

There wasn't any need for talk.

★

Nan, my daughter, arrived a little before three o'clock, driving down from college in Boston. She was a senior now herself. We were both special education majors and there were always a hundred things to talk about, compare. There was never enough time for all we had to say. Luke immediately recognized Nan as a friend and trotted beside her, helping carry things in from her car.

Within another half hour, Mark, Cal's youngest son, arrived with two high school friends and they all went off together to the small store in the village to buy more food. They took Luke with them without question, and later, with the afternoon light almost gone, I looked out of the kitchen window to see Luke riding high on Mark's shoulders as they came up the path to the house, the others carrying the bags of groceries.

Everybody helped with supper, spaghetti and salad and

192

french bread. Everybody getting in everybody else's way; there wasn't enough room in our little kitchen. I ordered everybody out; nobody went. I gave in to bedlam, confusion, and laughter.

After dinner we went back to the living room and built the fire high again. Luke sat close beside the flames, adding small sticks from time to time. The rest of us talked about soccer and exams and the news from the rest of the family. Nan and I huddled for a while to compare education notes and commiserate over method courses, and count the days of school that were left. We would both graduate in June. I was only twenty-two years behind. Never mind. It's almost done.

Somehow we got involved in a game of Fictionary — Nan and Luke and I on one team, Mark and his friends on another. Cal read out unknown words from the dictionary and we made up definitions.

Luke loved this game and whispered ideas to me, one after the other, while a small mouse ran up and down the stone wall above the fireplace.

At nine o'clock I took Luke's hand and we went back to his room. We opened his suitcase and he took out his pajamas and toothbrush while I turned down his bed. He undressed quickly, his back toward me, and I walked to the doorway to give him more privacy.

"Listen, Luke," I said. "Go get washed and brushed and then I'll read you a story before you go to sleep."

While he was in the bathroom I thought about how strange this must all seem to him. Was it scary to sleep alone in a big bed in a strange house?

Luke reassured me when he came back. He stood on the bed and traced the carved birds and grapes that made up the wooden headboard that was twice as tall as he was. He bounced gently up and down while his fingers examined the wood and there was nothing frightened about him. I remembered the nights he had spent watching over his father on the mountain. He'd been a lot more alone than this.

Suddenly Luke stopped his gentle bouncing on the bed. "Oh, oh, Mary," he said. "I forgot the present."

He brought me the flowered box and I opened it as he watched.

"Whitman's Sampler. My favorite, Luke. My father used to buy candy just like this on Valentine's Day. Thank you."

"You're welcome," Luke answered seriously, remembering to "mind his manners."

"Why don't you take it out to the living room to offer everyone a piece? Yourself too, except then you'll have to brush again."

I watched Luke from the hall, feeling a wave of love for my family as they praised him and patted him and kissed him good night without conscious thought, barely interrupting their conversation.

When we'd finished reading, I tucked the covers around Luke and kissed him myself.

"Do you think we'll see the deer tomorrow?" Luke asked. "We looked all over this afternoon, but we didn't see 'em."

"Maybe. Early in the morning is best. When you first wake up, look out this front window. That's where I usually see them, down under the apple tree in the middle of the meadow.

"Good night, Luke. Sleep well. I'll leave your door open. Cal and I will be coming to bed in a few minutes. Call if you want anything."

But we slept soundly all night long and the sun was shining on the tops of the mountains when I woke and turned and saw Luke standing in our doorway.

194

"Hey, Luke. Good morning." Then remembering the deer, I lowered my voice to a whisper. "Did you see the deer?" I asked.

Luke shook his head. "Not one."

"Well, come get into bed here. Your feet will freeze on those stone floors."

Luke climbed up over the footboard and I tucked him in between us, snug and warm.

Pancakes for breakfast, then Nan and Luke went out to look for deer. They saw a raccoon with only three feet, two spiders, one with a perfect web, and a snake, but no deer.

In the afternoon we went down to the lake and took turns playing tennis and fishing off the end of the dock. Nobody caught anything and most of the bounce had died in our summer tennis balls; but nobody minded. We weren't down there to win prizes.

Every once in a while I would realize Luke was gone and then suddenly he would come running down the road or up from the beach, in what I had come to think of as Luke's happiness run, wheeling, turning, happiness almost lifting him off the ground.

The hours ran out too soon. Everybody packing up, heading back to school and college, remembering suddenly all the undone homework, reports not written, books not read, the real world of Monday coming close. We hugged each other, kissing quickly, promising to call, to write, to see each other soon. Luke stood by the fireplace watching us.

After Nan and Mark left, we packed our own things, checked the fire, turned off the water. I looked for Luke and found him out on the stone wall in front of the house, alone.

"I think maybe I saw one, Mary. Look. See that deer?"

I peered into the dusky meadow, looking hard, wishing a deer into existence, but nothing moved.

"Time to go, Luke," I said as gently as I could. "Are you all packed?"

We rode silently for the first hour and a half, Luke sound asleep against my shoulder. Then a traffic jam and honking horns woke him. He rubbed his eyes and looked at me in the half light of the other headlights.

"I was dreaming about the deer. Like the one I saw in the meadow. Remember that one?"

"I remember the tracks we saw," I said, knowing how badly he had wanted to see it — how much I had wanted it, too. Now he was putting the deer there the only way he knew. "So anyway, we know the deer are there, and I remember you saw a mouse and a snake and a raccoon —"

"With only three feet, but he could still walk okay, and a spiderweb."

"Yes," I said, "and a fish. You saw a lot."

"At least six things. I'm gonna tell Frank tomorrow. Maybe tonight even."

Luke's voice faded and he was back asleep. Was he dreaming once again of the deer he hadn't seen? Or perhaps he had. Who could know for sure?

Well, my plan hadn't worked out. My hopes of having Luke see deer in another light, to understand that they were meant for more than killing, had flopped. I sighed, adjusted Luke's body so that I could lean against the window and then I, too, slept and dreamed of deer and boys and birds against the sky.

"We're here." Cal's voice woke me and I felt Luke squirm awake.

"Hey, sleepyheads, wake up. We're back in Falls City."

Luke stretched and sat up and I blinked my eyes to get them open. The light went on over Luke's front door and then his mother stepped into the light, peering out toward the car.

I rolled down the window.

"Hello. We're back," I called redundantly. "Luke was terrific."

Luke said, "I'm gonna tell Frank I saw a spiderweb and a raccoon with three feet and a mouse and a snake and deer tracks — and a deer. Right, Mary?"

"Right. You tell him what you saw."

"And I'm gonna tell about the fireplace and how you can light a hundred matches there, more'n a hundred and not hurt nuthin'. Right, Mary?"

"Right, Luke."

And then without thinking, Luke gave me and Cal too, a quick hug, casually, easily, as he had seen the other older children do.

Cal carried Luke's suitcase to the door while Luke ran ahead and I sat thinking how maybe Luke had learned even more than I had planned.

Mrs. Brauer had her uniform on under her coat. A black blouse, a short black skirt and a white frilly apron. She glanced nervously at the clock on the wall above the counter of the diner.

"I gotta be there by five sharp," she said, "or Joe has a fit. But I had to talk to you. Thanks for meeting me. I didn't want to come to school like this." She glanced down.

I nodded. "This is fine." I would have met her anywhere she suggested. I was so glad she'd called.

"Not that there's anything wrong with Joe's place. I don't mean that. I wouldn't work there if there was any

197

funny stuff going on, know what I mean, but still, you know how those teachers talk. I didn't want them gettin' wrong ideas."

Again I nodded, waiting. I had lots to say myself, but I wanted to hear her first.

Her coffee sat untouched in front of her and now she pushed it to one side.

"Luke liked being at your place last weekend. It's all he talks about now. Anyway, I figure that you had a real good chance to look at him and the thing I gotta know is, is Luke gonna be all right?

"See, Chuck, he's a friend of the family like a cousin sort of, stays at the house some. Chuck says Luke's like his father. Bad blood. Sick. Maybe even sick in the head. Chuck says maybe Luke'd be better off living with his father."

"I thought Luke's father was in the hospital," I said, trying to keep my voice even, friendly, not wanting to frighten her away.

"Well, in and out. Who knows? But he's got an apartment in the city and a wife with three kids. Seems to have plenty to spend on them, so Chuck says why not send Luke in there. That way he, Luke's father, will have to spend on Luke, too. Only way any of us will ever see a cent."

"Do you want Luke to go?"

This was what I had to know. I could understand the bitterness. I could even understand Chuck's wanting to get rid of Luke, there must be some jealousy and also it would be easier economically. But what about Luke? How would he fare with a stepmother who had sent him back to his grandmother's when his father went in the hospital this past summer? It didn't sound as if she'd been too eager to have him around then. There was no reason to think she'd changed. But how did Luke's mother feel? Did she love him? That was what I had to know.

I looked at her carefully. Tears were clinging to the black beads of mascara on her lower lashes.

She shook her head. "I just want him to stay with us. He was the first, you know. The first baby. He was so fat and cute, you wouldn't believe. And good too. Even Grandma said he was the best baby she'd ever seen. Never cried. Always did just what we said."

Mrs. Brauer touched her lower lashes with a paper napkin, blotting up the tears, careful not to smear the mascara. "I don't know what went wrong. Everything fell apart all at the same time. Frank and Alice came too fast, I guess, and I got sick and then Luke's father had some habits like — well, they got worse, and we split up and then the next thing I know the school is calling me about Luke — then the police are calling. I don't know. I don't understand it." Mrs. Brauer's voice quavered and she stopped to clear her throat. "You know what the police said? They said he was the rottenest kid in the neighborhood."

"Forget that," I said. "Luke isn't rotten. He's good and he's smart. He was just scared and angry and he didn't know how to tell anybody so he set some fires instead. But he needs you, Mrs. Brauer, Luke needs you more than anything in this world."

"Me?" She glanced down at herself again. "Why would anybody need me?"

I smiled at her. "Easy. Because you're his mother. You know more about him than anybody else. You've known him for, what — eight years?" I stopped, shocked, realizing I didn't know exactly how old Luke was. "See, I don't even know when his birthday is. But you do."

"May thirtieth."

I nodded. "And you remember what he looked like when he was born and when he first walked and what he said when he began to talk. Nobody knows all those things but you."

I had Mrs. Brauer's complete attention now. I hurried on.

"And you remember how he used to help with Frank and Alice when you were sick, do some cooking —"

"He did all the shopping, too," Mrs. Brauer said with pride. "I'd give him a purse with a little money and he'd get the things I told him. He always brought the money back if there was any left. He even got so he knew what things cost!"

"Yes. I'm sure he did. Luke's plenty smart enough, Mrs. Brauer."

"Then how come he got left back?"

Her voice sounded like Luke's now. It almost made me smile to hear how much alike they sounded.

"I don't understand it all," I said. "Maybe he didn't do as well on tests as he should have. Maybe he'd missed a lot of school over the years. Maybe he set fires because he was feeling mad and sad about a lot of things, your being sick, his dad leaving, Maybe he even felt like there was more to do than he could handle."

"I know that feeling for sure," Mrs. Brauer muttered under her breath.

"And so maybe he wanted to get back at the world a little, or maybe he just wanted to get away by himself sometimes. Anyway, I think he was thinking about a lot of other things instead of school work. And then when he came back this fall and found he'd been left back, it was too much and he forgot all the progress he'd made. But look, he's starting again. It will take awhile to come back, but at least he's starting."

"Maybe," she said. "Maybe so." Her eyes flicked toward the clock. "Listen, I gotta go in a minute. I mean if you're late, Joe is on your back the whole night and I sure don't need that. But just tell me this. What's going to happen now? Chuck says maybe he'll never get out of second grade. Maybe that's as far as he can go."

"Luke can get out of second, third, fourth, and fifth and sixth. Luke can graduate from high school and get a job and help you, and Chuck too, if he's around, to pay the bills. At least until he has his own family."

Mrs. Brauer was obviously taken back by the idea of a Luke that large. I took advantage of her silence and the extra minute it gave me.

"I can help him with his school work; I'm going to be at the school every day after Christmas. And I can show you how to help him, too. But I'm just a teacher, and there are hundreds of teachers in the world. But you're his mom. You're the only mother he's got. He needs you to love him, Mrs. Brauer."

"I do love him. I always have. It's just — hard. I mean, it's really hard now."

"I know. It's hard for Luke, too. And Chuck. But tell Luke you love him. Tell Chuck how much you love Luke and that you hope Chuck'll get to like him, too. But in any case, your apartment is Luke's home. It always has been and it always will be. Tell Chuck to give us till June. If you and Luke and I all work hard, as hard as we can, I bet by June Chuck is going to be proud of Luke."

★

I ordered another cup of coffee after Mrs. Brauer left. I hesitated between the pink packet of artificial sweetener and the white one of sugar. Cancer or diabetes? The world was full of wonderful choices.

I sat alone at the booth thinking about my talk with Mrs. Brauer. "Just give us till June. Chuck is going to be proud of Luke." I shook my head. Maybe if I don't graduate I can get a job giving pep talks to parents, or maybe the football coaches could use me during halftime. "Come on, team, you can do it."

What was I doing raising her hopes? And over and above that, suggesting that she stand up to Chuck and tell him she wanted Luke to stay with them?

How did I dare? What did I know? I sighed and stirred my lethal coffee. Maybe Luke wouldn't be able to satisfy the Child Study Team's requirements for third grade. Maybe they'd keep him back again or put him in a special class. Maybe Chuck would leave and they'd be worse off and Mrs. Brauer would blame me. Maybe I wouldn't be able to tootle "Twinkle, Twinkle, Little Star" on my recorder with a classroom of twenty-year-old kids staring at me. Maybe I wouldn't pass my exam.

I could use a pep talk myself.

Exams. Exams were less than a month away, before Christmas vacation. I'd been cutting a few classes and I sure hadn't contributed anything during class. But I had completed my assignments and nobody but Mrs. Karras had commented on my absences. Not even the week that I had spent with my father after my mother's death.

A familiar sense of loss ran through me and I put down my coffee cup and got out a pencil and a piece of paper. Lists helped. I'd make a list.

I was used to missing my mother now. I realized that it was something that would be a part of me for a long time. The thing was to keep it in proportion. My father seemed to be all right. He often drove to our house in the country on weekends and sometimes, if he had been visiting my mother's grave, he would show up at the apartment and stay for dinner. In any event, he would be with us for Christmas.

★

I drank my coffee and listed my courses on the piece of paper, the number of classes left for each, reports and projects due. If I alternated cutting, missed different classes rather than the same ones, and if Luke, and Lisa too, could tolerate my coming down at different hours on different days, I could get down to School 23 three times a week and work with Luke for forty minutes each time. If I could get Luke and his mother to agree to fifteen to twenty minutes of practice each night, I was sure Luke could be at least at mid-to late-second-grade level by January. After all, he'd been there the year before. I'd just have to plan his work carefully.

So much for Luke's classes.

So much for mine.

Enough of both for now.

I paid for the coffee and raced home.

"Look, Luke. Try this. A whole row of hills and valleys." I handed him the Magic Marker.

Luke bent his head over the paper and concentrated on hills and valleys.

We were working hard on academics now, and besides reviewing first- and second-grade work, I had decided to teach him third-grade script, or cursive writing, as it was called at School 23. I'd discussed it with both Lisa and Mrs. Karras, explaining that Luke's math was in good shape. He knew his addition and subtraction facts through twenty; he could add two columns, carrying the ones to the tens; he could subtract. He understood time and money. His reading was not as good, but he was working in a second-grade reader and his silent comprehension was fine. It was just difficult for him to read out loud. He omitted some words and put in others of his own. He also had a lot of trouble with phonics. He couldn't hear the subtle differences between the short vowels, and consequently the instruction to "sound it out" remained a mystery to him.

We worked on math and reading and written expression every day. Luke still dictated stories to me, but now he copied them himself and drew illustrations into a book that I had made for him. He loved doing this and his "eye-hand coordination" (a college term for the ability to move the hand and eye together smoothly) was so good that it seemed to me that it should be easy for him to learn to write rather than print, particularly if I could demonstrate it clearly.

The big advantage to cursive writing over printing, as far as Luke was concerned, was that it wasn't taught until third grade and if Luke learned to do this before anyone else in his class, it might raise his opinion of himself.

Luke finished his line of hills and valleys. "Okay," I said. "Now watch this. One hill, one valley. Right? Now watch what happens when I put a line through it — x."

"An x," Luke shouted. "You just made an x. Here, let me try."

"Pretty sharp," I said. "How about this one? It's a little harder. A hill, a valley and a loopy tail. Down and back up again — y. You can check the letters on the strip if you want."

I had found a small teachers' supply house in Falls City and had bought adhesive strips showing the alphabet in both block print and cursive. Luke had both strips fastened to a board that we laid out on the long table in the music room.

"I don't need to. That's a *y*. See." Luke wrote it quickly. "Show me more."

"All right. Can you make waves like this?" _ccccc_ "Another whole line? Okay. That's fine. Do one wave and you have a *c,* close it up and you have an *a.*"

Luke made hills and valleys and *a*'s and *c*'s and *x*'s and *y*'s on his paper and then, not able to resist, on the blackboard as well.

"Tell Mr. Foley to leave it there, all right? You write right beside it. DO NOT WASH. That's what Miss Eckhardt does. See, I'm maybe gonna show it to her. All right?"

"Yes, Luke. That's a good idea. Here's your notebook with your work for home. Four math problems, two stories in *Getting the Main Idea,* and your handwriting page. How's that?"

Luke nodded. "Okay. Boy, wait'll I show Frank I know how to write. I mean really write."

Our plan for Luke was going well. I met with both Lisa and Mrs. Brauer at the end of each week, reviewed what we'd each done, and planned for the next week.

In Lisa's class Luke was doing the work and handing it in. He still had no friends and rarely spoke, but Lisa was pleased and said so to Mrs. Brauer. "I've got him in my top math group now. Would you believe that?"

Lisa and I planned Luke's work together, deciding what he should do in class, what he should do in his sessions with me. Neither of us could figure out why Luke had made such a bad impression on the Child Study Team at the end of last year. The only possibilities were that they had tested him after school or on a Saturday and Luke had been nervous and anxious and his basic knowledge had been too shaky to stand up under the pressure of testing, or else they had not tested him at all and just gone by old reports.

I prepared his homework and the tasks I sent home with Luke were ones that I was sure he could do well. He could use the practice and just as important, he needed to look good in front of his family.

Mrs. Brauer was doing her share, too. She didn't leave for work until five so she made it a point to have some milk or juice ready for Luke when he got home from school and then sit with him for fifteen minutes while he showed her what he could do. She didn't attempt to teach or explain. If Luke got mixed up they just skipped it and Luke brought it back to me. Mrs. Brauer was amazed at how much Luke knew. She didn't have to try to praise him to make him feel good. Her honest surprise delighted Luke and prompted him to learn even more.

My three sessions a week with Luke were divided between academic skills and something nameless. Academically, I tried to give him as many successes as possible, gradually shoring up his weaknesses. Once again, I learned more from Luke than from my courses. What he taught me all over again was to teach to his strength first, remediate his weakness later — ninety percent to the strength, ten percent to the weakness in the beginning. Which was why I was concentrating on increasing his sight vocabulary, giving him massive doses of sight words each day. He could remember what he saw. We worked only a little on vowel sounds and word analysis skills. It was also why we ended each session with a few math problems. He always walked out feeling good.

The something nameless? I don't know. I couldn't call it

therapy. I didn't even have a bachelor's degree in anything. And yet, I knew that Luke had to have a place where he could talk about what he was feeling. He couldn't do it in class or at home, so I tried to make room for this during our time together. I knew it wasn't enough, fifteen minutes, maybe, out of the forty, three times a week. But I had already learned that there was never enough time.

I still asked Luke about the best thing and the worst thing at the beginning of each lesson. This often triggered a thought and because Luke trusted me, he was very honest. His best things now were mainly his school work, sometimes a trip with the neighbors, once a shopping trip with his mom to get new sneakers. His worst things were abundant — the shrimpy babies that made up second grade and the embarrassment of being seen with them; the spankings he got; sometimes no dinner; Wendell's taunts; nightmares; his mixed feelings toward Uncle Chuck. Sometimes Luke would get down the ancient family of dolls that had been part of my teaching equipment for years and ask me to play the part of his mother or Chuck or Mrs. Karras, while Luke played himself or sometimes his mother or brother.

Did it help? Who could say? Nobody knew we even did it. I just crossed my fingers and added up each day that he came to school and each day without phone calls from the police.

★

Luke was doing better, but my own life was not so peachy. Exams in Education of the Mentally Retarded Trainable, Language Arts, Teaching Elementary School Math, Teaching Elementary School Science, Methods and Materials for Teaching Music were scheduled for next week. The only exception was the seminar in Special Education. There I was supposed to write a report on what I'd learned in student teaching. My student teaching was scheduled for the next semester, but I'd written most of the report anyway. Mrs. Karras said she'd sign it. They'd probably never notice.

But I was worried about the others and was up at five each morning rereading text books. What did I know about teaching elementary science? Our professor was a nice elderly man who showed us films each day. I'd learned how to build a terrarium, but suppose he asked about electricity or earth science on the exam? And it was almost as bad in all the other subjects. What I'd actually learned about teaching reading and math and language arts, I had learned from teaching Luke — and the children I had known before him.

Besides my own worries about exams, I was very discouraged about the education young teachers were getting and it was not until later in graduate courses (still at Union State) that I experienced the pleasure and excitement I had always associated with learning. Someday, some way, I vowed to do something about the education of teachers-to-be.

What's more, Cal was obviously getting tired of my short-order cooking and the mention of roast lamb or hollandaise sauce crept increasingly into his conversation. Once when he asked if I planned to do a wash that day, I snapped that he went by the laundry room as often as I did — and then I burst into tears.

And there were the children, our own ever-present children. Seven was a bigger number than I'd realized. Now there were comments about a lack of letters and cards. To compensate, I called as often as I could and told them all not to worry about calling collect if they needed us. Our phone bill skyrocketed. Once again I wondered if I would really make it through to the end. And if I did, if our family would still be intact.

★

My last exam was Methods and Materials for Teaching Music. I had practiced and practiced "Aura Lee" and "It Came upon a Midnight Clear" both at School 23 and also on the Sunday school piano on weekends after church was over. I played "Twinkle, Twinkle, Little Star" on the recorder every night ten times, in the bathroom with the water running. I didn't think Cal needed that on top of everything else. I knew exactly which fingers to put where, but sometimes, for seemingly no reason, a shrill squeal came out instead of the correct note. I would just have to hope, and as the music clerk said, control my breath.

There were eighteen of us in music class. We performed our solos in alphabetical order as Mrs. Oliphant called off our names. The kids were as nervous as I was and I'm sure it was just as hard for some of them.

Lewis, the boy ahead of me, got up from the piano after playing "When the Saints Come Marching In" with left-hand chords and took a handkerchief out of the back pocket of his jeans and wiped the sweat from his forehead.

"That was very good, Lewis." Lewis nodded his thanks. He was big and black and a guard on our winning football team. He wanted to be a high school coach; it seemed unlikely to me that he would ever need to play the recorder. Not so to Mrs. Oliphant. "Let's see now, Lewis, you were assigned 'Twinkle, Twinkle, Little Star' on the recorder. Class! Shhh!" Mrs. Oliphant tapped her pencil on the side of the piano. "We need quiet so we can hear Lewis properly." Sweat covered Lewis's brow again, but both hands were on the recorder and he could not wipe.

Someone giggled and again Mrs. Oliphant tapped the piano. The room was still. "You may begin now, Lewis."

All of a sudden I realized Lewis was playing my song. He couldn't do that! "Twinkle, Twinkle, Little Star" had been assigned to me! That was the one I'd practiced. I started to raise my hand, then thought better of it. My whole upper body was as damp as Lewis's forehead. Lewis played through to the end without a mistake. His version sounded much better than mine ever had.

"Thank you, Lewis. You may sit down. Let's see now. MacCracken. Uh, yes. Are you ready, Ms. MacCracken?" Mrs. Oliphant called everyone else by their first name — me she called Ms.

I nodded and went up to the piano and played "Aura Lee" without a hitch. I missed two notes in "Midnight Clear," but managed to keep going and Mrs. Oliphant did not comment.

I stood beside the piano, holding my recorder and my breath. Maybe both Lewis and I had been assigned "Twinkle."

Mrs. Oliphant studied her list. "Your assignment for the recorder was 'A Tisket, A Tasket,' Ms. MacCracken. Are you ready now?"

"Excuse me, Mrs. Oliphant. My assignment sheet says 'Twinkle, Twinkle, Little Star.' " I could not believe I was having this conversation.

"Well, mine says 'A Tisket, A Tasket,' Ms. MacCracken."

"I have practiced 'Twinkle,' Mrs. Oliphant."

"Do you have your assignment sheet with you, Ms. Mac-Cracken?"

"I believe so, Mrs. Oliphant."

"Then get it. Immediately."

I went back to my seat and rummaged through the pile of books beside my chair until I found my zippered notebook. I opened to the section marked "Music" and there in the slotted pocket was the assignment sheet. It said: "Final Examination: piano — two solo renditions of your choice from *Musicale*. Recorder — one solo rendition of 'Twinkle, Twinkle, Little Star.' "

Thank God.

I handed the sheet to Mrs. Oliphant.

She read it and then handed it back. "You are correct, Ms. MacCracken. Proceed."

I finished the first bar and started on the second. My breath must have become uncontrolled because the note slid away into shrillness. I tried several times to get it back, but no luck. Coughs and giggles filled the room.

"All right, Ms. MacCracken. You may sit down."

I looked at Mrs. Oliphant desperately. I could not fail Methods and Materials for Teaching Music. Without it, I couldn't graduate or get certification. I took a deep breath.

"I would like to try it one more time," I said.

Mrs. Oliphant looked at me steadily.

"All right. Permission granted," she said. I never understood whether she imagined herself in kindergarten or the army.

I blew out and then raised the recorder to my lips and began again, remembering to blow down over my lower lip rather than directly into the hole. I closed my eyes; blocked out Mrs. Oliphant and Lewis and the other sixteen kids.

I played it straight through without a mistake.

The class clapped when I finished and I smiled my thanks, but never, ever will I sing or play that song again.

★

My father was supposed to arrive on the morning of Christmas Eve, but somehow he got confused and arrived two days early. Nan was home from college and was making his Christmas present, a felt banner, on the floor of the living room when he rang the doorbell.

We had decided to stay at the apartment for the holidays because many of our children were flying in and then out at odd hours of day and night and from the apartment we could get to all three airports, Newark, La Guardia, and Kennedy. There was no airfield near our house in the country.

It was a crowded, confusing time. Happiness and sorrow mixed together. Sue was there and Nan and Steve and his wife, Margie, and Cal's Karen and Mark. Michael and his family were in California, Joan was in medical school in Colorado.

We put up the tree on Christmas Eve afternoon and it looked beautiful against the glass doors to the terrace, the New York skyline a perfect backdrop. Silently, I wondered if anyone else could hear my mother's voice saying as she did each year, "You know, I think it's the prettiest tree we've ever had."

27

January 5. The first day of the last term of my senior year! My marks had come over vacation and I'd passed everything with respectable grades, even music. My undergraduate days were almost over. I was going to make it! Come June, I'd be a certified teacher.

I stopped by Professor Foster's office for a final briefing on student teaching. He went over the various reports that Mrs. Karras and I were required to write and said that he'd be down from college once or twice.

"You understand, Mary, that your student teaching experience will be for twelve weeks rather than the usual six."

I nodded. "Yes, I know. It's because I'll only be at School Twenty-three in the mornings so that I can take History, School in Contemporary American Society, and Philosophy of Education in the afternoon."

"That's right. Usually our seniors have finished all their three-credit courses by spring term so that they only have a seminar or two to go along with their student teaching. Of course, they also spend a good bit of time interviewing.

"Which brings us to your plans for next year. Do you know what you're going to do?"

"Teach," I said, smiling at him. "That's why I'm here."

"We'll need to get you lined up for campus interviews then. Also you should complete your resumé and bring it in for me to go over. I guess that's it for now. Good luck at Twenty-three."

★

Mrs. Karras was waiting for me by the front door when I arrived at nine o'clock.

"Ah. Good, Mary. I was worried you weren't coming."

I smiled at her. "Not a chance." But I heard what she was saying and resolved to get there earlier the next day.

I followed her into the music room and she spread a sheet of paper in front of me.

Student	Grade	Teacher	Time Slot
Louisa	1	Parnell	9:00–9:40
Luke	2	Eckhardt	9:45–10:25
Bobby	3	Novak	10:30–11:10
Maureen	2	Bianca	11:15–11:35
Harold	5	Kraus	1:00–1:40

I studied the list. "It's fine. Except for Harold. I have to be back at college for a one o'clock History course. Professor Foster arranged it so I'll student teach mornings for twelve weeks instead of six and take the last required courses in the afternoon. I'm sorry. I assumed he'd checked it out with you."

Mrs. Karras nodded. "I guess I knew that. I guess I was just hoping. Harold needs help so badly. Now, shall we get the children?"

I looked at her. "I don't know them."

"I know, Mary," she said. "Before, for the mental health project, the psychologist tested the children and there was a file of sorts for each one. Well, there's no time or money for that now. Besides, there's no better way to get to know them than to see them. And I'd be interested in hearing what you think about each one, without having read anybody else's opinion."

Mrs. Karras brought Louisa to the music room, introduced us, and left. Louisa had glossy dark brown skin, round cheeks, and four or five pigtails that stuck out all over her head in different directions. She wore a bright pink dress and looked like some kind of ice cream sundae. What could be the matter with Louisa?

"Louisa," I said. "Let me help you wriggle up here onto this chair. It's kind of big."

Louisa's feet swung back and forth six inches off the floor. I'd have to see about getting some smaller furniture.

"Louisa, can you tell me your last name?"

"Uh-huh. Hit Louisa Mae."

Hit Louisa Mae? Who would hit her? Then I realized what she was saying. I was going to have to listen carefully.

"Louisa Mae what?" I asked gently.

"That hit. Louisa Mae."

"Do you know where you live?"

"Falls City."

"Good, Louisa. Should I call you Louisa or Louisa Mae?"

"Louisa Mae. That my name. Nobody call hit right."

"Do you know what street you live on?"

Silence.

"How about your telephone number? Do you know that?"

"Hain't got no tefone."

"Do you know your daddy's name?"

"Hain't got no daddy, neither."

These questions were for the birds. At least they weren't for Louisa Mae. I put my pad and pencil down and went and got some crayons and unlined paper.

"Louisa Mae, let's pretend we've got a million dollars."

"Hoowee." Louisa Mae's eyes were round as silver dollars themselves.

"You can buy anything you want. Draw me a picture of what you'll buy."

Louisa Mae knelt on the chair and drew a large round circle and then a smaller one and then put her pencil down and looked at the ceiling. I was beginning to realize she never looked directly at me. Always a little to the side.

I waited. She continued to look at the ceiling. Finally, she looked back at the paper. "That hit," she said.

"Okay. Can you tell me about it?"

"Hit Baby Hug Me. Seen hit on TV. Kin I go?"

"In just a minute, okay? Draw me one more picture first. Draw me a picture of your best, best friend."

Another circle. Two lines. A smaller circle between the lines. Down went the crayon. Eyes to the ceiling.

Again I waited.

Slam! Louisa Mae hit the table with her hand. "That hit! I mean hit!"

"Okay. Fine. Just tell me who it is."

"That Clara. That her legs and that her pee-pee 'tween um."

"Okay. I see. Thank you, Louisa Mae. I'll walk back to class with you now."

Maybe Clara was a boy or a hermaphrodite, I thought as I walked beside Louisa Mae. Or maybe she meant Clarence.

★

Luke was sitting in the music room waiting for me when I got back from Louisa Mae's classroom. I was not proud of my first interview. Oh, well, at least I'd see her again tomorrow and the next day and the next. I loved the fact that we had so much time.

"You're late," Luke said, eyes on the clock.

"I'm sorry." I smiled at him. "How are you? Did you have a good Christmas?"

"Yeah. Okay. It was a long time ago. How come you're here in the morning? How long've you been here anyway?" Luke looked at me suspiciously.

"Since nine. Remember, I told you that I'd be here every day after Christmas. Well, here I am." I pulled Mrs. Karras's sheet of paper over in front of me. "And I'm going to work with you every day, every school day from nine-forty-five to ten-twenty-five. See?" I pointed to the time written by his name on the paper.

Luke studied it. "Nine-forty-five to ten-twenty-five. Forty-five. Fifty. Ten o'clock. Five, ten, fifteen, twenty, twenty-five." Luke counted on his fingers. "That's not as long as before," he said.

"No. Not quite. But it's every day. That's five times instead of three." I paused. It was not like Luke to be cranky. "Is anything the matter?" I asked.

216

"Nope."

"Okay, then do you have a best or a worst thing?" I got down the plastic dishpan with his name on it that had replaced the worn carton. I took out his notebook. The last entry was for the day before Christmas vacation. I had not made a plan for today, it had seemed too far off. We'd just have to make it up as we went along.

Luke was still staring at the sheet of paper Mrs. Karras had given me. "Who's Louisa?"

"A little girl from first grade. I don't know her last name."

"Oh, I know her. Louisa Mae West. She lives in the cellar of the house across the street from the project."

"In the cellar?" I couldn't help myself.

"Yup. Her grandma and uncles live upstairs."

"Oh. Well, never mind Louisa Mae. Tell me about you. Your best and worst."

Luke was not to be diverted. "Who's Bobby?"

"Luke," I said. "We talked about this before Christmas. Remember? I explained about student teaching, how everybody that wants to be a teacher has to do it and that I was lucky because my student teaching was going to be here at Twenty-three. Usually you do student teaching in a classroom, but instead I'm going to work here in the music room with four children, and you're one of the four."

"Who're the others?"

I read from the sheet: "Louisa, Bobby, Maureen."

"Maureen Barber? She's the biggest baby."

"I don't know her last name. Mrs. Karras forgot to write it down, but I'll let you know. And maybe later there will be a Harold somebody." I figured I'd better tell him about all of them at the beginning.

Luke flicked his thumbnail against the green plastic dishpan. "How come you gotta see so many kids?"

"That's the only way it will count for student teaching."
I tried to think while I talked. Luke's jealous. Finally I
understood. I should have thought of this. I'd promised
myself to make this room a safe place for Luke. A place
where he could grow. And now, without warning, I'd
dumped three kids on him, plus Harold, whatever we were
going to do about Harold. Luke had a right to be jealous. I
remembered how carefully I'd prepared Susan, my oldest
child, for the new baby.

What had I told Sue? I couldn't remember what I'd said.
Only her delight when I'd had twins, Nan and Steve. At
two and a half, she was sure I'd done it just for her so we'd
each have a baby of our own to "salt" (read powder) at
bathtime. I suppose what I'd done unconsciously was to
make her feel special, let her know that her place was
unique, hers for all time. Also tried to include her in, not
out, as much as I could, while I cared for two new babies.

I sat looking at Luke, trying to think how to tell him
he'd always be special. No one in the world could ever take
his place. How could I translate that into the right words
for Falls City and Luke?

Luke scratched at the table, his head down so I could
hardly hear him when he spoke. "You gonna take all those
kids up to the country, too? So they can all see the deer an'
everything?"

I wanted to put my arms around him. But instead I took
the handwriting paper out of his dishpan. "No, I won't
take them there. The house is closed for the year now,
anyway. I guess you're the only one from School Twenty-
three who'll ever see that house."

Luke pushed the handwriting paper aside and picked up
the crayons I'd had out for Louisa. He pulled an unlined
piece of paper toward him. "I remember what it looked
like," he said, beginning to draw. "It's made out of stones,
great big stones, see, like this. And it's got this funny kind

of green roof. I forget what it's called. And then here's the chimiley."

"That's exactly right, Luke. That's just the way it looks."

"And then, see, out here's the meadow," Luke drew a long rectangle in front of the house. "And here's the wall. That's stones too, and here's the woods." He drew lots of spiky trees beside the rectangle. "And right here in the middle of the meadow is an apple tree."

Luke drew a round bushy apple tree and then, of course, under the apple tree he drew a deer with antlers sticking up from his head. "And here's the deer I saw under the apple tree. And that's the way it is."

Luke pushed the drawing over in front of me. I smiled at him. "Yes," I said. "That's just the way it is. Let's tape the picture up here so that the others can see what it looks like and maybe sometime you can even tell them about it."

"Yeah. Maybe. And maybe sometime I can help you with that Louisa Mae. She lives right across the street, you know."

★

Mrs. Karras put her head in the door. "How are things going?" It was clear that when the project belonged to Mrs. Karras, she made sure she knew what was going on.

"Okay." I hoped she wouldn't bring the next child until Luke was gone.

Somehow she understood what I was saying and answered, "Fine. You're on your own now."

I finished with Luke and walked back to Lisa's class with him. I waved to Lisa and touched Luke's shoulder before he went in the door. Lisa called out, "Luke's earning stars in here now." I signaled back an A-OK, impressed once again with the resiliency of these city kids.

Mrs. Novak's third-grade class was on the second floor

and the list said that was where my next child, Bobby, was. I watched through the door for a second to be sure I wasn't entering at the wrong moment and then introduced myself to Mrs. Novak and asked if I could take Bobby.

"Bobby who?"

I wished she would talk a little more quietly.

"It doesn't say. I'm sorry. I'll find out. Be right back." I should have known better.

"Wait. Never mind. Any Bobby that needs special help has got to be Bobby Ferraro. The two other Bobbys I got are both good."

Her voice boomed through the classroom while I cringed. "Bobby Ferraro. Go with this lady. Take your pencil." She peered at me. "How long will you keep him?"

"Till eleven-ten."

"All right. But be sure he comes straight back here. No wandering into the lavatory. You know what goes on in there."

I didn't. But then I was beginning to see that there was a lot I didn't know about School 23. I walked straight to the door, opened it, aware of another small body in front of me, but I didn't look down until I had closed the door and we were in the hall.

Bobby looked like a little rat. He was very thin, with a sharp pointed face and dark blond hair that was slicked down tight to his head. He followed me obediently down the stairs and through the halls to the music room.

Once there, I introduced myself.

Bobby came over and pumped my hand. "Glad to meet-cha. You the one that's going to be my tutor. Mrs. Karras told me I was getting a tutor yesterday when I was in the office."

"How come you were in the office?"

Bobby shrugged. "I got sent there."

"For what?"

"I don't know. For talkin'. Or gettin' out of my seat. Something like that. I get sent down most every day. What are we gonna do in here, anyway?"

I was beginning to feel tired and the day wasn't half over. I shrugged myself. "We can do whatever you'd like to do today. Tomorrow we'll have a plan."

"Anything I want? You got some cards?"

"Yes." I went and got them out of the drawer in the file cabinet. I remembered reading about "non-directive therapy," letting the child lead the way. That's what I'll tell myself I'm doing, I thought.

"You know how to play any games like Black Jack, Poker, War?"

"I know Poker and Black Jack."

"You do?" Surprise tinged Bobby's voice. "I'll deal. Black Jack."

"We don't have poker chips," I said.

"We'll tear up paper and use the pieces for chips." Bobby was resourceful. I could see that.

Five minutes into the fame and I caught Bobby palming first one ace and then another. I called him on it, forgetting to be non-directive, and he cheerfully put the aces back. Bobby's approach seemed to be take all you can get. If you're dumb enough to be cheated, you deserve it.

We played six hands before Bobby lost the deal. I took the cards and shuffled them idly back and forth. Suddenly I realized that Bobby was fascinated. I flipped a little faster, showing off, dividing the pack in two, letting the cards fall together alternately, arcing them upwards with my fingers, then pressing my thumbs downward, making the cards flutter back into place.

221

"Where'd you learn how to do that?" Bobby wanted to know.

"I used to play cards with my cousins on rainy days in the summer when we couldn't swim or fish."

"You know how to fish?" Evidently in Bobby's eyes women didn't fish. "What kinda fish you catch?"

"Perch, small-mouth bass, pickerel. Once a muskie."

"Trolling or still fishing?"

"Mostly trolling. But sometimes we'd anchor off a shoal."

"You use worms?"

"No, minnows. We seined for them in the bay. Shiners, small perch minnows. Perch minnows were especially good when we were out for bass early in the morning." I stopped, caught up in my own thoughts. Memories of seining with my father. Why did I think it was all right to fish but not to hunt deer? Was it because the people I loved fished rather than hunted? Was it just that I'd had a different kind of model than Luke had had?

I missed the first part of Bobby's sentence. ". . . five sunnies. And I cleaned 'em all myself too. You know how to clean fish?"

"Not too well. My dad usually cleaned them."

"Yeah. Well, I can clean any ole fish. You know what else? I can skin rabbits too."

"No?" Remember the fish. Don't make a judgment.

"Yep. When me and my brothers go camping we lotsa times shoot rabbits and skin 'em."

"How many brothers do you have?"

"Eight. There's nine of us Ferraros."

Mrs. Karras appeared. "Well, Bobby. Hello. It's nice to see you somewhere other than the office."

"Yes, ma'am," Bobby answered.

I looked at the clock. Eleven-ten exactly. "Come on, Bobby. We have to go. I promised you'd be back by ten after."

"I want to talk to you before I go," I said to Mrs. Karras on my way out.

Bobby trotted beside me through the halls.

"You gonna show me how to do that shuffle?"

"Sure. I'll show you tomorrow. Here's your room."

"Okay. Listen, I'll come down myself tomorrow."

"Fine with me, if it's all right with your teacher."

"She'll let me, if you gimme a note to take back saying I got there on time. She just doesn't want me smokin' in the head." At least life was clear and understandable to Bobby.

Mrs. Karras was sitting in the music room with a pretty little blond girl when I got back.

"I know I said I was going to leave you on your own," she apologized, "but you seemed to be running a little late and I didn't want Maureen to miss her turn."

I smiled at Mrs. Karras. "That's okay. I can use all the help I can get. Hi, Maureen. I'm Mary. Mary Mac-Cracken," thinking it would be wonderful if it turned out that Maureen was into poker too.

No such luck.

Maureen pushed the cards away. "My mother says cards are a waste." Her voice had a nasal, whiny quality.

"Does she? Is she a Presbyterian? I was never allowed to play cards on Sunday, but that was because my mom's dad was a Presbyterian minister."

"What's a Presbetearn?"

"Presbyterian? It's a kind of religion."

"Like Catholic? I think that's what we are. But we don't go except Easter and Christmas Eve."

"That's my favorite time. Christmas Eve. We always go to the midnight service. Last year it was even snowing."

Maureen clucked. "I know. I had these new boots? But Jimmy wouldn't let me wear them. He is sooo mean."

"Who's Jimmy?" I asked, more because she seemed to

want me to than for any other reason. I was leery of moving too fast after Louisa Mae.

"He's my mother's boyfriend. But we're not supposed to talk about him. And if we have to, we're supposed to call him Uncle Jimmy, so people'll think he's a relative. But it's silly; everybody knows he's a boyfriend."

Maureen had the makings of a realist as well as a truly great gossip.

She crossed her legs and smoothed her skirt as she continued. "He really is terrible. You know what he did yesterday? Jimmy, I mean. I didn't eat my cereal fast enough, so know what he did? He just picked up the whole bowl and smushed it in my face. And last week" — Maureen swallowed; she was talking so fast her mouth was dry — "know what he did last week? I didn't eat my supper. So he saved it all night in the refrigerator and then he made me eat that and the cereal. And once he strapped me in the baby's high chair and kept me there until I cleaned my plate."

Poor Maureen. Also poor Jimmy. Maureen had just met me and was telling lurid tales. What did she tell the neighbors?

"Well, my mother says she will never have any children with Jimmy. She may marry him, probably not, but even if she does, she will not have children with him. See, we are her children and not Jimmy's so she has more to say. If the children were part his, she couldn't control him at all."

"Yes," I said. "I can see that." I felt full. I needed time to digest all that she said. But there was no stopping Maureen.

"My mother was going to sign permission for me to be in the program last year. The one with tairipic tutors. But you know how it is — promises, promises. My mother says that program never even got off the ground."

"How old are you, Maureen?" I asked, thinking maybe she'd answer a hundred and two.

"Seven, going on eight. My mother says it's not that I'm dumb, it's just that I don't put my mind to it — that and the allergies."

"Allergies?" What now?

"Oh, yes. I'm allergic to almost everything. Cats, chocolate. Dust even. That's why I have shots every week. The nurse maybe is going to teach my mother how to give me the shots so it don't cost so much."

A bell sounded throughout the school.

"That's the first bell for lunch. I'll be in tomorrow." Maureen slipped out of her chair and was gone.

I sat down at the table waiting for the whir of Maureen's words to be gone so I could think.

Louisa Mae, Bobby, Maureen. Why had Mrs. Karras picked them out? Luke — I knew Luke. But it had taken time. How could I possibly help these children in three months' time? And what about Harold? I hadn't even met him. Suppose it had only been for six weeks? That would have been worse.

Again, none of these children seemed so terrible to me. Where was the hostility that I had read so much about? These kids seemed to crave attention rather than reject it. Maybe the secret was getting them while they were young. But even so, how could I help them in so short a time? And yet, what all these kids seemed to want most was somebody to talk to. Could it possibly be that simple?

Thinking about student teaching reminded me of college. I had History at one o'clock. If I was going to see Mrs. Karras first, I had to get going.

"Okay," I said to Mrs. Karras. "I know you only have a minute and so do I, but now that I've lived through trial

225

by fire, how about telling me what you do know about Louisa Mae and Bobby and Maureen?"

Mrs. Karras smiled. "To tell the truth, I really don't know much about them. Louisa Mae just moved in with her grandmother, who registered her. Her first-grade teacher reports that Louisa doesn't know the alphabet or numbers, but more disturbing are quote, the signs of immaturity, unquote. That means she wet her pants the other day."

"Wait till I show you her drawings."

"What I want you to do is keep an eye on an unknown commodity. I don't know what we're dealing with in Louisa.

"Now, Bobby. I can tell you a little more about him. There are nine brothers. Bobby's next to last. Every single one has been a troublemaker. Bobby has several arrests for breaking and entering, usually with one of his brothers. None of them are too bright. I do have Bobby's IQ somewhere, because he was tested by the psychologist at one time. I'll look it up for you.

"With Bobby — just get him through. He's old for his class, anyway. I think they had him in two different kindergartens, but, anyway, no teacher wants him twice. As soon as class lists go out you can hear them yell, 'Not another Ferraro!'

"Maureen is something else altogether. She spends half of her day in tears, the other half whining and complaining. That's on the days she's here. There's no doubt in my mind that she's a very bright little girl. She should be enjoying school. She should be one of the ones to make it out of this life. But not the way she's going. I honestly don't know what to tell you to do with her. She's on the waiting list at the clinic, but you know what that's like. They don't have room for any new cases this semester. So there goes another year."

Mrs. Karras got up. "Mary, I don't expect miracles. You know me well enough for that. You don't know how badly these kids need somebody to talk to. If you don't do any more than that, I'll be satisfied."

"Mm-hmm," I said. "Sure you will."

But I didn't really mind. Mrs. Karras loved her school. All she was trying to do was get as much help as she could.

★

The history professor didn't know it, but the colonists' revolt against England seemed dull beside School 23, and Philosophy of Education and School in Contemporary American Society couldn't even place.

I arrived at School 23 at eight-thirty the next morning carrying three marbleized notebooks, clay, salt, an old cigar box, more Magic Markers, index cards, the Spache, and the WRAT. No getting caught short today. Today I'd have a plan.

I was greeted by Mrs. Karras. "Good morning, Mary. Coffee?"

"Thank you. No time to talk, though."

I took my mug of coffee and closed the door to the music room. The clay, salt, and cigar box were for Louisa Mae. The index cards and Magic Markers for Bobby, the tests for Maureen. I had what I needed for Luke.

"Good morning, Louisa Mae," I said as Mrs. Karras delivered her at two minutes of nine. "How're you today?"

Louisa Mae's pigtails were slightly atilt.

"Grobby," she said.

I could not decipher "grobby," but it did not sound positive.

"I'm sorry."

Louisa Mae squirmed herself onto the chair. "Sent me home. Hain't right. Called me a 'mother—,' you know. Cain't call me that. Hit him."

"They sent you home? Yesterday? Oh, Louisa Mae, I'm sorry. Who did you hit?"

"Him," she said with finality. Was that a personal pronoun or a name? Who could tell?

I began to divide the clay into separate colors. Red, yellow, white, green. I tore off small pieces and rolled them back and forth against the long table. My plan was to soften the clay and then use it to make letters for Louisa Mae; a clay *B* might be more memorable than one written on a piece of paper.

Louisa Mae picked up the piece of white clay I had rolled out. "Cigarette. Burn you cigarette if you don't mind. Ahhhh. Ahhhh." The horrendous squeal filled the room. I sat absolutely still watching Louisa Mae. Now she took the clay and hit it with her fist. "You'll get hit now." Bam. Bam.

I began rolling out the red clay. Louisa Mae grabbed it and smashed it on top of the white. "Going to the hospital? Nooo. Nooo. I be good. Not operation."

My God. Dear God. Is this child abuse? How can I possibly teach this child letters and numbers with all that's going on inside of her?

Suddenly Louisa Mae threw the red and white clay across the room. "Hey!" I said. "Wait a minute now."

But Louisa Mae wasn't waiting. She had thrown the cigar box and had hold of the salt when I pinned her arms.

228

"Now just a minute, Louisa Mae. You don't throw things in here."

She turned her head back and bared her teeth, trying to bite my arm. But she was an amateur compared to twelve-year-old Alice whom I had taught four years before.

"No throwing. No biting," I said. "Let's get the clay." I kept my hold on Louisa Mae and propelled her to the center of the room where the wad of clay had fallen.

"Pick it up and put it back."

And, amazingly, she did. Then she slid down under the table.

"Gonna sit my house now," she said from under the table.

"All right. I'll sit with you."

Louisa Mae and I sat together under the table. I prayed silently that Mrs. Karras would not do one of her routine checks at this moment.

Then Louisa Mae said, "Wanta draw."

"All right."

We came out from under and I got the crayons and paper while she waited docilely. More round circles. Ovals. None connected.

Louisa Mae got up. "Gonna draw on de board."

"Okay."

More circles. Then a rectangle. "Hit chimley," she said. "Here smoke." A long wiggly line came out of the rectangle. "Smoke go sky."

"Yes, smoke goes in the sky."

"To God."

Oh, now, Louisa Mae. Do you have to bring in God?

But she was sure. "Drawin' God now," she said, as huge circles covered the board. Then she stopped and looked at me. "How many feets do God have?"

Now who could answer that?

★

Luke watched from the doorway as Louisa Mae drew little circles up and down the board, hopping with excitement.

It was time for her to go, but I waited one more minute, hoping for a natural break rather than interrupting her — and got it.

Louisa Mae put down the chalk and looked almost in Luke's direction. "Dere's God's feet, boy," she said with pride.

When I got back from returning Louisa Mae to her classroom, Luke was erasing the board. God and his many feet were almost gone.

"Thank you, Luke." I sat down on a radiator cover near the board and watched. It was a pleasure just to look at him. He was tall now, a head above the other second graders, and very handsome. Slim, graceful. He rarely laughed or even smiled, but his interest in everything around him was so intense, he lit up the room when he walked in. In the turbulent sea of Louisa Mae, Maureen, and Bobby, I was grateful for Luke. We knew each other and what we were trying to do.

Luke erased the last of the small circles and then brought his dishpan of materials to the long table. I sat beside him and smiled a welcome.

"I am so glad to see you. How are you?"

Luke shrugged, getting out the teachers' guides to correct his work as well as the graded sight-word list.

"Okay, I guess." Luke put his arms on top of his books instead of opening them.

I waited. There was obviously something he wanted to say before we started working, something that wasn't easy to say. He was having difficulty finding words. Finally, "You know that little black kid that was just in here?"

"Yes. Louisa Mae."

" 'Member I told you she lives across the street?"

I nodded.

"Well, last night when I went out to get Frank and Alice to come in for supper, she was out there running down her side of the street, screamin' and yellin'."

Luke paused and then looked at me squarely.

"She didn't have nothin' on but her underpants and it was freezin' out there."

"Thank you for telling me, Luke. I'll try to find out what's going on."

"Not even any shoes. Her feet must have froze. One of her uncles came out and grabbed her and stuck her under his arm and took her back in."

I shook my head. "I don't know what's happening, Luke. I'll talk to Mrs. Karras before I go back to college. Thank you again." I changed the subject to focus on Luke himself. "Any trouble with your homework?"

Luke shook his head. He was still moving steadily ahead: he'd mastered cursive writing and now, after we had edited his first drafts, he copied all his work in what he called "real writing." I was beginning to show him the similarities between addition and multiplication, nothing much. Just that 2×3 meant that there were two threes and 5×3 meant there were five threes. Anybody who could add fast could do multiplication. Luke couldn't believe it could be that simple.

In fact, he had a hard time remembering why any of the work had once seemed so impossibly difficult. His reading was improving now almost as rapidly as his math. Again it was no miraculous trick on either Luke's part or mine. We simply added five new words on index cards to his word bank each day.

In order to make the words more visually memorable to Luke, I printed each one with a different colored Magic

Marker and he traced the letters with his fingers as I wrote them on his back with my finger, saying each letter out loud together. Then Luke used each word in a sentence. His mother reviewed them with him at night and listened with pride as he read her stories made up of the words he'd learned. There were three or four hundred words to each grade on the word lists I'd made from the backs of the school's basal readers. Luke had known all the first-grade words and most of the second when we started this year, so it was easy to keep building on his solid base of sight vocabulary.

He still had difficulty figuring out words he didn't know. He often couldn't remember the sounds of vowels or blends or how to break a word into syllables. His comprehension and understanding of what he read were high; his word attack skills were low.

Luke and I were at the board reviewing the short sound of *e* when the door opened and I turned to see Bobby Ferraro's ratty little face peering into the room. "Can I come in?"

"Uh, yes, sure, Bobby." The clock showed I was already five minutes into his time. "If you'll sit down over there I'll be with you in a minute."

But Bobby was already with us at the board. "Hey, Brauer, I dint know you got tutored, too. Those your words? Hey, man. I can read those. Those are easy." He read down the list: "*Bed — fed — led — red — Ted.*"

Luke said nothing. Then he looked at me. "Can I still read one page from *Golden Bridges?*"

"Of course." *Golden Bridges* was the third-grade basal reader. We always ended with one page of this now because it was composed of the sight words Luke could remember so well and was an antidote for the difficult phonics and word attack skills. I still felt it was important to end each session with success.

I turned to Bobby. "Would you write a sentence for each of those words on the board while I do this one last thing with Luke? The paper's over there in that drawer and there should be a pencil there, too."

I went back to the long table and sat down beside Luke. He already had the book open and began to read.

At the end of the first paragraph he looked up. Bobby was standing in the middle of the room listening to Luke with his mouth open. Luke, the school dummy, left back in second grade, was reading the third-grade book with ease.

I let Bobby stand there. Who cared whether he copied the words or wrote the sentences? What he was doing for Luke in that one minute was worth more than all the praise I could give him in a year.

Luke closed the book and looked at me, waiting for my comment. But I waited for Bobby. He closed his mouth, then opened it again. "Jeez," he said, "how'd you learn to do that?"

★

From that time on Bobby and Luke shared part of each other's time. Bobby came early, Luke stayed late, so that they were each getting almost an hour a day.

They were good for each other. Luke's mind was quicker, his ability to grasp concepts better, but Bobby had his own strengths. For one thing, he had an almost perfect ear. The slightest variation of a sound was blaringly apparent to Bobby, so that phonics and word attack skills were a snap for him. He shone in one arena, Luke in another, and they developed respect for each other.

They helped each other in other ways as well. Bobby was rooted in reality; his family was poor and evidently boisterous and unruly, but there was also a knockabout cohesiveness to them, a sense of family. Whatever Bobby's problems were, they didn't seem bad enough to cause him to run away, either mentally or physically.

In another discussion of the troublesome short *e,* the word *pet* came up. Bobby immediately began to tell us how his pet bird had died. He had put it in a cereal box and buried it in the woods. "I cried somethin' awful."

Luke said, "Not me. I never cry. Last year my dog — we had a big, big, dog then, almost all Saint Bernard — got hit by a car and died right in the street. I didn't cry or nuthin'. My mom and I just got the wheelbarrow from Mr. Berkus and pulled on that big ole dog till we got him in it and then we wheeled him down to the dump."

I loved watching Luke and Bobby. They worked well together. They listened to each other. They played together both inside and out of school. Best of all, the Ferraro brothers now included Luke in their fishing and camping expeditions. He thrived in their company and developed a capacity to deal with life rather than running away to fantasy. I missed his flights of imagination, but I welcomed his new strengths. Most of all, I welcomed Bobby.

For the first time since I'd known him, Luke had an honest-to-goodness friend.

All senior classes were canceled for two days. Campus interviewing was in full swing. Longworth Hall had been cleared of teachers and in their places sat interviewers from various schools and institutions questioning seniors one at a time.

I had signed up for five different interviews — three were for teaching positions in special ed, one a kindergarten class, one "open." I wasn't sure what "open" meant, but it sounded possible.

We sat outside the classrooms waiting for our names to be called. Ten to twenty bodies in a row, turning restlessly on the wooden benches, leafing through our resumés. The wait was usually thirty or forty minutes, the interview five or six.

On the second day, as I twisted back and forth on the bench between two sets of jeans and long straight curtains of hair, Amy Schwarzenbach's rangy figure loped by.

I was off the bench in a second. "Amy! Hey, Amy! Wait a minute."

Amy paused, squinting her eyes in my direction.

"It's me," I said. "Mary. Remember swimming and TSS? How are you? I haven't seen you for months. Ian either. How are you doing?"

Amy shrugged and nodded. "Okay, I guess. Except it's a long time between letters."

"Letters?"

Amy nodded again. "Ian's in Vietnam. You didn't know? He got called last summer. I tried to get him to go on up to Canada. But you know Ian. He just said if he kept his hat on, the enemy'd never know he was there. But I don't know, Mary, I think they make them wear helmets, don't they?"

I wanted to cry or maybe yell. How could they do that? Make Ian part of that war. Out loud I said, "I'd put my money on Ian. I bet he's got his hat on under the helmet."

Amy touched my shoulder. "Thanks, Mary. I gotta run. Would you believe I'm helping Hogan coach the swim team? See you."

I sat back down. The hair curtains on either side were

misty now. Why did people keep saying "See you," particularly when they didn't?

★

Each of my interviews was a carbon copy of the others.
First an inspection of my folder, which contained my
resumé and credits. Next, a description of the job and then
the same question. "Why do you feel you are qualified for
this job?"

The first time I was asked, I had no answer. I had never
had a job interview of any kind before and I felt both
nervous and shy. Why did I feel I was qualified for the job?
Why did they ask that? The only qualifications I had were
inside the folder and the interviewer had already read that.
Was I supposed to have some other hidden qualifications,
or was it a memory test to see if I could remember what I
had written down?

I went to see Professor Foster.

"It doesn't matter much what you say," he said. "They
want to see what kind of person you are. Just project your
personality."

I looked at him and shook my head. "I came back to
college for two years because I needed the credits to be
able to teach, and at the end, the thing I'm supposed to do
in order to get a job is 'project my personality.' "

"Don't be bitter. Doesn't help," Professor Foster inspected me carefully, then grinned. "And one more thing.
You might try wearing a little tighter sweater."

He ducked before I even threw the book.

★

I did try to talk more and it seemed to work passably
well. At least two of the interviewers said they'd be in
touch to arrange a follow-up interview. Well, actually only

one. The second man changed his mind at the last minute.

"Uh . . . now . . . did you put your age down in your resumé?" He was suddenly leafing through pages.

"Yes. On the front. Forty-five."

"Forty-*five?*" He cleared his throat, lowering his voice from the crescendo. "Yes. Well . . . excellent. We'll be in touch."

But I knew he wouldn't. I limped back to School 23 feeling older than I ever had before.

I stopped in Mrs. Karras's office to catch up after missing a day and also to tell her about Luke's remarks about Louisa Mae.

"She lives in the basement?" Mrs. Karras echoed. "What makes Luke think that?"

"I don't know. I didn't want to press him, but then he told me about seeing her outside in her underpants and I thought you should know."

"Yes. You're right. I'll have the social worker or someone check up. Incidentally, Mary, Luke is doing so well. Lisa was showing me some of his work when I was in her class the other day."

I sensed happiness and the return of youth.

Never planning to ask, I asked, "Do you think I could teach here next year?"

Mrs. Karras shook her head. "Much as I'd love it, I'm afraid there's not a chance of getting money to continue the program."

"I know. But maybe I could teach, just teach, in one of the classrooms."

Mrs. Karras got up and walked to the window. She stood looking out for a while and then turned and, still standing in front of the window, spoke to me from there.

"Yes. You could do that. I'm sure one of the teachers will have a baby or get sick or retire between now and

September, and I could hire you. But is that what you really want, Mary? I think you should think about it very carefully because what you do this coming year will set the course for the rest of your life. Certainly, you could teach a regular class. You'd probably have a ball. But what about the other kids — emotionally disturbed, learning disabled, socially maladjusted, whatever the labels are, the kids most people think are bad, difficult, dumb, different, unable to learn, in trouble of one kind or another? Are you sure those aren't the children you want?"

I nodded. I knew she was right. "Okay," I said. "Thank you. I will think about it. Listen, one more thing I wanted to ask. Would it be all right if I took Luke and Bobby down to the library and let them get library cards?"

Mrs. Karras chuckled. "Of course. That's a fine idea. They're residents of this town. They're entitled." Then she laughed. "I'll bet Bobby will be the first Ferraro to have a library card."

★

Maureen was standing outside her classroom door crying as Luke and Bobby and I headed for the front door. We couldn't just walk by her.

"Wait. I'll just be a minute," I said to the boys.

I squatted down next to Maureen. "What's the matter, babe? Why are you crying?"

Maureen shook her head, unable to speak, sobs mixing with hiccups.

Across the hall Bobby pointed his finger and sing-songed, "Crybaby. Crybaby. Maureen is a crybaby."

"Cut it out, Bobby," I said sharply and handed Maureen a wrinkled but clean piece of Kleenex from my pocket.

Maureen wiped and blew and then sat down on the floor and began to wiggle her right foot out of her shoe. Be-

238

tween sniffles she said, "I got it for you. Jimmy spanked me somethin' awful when he saw me copying it, said we didn't give our phone number to no friggin' do-gooder lady, but when he left for the station this morning, Jimmy's a policeman, you know, and Mama was curling Diane's hair, I copied it down again and put it in my shoe so nobody'd know."

Maureen handed me a small, crumpled piece of paper with her phone number written in large penciled numerals.

A routine question that I asked all the kids. "What's your address? Do you know your phone number?" And it had created a family crisis and earned Maureen a spanking. The families of children like Maureen and Luke lived closed lives, full of secrets and deceit. It was necessary for survival. Any probing from the outside might cut off desperately needed welfare funds or reveal long-hidden police records or hospitalizations. To enter the world of these city children would be a long, slow journey. Mrs. Brauer had just begun to trust me. Would I ever reach someone like Jimmy or Luke's Uncle Chuck?

I smoothed out the slip of paper and folded it carefully and put it in my pocket. I looked at Maureen, her nose clogged from allergies and tears, sitting, damp and miserable, on the hall floor. There was no way I could leave her there.

"Thank you, Maureen. I'll copy your phone number in my book and tear up the paper as soon as we get back. Come on, now. You'll need your jacket. We're going down to the library."

Across the hall Luke and Bobby groaned in unison.

Maureen scurried to the coat closet in her classroom as her teacher pulled me to one side. "Take her with my blessings. She's worse than all the boys together at disrupting the class. All those tears and crying and moaning. You know why she's carrying on like that? Because she didn't get picked for the spelling bee, that's why. What else can I do with her besides put her in the hall?"

I nodded. Maureen would not be a joy, particularly in a classroom of thirty.

When Maureen and I joined Luke and Bobby, Bobby made a definite point of holding his nose and gazing at Maureen. I made an equally strong point of holding the hand that had held the nose and holding it hard.

"Jeez," Bobby said. "I was just havin' fun."

"Okay," I said, letting go. "Let's all have fun."

Bobby and Luke dashed ahead and Maureen and I followed, our progress slowed by the fact that Maureen walked with her face buried against my leg.

But even so, I was aware of feeling good. Feeling better. It was almost like having a class again. A class meant the kids I taught. And that meant Louisa Mae. We couldn't go without Louisa Mae.

I herded Luke, Bobby, and Maureen toward first grade. Maureen now joined loudly in the complaints about having to take Louisa Mae.

"I bet you already saw her today. She shouldn't get to come twice. That's not fair." I could stand tears and temper tantrums, but the whine in Maureen's voice went through me like fingernails on a blackboard.

"Maureen," I said, squatting beside her once again. "May I tell you how I perceive you?"

Maureen nodded, not having a glimmer of what I was talking about.

"That's not fair," I said in near-perfect imitation of Maureen's whine. It was so unexpected that Maureen laughed.

"You sound funny," she said.

"Yup," I agreed, "and so do you, when you talk like that. Try to keep your voice down more. Like this, okay?"

Louisa Mae's teacher was even happier to give permission than Maureen's teacher had been. Louisa Mae had poked one of the boys in the eye and had been relegated to the chair in the corner. The only trouble was that she insisted on covering her head with her dress, which sent both boys and girls off into shrill giggles.

At last we were off, Louisa Mae and Maureen holding my hands, Luke and Bobby scouting in front.

We were going to have to hurry. I could hear the big old clock in the city bell tower striking eleven and we had to be back before twelve for lunch.

But the library was only six blocks from the school and Luke was used to our walks and stayed at Bobby's heels, keeping him in line. I kept the girls' hands enclosed in mine and we arrived at the library intact.

I was unprepared for the inner vastness of the library, an ordinary-looking stone building from the outside that I had passed many times. But inside, everything was dark wood, empty space, and walls of books and silence.

One elderly man sat at a table on the right, nodding over the newspaper. The only other living person in the building seemed to be a librarian who sat at a large desk, blocking the entrance and exit. There was no way to get in or out except by squeezing past her desk. We were obviously going to have to speak to her.

"Good morning," I said. "We've come over from School Twenty-three. As a special treat. Do you have a children's section?" I asked.

"Yes. Over this way," she waddled ahead of us, talking without looking at us. "Nothing fancy. We don't have the money for all that software hullaballoo, and we don't have many children nowadays. But in its time, it was a pretty fair collection."

Bobby waddled after her, somehow making his skinny body look as fat and awkward as hers.

Up until now the children had been quiet, hushed by the large, unfamiliar room, but now that we were in motion again, awe was receding. My hands were full with the girls and I could only hope the librarian would not turn around suddenly and discover Bobby.

The children's section was not inviting. There were no books on display or out on the tables. In fact, most of the books were without labels and their dull black, blue, and green spines lined the shelves monotonously. It was very different from other children's libraries that I had known and I sighed even as I thanked the retreating back of the librarian. A disappointment. A waste of the children's time and mine. Well, at least there would be no trouble in getting back by twelve.

But I had forgotten that these children had no other libraries to compare this with, that there were probably very few books of any kind in their homes.

Luke, Bobby, and Maureen were all on their knees pulling books out, pushing them back in. Many of the books did have illustrations on their front covers and Luke was studying a cover that had a picture of a small brown deer and other animals in a forest. Bobby skipped around the room, taking a book from here, a book from there, piling them on the table.

"Crimminee. Look at these things. They got books about everything in here. Lookit that." He pointed to his pile. "Rudolph. Snoopy. They copied all the good stuff on TV and put it in these here books."

Maureen was sitting on the floor reading, oblivious to the rest of the world.

I sat down on one of the chairs and pulled Louisa Mae onto my lap, watching in wonder. These children were like sponges, soaking up whatever they came in contact with.

Louisa Mae tugged my arm. "Hain't got no book."

"You're right," I said. "Let's find one for you."

Luke came over to my side. "Come on, Louisa Mae, I'll show you where the pitcher books are." Luke led her to a low shelf where the larger picture books were stacked and took out the top one. "Here's a train," he said. "Wanta book about a train?"

But Louisa Mae ignored him, digging through the books till she found one with a picture of a doll.

"Hit Baby Hug Me," she said.

I had been so busy watching Luke and Louisa Mae that I hadn't seen the librarian arrive.

"The children are only allowed to take down one book from the shelves at a time, Miss. Not create a mess like this. We don't have all the money in the world, you know, to hire people to clean up after children."

"Okay, kids. That's enough. Put the books back. You can each pick one book and then we'll get you a library card and you can check it out."

"Library card? Can these children read? You have to be able to read to have a library card."

"They can read."

"Well, are they legal residents? That's a requirement, you know. We don't issue books to out-of-towners." The librarian was becoming distraught with the thought of parting with four of the ancient books.

"Yes," I said. "They all live here." Although suddenly I wasn't so sure about Louisa Mae.

Back at her desk she got out cards. "All right. One at a time now."

"Bobby Ferraro. Twelve forty-four Prospect."

Good, Bobby, I thought. You sound like a pro, giving your address without being asked.

"I'm going to take this here book on magic." Who would have guessed Bobby was interested in magic?

"Well, who's next? Hurry along now." The librarian tapped her stamper on the ink pad.

Luke whispered to me, "I don't think Louisa Mae knows her street. I got her doll book here, but she'll start to cry or curse if that lady don't let her get her book."

I nodded. "See if you can get two, Luke."

Luke stepped up to the desk. He looked so small beside the large librarian and her desk. "Luke Brauer. Eight thirty-four Cherry, apartment three A. These two, please."

The librarian eyed Luke, started to say something, then glanced over at me and changed her mind. She wrote out Luke's card, stamped his books, and put his card in a file on her desk.

"Go ahead, babe," I whispered to Maureen. But she shook her head. "I can't, Mary. Jimmy would whup me good if I gave my name and address to a perfect stranger."

"It's okay," I insisted. "It's all right to have a library card." It was more than all right for Maureen. It was important. I had watched her for those few seconds as she sat reading on the floor, completely engrossed in the book. Here was a whole other world for her, where she wouldn't need to whine and allergies would fade. "Go ahead, Maureen," I urged again. "Get your card."

Maureen inched forward.

"What's your name?"

"Maureen. Maureen Barber," her voice a whisper.

"Yes. Well, where do you live?"

Silence.

"Speak up."

244

"Thirty-nine Fairview," Maureen whispered, her breath rattling in her throat.

"Okay," I said. "That's all. Thank you." I whisked the children out the door.

Luke took Louisa Mae's hand as soon as we were outside. "Here's your book, Louisa Mae. Come on and carry it. Come on." Over his shoulder Luke said to me, "I'll tend her, Mary. You watch out for the other two."

I glanced at my watch. Ten of twelve. "Hey," I yelled, "we have to run. Come on now."

I grabbed Maureen's hand and set off full tilt. Luke ran beside me, tugging Louisa Mae along with him. Bobby ran in circles around us, raising his book over his head and shouting for no reason at all, "Yay, team!"

We were in the front door as the first lunch bell finished ringing and Luke and Bobby dashed for their classes. I deposited Louisa Mae and then trotted beside Maureen to her classroom.

Her cheeks were pink, her eyes shining. No tears or whining now. Outside the room Maureen reached up and pulled me down and whispered in my ear, "I love you," and then sat on the floor, took off her right shoe, and stashed her library card safely in her sock.

Mrs. Karras was waiting by the front door when I arrived that first Monday in April.

"Well, she's gone," she said.

"Who's gone?"

"Louisa Mae."

I pulled my jacket back on, suddenly cold. "How can she be gone?" I asked without logic. "She was here last week."

"Well, she's gone now." Mrs. Karras was as angry as I'd ever seen her. "She was here Monday and Tuesday last week, but as you know perfectly well, she was out the rest of the week. The nurse made a routine call on Thursday and the grandmother said Louisa Mae was sick, had the flu. Lies, lies, lies. Why can't anybody tell the truth anymore?"

"What happened? Where's she gone? Why do you think she has gone?"

"I don't think. I know she's gone. On Tuesday I called myself. This time nobody answered. I just got this very strange feeling that something was wrong. You know, the social worker never did get in that house. Somebody always put her off with one excuse or another.

"Anyway, after school Friday, I got hold of the truant officer and went over there. Nobody answered the bell, so then we went around back, to try the kitchen door, and there was the grandmother, standing in the kitchen stirring something on the stove. We could see her clear as day, through the glass windows in the door, so she had to let us in.

"Then she tells us that Louisa Mae doesn't live there anymore. Louisa Mae's mama had thought she'd move back home to Falls City, but now she'd changed her mind and gone on out to Chicago to stay with her sister."

"Chicago? Will Louisa Mae go to school in Chicago?"

"Who knows! Who —" Mrs. Karras stopped mid-sentence and walked back to her desk and sat down and wearily put her head between her hands. After a minute she looked up at me. "You know, I almost said 'who cares.' That's the first time I've ever felt that way." She rubbed her temples. "It's the waste that makes me so damn mad.

Waste of her teacher's time, my time, your time. What good did it do? You could have been working with Harold all along if we'd known Louisa Mae was going to skip. And I tell you, I wouldn't be surprised if that grandmother didn't know all along that they weren't going to stay here for good, and just used us for baby-sitting."

I walked out and across to my room. I thought of it as my room now, rather than the music room. I didn't want to hear about Harold or the grandmother. I wanted Louisa Mae. How would I ever find out what "grobby" meant or why God's feet were so important? Or even more important, why she had been scared of the clay and called it a cigarette. I closed my eyes. "God, watch out for Louisa Mae in Chicago, okay?"

Someone rattled my door and I reluctantly opened it. Mrs. Karras. I sighed and then realized that Mrs. Karras wasn't alone.

"Mary," she said brightly, "I'd like you to meet Harold Mills. He's in fifth grade, Miss Kraus's class . . . or maybe you've already met."

I couldn't believe she was doing this. "Hi, Harold," I said to the pale pudgy boy who stood beside her. "Have a seat." I glared at Mrs. Karras. "May I speak to you in the hall?"

Outside the door I hissed, "What are you doing? The body's not even cool yet and already you're dragging someone in on top of it. Did you care about Louisa Mae at all? For that matter, do you care about me or anyone in the world? Or only School Twenty-three? A school is made of children, you know."

"I know. I know it all too well, and you've got to learn this, too, if you're going to survive. Schools are made of children and children come and go." Her voice grew gentler and she touched my arm. "Most schools aren't like the one you taught at before. There your children stayed for two or three years at a time, often in the same class. You had the luxury of long periods in which to help those children.

"Well, it's not like that here in the city. You do what you can with what you have. A child comes, a child goes. You have to hope you touched them for a second. There are too many kids who need help to waste even a minute." Mrs. Karras turned and headed back to her office. I knew she was right. Without Mrs. Karras there wouldn't even be a place like School 23.

I went back into my room. Harold was slouched against the file cabinet, eyes on the floor. I had absolutely no idea how to get started.

I sat down at the long table and studied him, but nothing came. Then for no particular reason, I remembered the House-Tree-Person test, the same test Jerry had had me give Luke in my beginning sessions with him. Jerry was no longer around to interpret, but perhaps Harold would enjoy the drawings as Luke had. Harold certainly seemed to be nonverbal. At least at the moment.

I got up and collected paper and pencils. "Harold, would you come on over here and sit down?"

Harold hesitated, but then shuffled across the room.

"Do you like to draw?"

Harold shrugged.

"Well, here's a piece of paper. Please draw a picture of a house. The best house you can."

Surprise made him look at me. "What kinda house?" His voice was very soft and there was some sort of odd lisp, almost a hiss, on the final *s* in *house*.

"Any kind you want."

Harold shrugged again and began to draw. He worked quickly and produced a tall skinny house without a baseline, reaching upward from the bottom of the page. The house had nine tiny windows, a wobbly drainpipe, and a toppling chimney.

Harold pushed it toward me. "Is this all right?"

My turn to be surprised. I had expected sullenness rather than eagerness to please.

"That's fine. Now draw a picture of a tree, okay?"

I had no training at the time to attempt interpretations of drawings and I still feel interpretations of children's drawings should be done with caution. Too often, too much is read into them. But at least Harry and I were doing something together and Harry seemed to be involved.

The picture of the tree was bare, without leaves or roots, only a round hole bored into the tree halfway up. The tree, like the house, began at the bottom edge of the page.

"Okay. One more. Draw a person, the best picture of a person you can."

Harry said, "Thass hard." The hiss was more evident and there was something almost girlish in the way he spoke.

"Well, just give it a try," I said. Suddenly I realized I was interested. I wanted to see what kind of person he would draw. I shook my head. Where had my resentment gone? Ah, Mrs. Karras. How cagey you are — but God, please remember Louisa Mae, all right? Chicago's a long way from here. . . .

When my thoughts came back to Harry, he was still working on his picture, spending far more time on this than either of the other two.

Finally he was finished. It was a picture of an odd-looking man or boy with a tiny head, even smaller arms, and big feet. The wispy arms and almost invisible hands were holding a heavily penciled barbell with large weights on both ends.

"Know what he'sss doing? He'ss lifting weightsss. You know what weightsss are?"

"Mm-hmm. My son has some, but I've never used them."

"Me neither. But with that many poundsss" — he pointed to the picture — "it'd be very, very, heavy."

"Yes," I agreed. "It would be very hard to lift."

Later on I would learn more about the House-Tree-Person test and consider it a valuable part of a diagnostic evaluation, although I would always feel it was important not to draw too many conclusions from this, or, for that matter, from any single test. But even in my first meeting with Harold, even with my limited knowledge, I could see how insecure and "wobbly" he felt — and he did seem to be saying he felt weighted down by heavy burdens.

★

It was twenty after twelve by the time I had finished my time with Maureen and packed the last items in her dishpan and put it back on the shelf. At the end of the morning I wrote a brief summary of what each child had done that day in their notebooks, so I could keep track of their progress and plan for the next day. Useful, but I was barely making it back in time for history.

I grabbed my canvas tote and jacket and headed for my car, fishing in my jacket pocket for my keys. Not there. Where did I put them? In my bag? Not there either. Back to my room. Had I left them on the shelf? Not there. Come on. Come on. You don't have time for this, Mary. Maybe in the car. Back out the door. Down the steps. Across the street. I shook the door handle. Locked. And sure enough, there were the keys dangling from the ignition. Oh, boy! I kicked the tire in frustration and heard echoes in my head. "You must be so patient, Mary, to teach those children." Patient? Me? They should see me now.

Well, at least I know what to do. Back into school to the office. I took a wire coat hanger from the rack and untwisted it, forming a small loop at the end as I had seen Cal do one day in the parking lot when he was helping a woman who had locked her keys in the car.

But I hadn't counted on the children. It was past twelve-thirty and they were coming back from lunch, assembling on the black macadam. I went around to the far side of the car, feeling foolish, trying to be as inconspicuous as possible.

I slipped the wire between the top of the window and the roof. The worn canvas convertible top gave under pressure and the wire slid in easily. I aimed the loop for the little knob that locked the door. If I could just lift that up I'd be in.

The loop went over, but then when I tried to lift, it slipped off. Steady. Concentrate. Get it on again. Keep pressing hard. Lift. The lock clicked and I grabbed the door, pulled it open — and looked up to see a dozen or more children peering at me from the back of the car. Front and center was Bobby Ferraro. "See," he said to what were obviously three other Ferraros, "I told you."

"Hi, Bobby," I said climbing in behind the wheel. "I'm late. Got to hurry. See you tomorrow."

But Bobby clung to the side of the car. "I told 'em you could fish and play poker and they wouldn't believe nothin'. But now they've seen you pickin' locks." Bobby shouted with pride. "Now they gotta believe me."

I felt as if I'd just received the Nobel Prize. Who cared if I was late for History?

31

April slid by. My courses at college were almost over. I still had to write a long term paper for History, chronicles of court cases for School in Contemporary American Society, and another paper for Philosophy of Education. Classes for seniors ended in mid-May. Graduation would be June 6. I knew I wouldn't go. Especially since Ian wasn't there. How could I walk the aisle in cap and gown with Ian in Vietnam? Besides, that belonged to another time of life. What mattered was the certification, the right to teach as a "real teacher" rather than as an aide.

I still didn't have a job, but somehow that didn't worry me. More and more the thought of working on my own, testing as well as teaching, was turning over in my mind. In fact much to Cal's surprise and my own, I drove out to college one Saturday morning and took my graduate record exams, just in case.

The core of my life was School 23. Bobby Ferraro flourished, down to once a week in the office. He still lied, copied, fought after school, came in with a bruised lip from "talkin' back" at home, but that was his life-style. Nothing was going to change that, but he was going to pass this year, much to his teacher's relief. And I loved Bobby. I was a pushover for his tough, sinewy survival techniques, his charm as a raconteur, his capacity for delight (he was in heaven for three straight days when the circus was in town), and his occasional unexpected openness.

"Do you have a best thing, Bobby?" To my surprise, Bobby's face turned deep red, but he nodded and came up close to whisper to me.

"Don't tell nobody. But the crossing guard kissed me today."

"Mrs. Renato?"

Bobby nodded.

I smiled at him. "She's nice, Bobby. You're lucky." Mrs. Renato was fat, fifty, and friendly. She knew better than most psychiatrists what these kids needed. I was always caught by surprise by how what seemed a tiny gesture was a treasure to be secretly cherished in School 23.

Harry lugged a suitcase in to show me the matches his father had brought him from bars across the country. His father didn't live at home anymore. He was evidently a strange, violent man with a drinking problem. Harry told of session after session when his father had tossed the landlord down the stairs and broken his ribs, or thrown knives across the kitchen at his mother. They lived apart now, Harry at home with his mother and two sisters. But his father still came to visit and when his car pulled up outside, it was Harry's job to hide the liquor behind the attic fan and then run before his dad could make him tell where he'd hidden it. Still, he loved his father and treasured each memento that he brought him.

★

Maureen was writing poetry. All through April and now into May, poems poured out of Maureen. No stories or illustrations for her. Instead she wrote sad, wistful little verses.

> *I used to like jelly,*
> *But now I don't.*
> *I used to like bubbles,*
> *But now I don't.*
> *Because what does it matter.*

She was a strange, unhappy little girl. Part of her seemed an old woman burdened with care, resigned to trouble, another part of her was three years old. One day in the middle of May she asked if she could stand on a chair. I agreed and held her hand to steady her as she climbed up. Once there she took a flying leap, twined her arms around my neck and her legs around my waist, and begged me to carry her to her classroom.

"We'd look pretty silly to the other kids, wouldn't we?" I asked, still holding her.

"Don't care. Don't care," Maureen wailed.

We compromised with once around the room and as far as the door.

The next day Maureen told me calmly that she was "finding solutions to her problems." She said she knew she wanted too much attention, but she was "working it out by writing," she said, as she smoothed her skirt.

★

Louisa Mae, Bobby, Harry, Maureen. I had only vignettes of their lives. But Luke I knew.

On his birthday his mother and Chuck gave him six ducks. They got them cheap, Luke said, 'cause they were left over from Easter and the pet store wanted to get rid of them. Luke named them Jimmy, Jesus, Patrick, Speedy Gonzales, Road Runner, and Louisa Mae.

"Louisa Mae?"

"Yeah. 'Member her? That little black kid that used to live across the street."

"I remember," I said.

"You ever hear about what happened to her?"

"No, Luke. I never did."

"I didn't think so. But this one little ole duck just kinda reminded me of her."

254

I silently blessed Luke for remembering.

A few days later Luke reported that all the ducks were dead. He had buried each one in a separate box out in the field near the brook that he crossed on his shortcut. We went out to look at their graves. Crosses made of two sticks marked each grave.

Luke and I sat quietly in the field. The grass was still wet and the early morning sun shimmered in each drop, turning the field grass into diamonds. I touched a blade with my finger and the drop disappeared and diamonds vanished, leaving only grass.

I looked at Luke. He was up, moving around, collecting a few black-eyed Susans, laying them on the graves. It was more than a year now since he had first brought me here. A lot had happened in a year. And now it was almost over. I couldn't come back again next year. I had to get a job. That's what going to college had been all about. There would be no point to becoming accredited if I continued to volunteer, but how could I leave Luke? Why was leaving always the hardest part?

Luke sat down beside me and sliced a piece of field grass down the middle with his thumbnail, put it to his lips, and blew a long, loud whistle.

"You know what, Mary? Don't tell my mother, but they shouldn't never have bought those ducks."

I nodded. I had thought so at the time, but hadn't wanted to spoil his pleasure.

"It wasn't their fault, though. The pet store shouldn't have gotten 'em ever. I don't know how they kept them alive so long. But ducks aren't supposed to be in houses or pet stores neither. Ducks are supposed to be in ponds and lakes or maybe in farmers' yards."

I nodded again without speaking, and tried making a

whistle of my own. It looked all right, but it didn't work. Until Luke picked it up and blew another shrill blast.

"I think," he said, "it's better they're dead. It's like they're more freer."

I nodded one last time, then slit another piece of grass. Over the lump in my throat I blew one note on my field-grass whistle.

"Guess what?" Mrs. Karras said when I arrived the next morning. "The Child Study Team is here and they have Luke in the music room, so you'll have to take Harold someplace else today." She steered me toward her office.

"Why? I mean, what are they doing to Luke?" My heart was pounding.

"Testing him. I guess to see if he can pass this year."

"Oh, no." I slumped down on the wooden chair opposite her desk. "Why didn't they tell us? I could have reviewed things with Luke. I could have showed him tricks to help make test-taking easier. You know what we did yesterday? Luke and I put flowers on the ducks' graves."

"Ducks?"

"Luke's ducks died. You know, he named one Louisa Mae."

Mrs. Karras squinted her eyes at me. "You all right?"

"Yes. Sorry." I knew I was rambling, trying to find base, to think what I could do to help Luke.

"Listen," I said. "I could skip seeing Harold this morning and go talk to the Child Study Team now if you want. I could tell them about the progress he's made. . . . I could come back this afternoon and see Harold. There aren't any classes today, anyway — just graduation."

Mrs. Karras shook her head. "I offered. But they said they want to make their own decision. I offered to talk to them, have you talk to them. But they said no, the only one they wanted to talk to was his classroom teacher, after they finish their testing.

"Bernie Serino evidently called the head of the Child Study Team and said he wanted to see it in black and white — raw scores, standard scores, percentiles, the works, on any child they were thinking of retaining or putting in another program."

"I bet Norm Foster had something to do with that. Well, at least Lisa will say something positive, don't you think?"

Mrs. Karras nodded. "I'm sure she will. Although I'm just not sure how much weight they'll give her opinion, compared to their testing scores.

"Did you say graduation was today?"

My turn to nod.

"Not going?"

I smiled and shook my head. "They're mailing me my piece of paper, that's what I really need."

The secretary put her head around the door and spoke to me. "Harold Mills is here. He insists he has an appointment with you now. What should I tell him?"

I grinned, happy with the thought of Harry coming to the office to look for me.

"Tell him he's absolutely right. I'll be there in a minute."

I turned back to Mrs. Karras. "I'd rather be here than at graduation any day. You've made this a pretty special place for kids, you know. And for me too. I don't think I ever would have graduated without School Twenty-three."

"I just wish we could keep you forever," Mrs. Karras said.

We both got up at once. Enough sentiment for one morning. "How long do you think they'll keep Luke in there?" I asked.

"Who knows! But I'll let you know if I hear anything. Where do you plan to be?"

"I don't know. Wherever Harry and I can find a spot, but I'll keep checking back here."

By eleven o'clock the door to the music room was still closed. "Is Luke still in there?" I whispered to the secretary.

She nodded her head.

"Oh, God," I said under my breath. It was more a prayer than anything else.

What kind of tests would they give him? Who were "they," anyway? How scared was Luke? If I had quaked with terror playing my recorder for Mrs. Oliphant, how must Luke feel in front of a team?

★

I walked Maureen back to her room at 11:55 and the secretary motioned me to her desk. "Mrs. Karras is in with them now, she said to tell you Miss Eckhardt was joining them at twelve. I'm supposed to go get sandwiches at the deli — anyway, Mrs. Karras says for you to check back here around one, one-thirty, if you can."

"Okay. Thank you. I'll be here."

I walked out to my car and sat down watching the kids race down the steps as the bell rang. I was hoping to see Luke, maybe not bother him — he'd probably need some time to himself after that much pressure — but just get a glimpse of him, make sure he was all right.

The school emptied quickly, but there was no sign of

him. I turned on the engine and drove down the streets of Falls City thinking about Luke. There was no way they could leave him back again. No matter how he tested, even if he'd got nervous and goofed, Lisa had his workbooks, she could show them to the Child Study Team. And they couldn't put him in a special class; none of the labels would fit. I was sure of it.

I finally pulled the car to one side and turned off the engine. For somebody so sure that everything was wonderful, I did seem to be a little shaky. I'd just sit here and wait it out and try to eat my apple.

When I got back, the door to Mrs. Karras's office was opened and she was alone behind the desk.

"Well, what did they say?" I asked.

"You won't believe it."

My heart was sinking. "What? Please. Hurry up. Tell me."

"They not only gave me permission to pass Luke, but to skip him to fourth grade, back with his old class."

"You're kidding!"

"You know I wouldn't do that. That's exactly what they said. The learning disability specialist gave him some reading and arithmetic tests and couldn't believe how well he did. The psychologist had him do some drawings and talked to him and says that his — wait a minute, I wrote it down — 'his social and emotional behavior has matured,' and the social worker went out to Luke's house and came back and said the 'stability of the family unit' seems to be improving. Then Lisa came in and showed his class work and I showed his folder with no arrests since November and almost no absent or late slips. They said they'd have the report typed and sent up, but they signed the promotion sheet for fourth grade right here."

I couldn't believe it. "To fourth grade?" I repeated.

"That's right."

I grabbed Mrs. Karras from behind the desk and waltzed her around the room. "We did it. We did it. We did it."

Then I stopped and held Mrs. Karras at arm's length. "Does Luke know?"

Mrs. Karras shook her head. "I thought you should be the one to tell him."

"Now? Right now? It's only one-thirty."

"Why not? You both deserve a holiday."

One more quick hug. "Thank you. I'll call you —"

I was backing out of her office as I was talking and when I hit the secretary's office, I began to run.

Lisa was having a party. Somebody's birthday. The class was in a circle on the floor. Balloons and paper streamers were all over the room, but I couldn't wait. I knelt beside Lisa and whispered, "Can you believe it?"

"I'm just beginning to. Want a cupcake? It's Terry's birthday."

I shook my head still kneeling beside her, still whispering, "Have you told Luke?"

"Are you kidding? Nobody gets to do that but you. Mrs. Karras and I agreed on that."

"Thank you, Lisa. Can I take him now?"

★

"How come they gave me all those tests this morning?" Luke demanded immediately.

"To see how you're doing, how much you've learned. Those people were the Child Study Team. What was it like?"

Luke shrugged. "Kinda scary. There were two of them, a lady and a man, asking all kindsa questions, making me read books and tell about 'em, and draw pictures. And then they gave me one of those old rats, like we did with the arithmetic and everything, remember? Only they didn't have any points or stars like we did. Just a lollipop."

"Well, you sure must have done a terrific job."

"Yeah? What'd they say?" Luke peered at me intently.

"They said you passed everything, and not only passed, you did so well they're going to skip you into fourth grade."

Luke squinted his eyes at me. "Whatta you mean?"

"Next fall when you come back, you'll be in fourth grade."

"What about third? I haven't had third yet."

"Doesn't matter. The Child Study Team says so. Mrs. Karras and Lisa say so, too. They say you learned both second and third this year — so, wham! Right into fourth."

"Regular fourth? Like where Bobby will be?"

"That's right," I said. "Exactly right."

Luke and I were both standing up now. Luke was beginning to hop a little, just a little, Up and down. Up and down.

"Let's celebrate," I said. "What do you want to do?"

"Everything. Everything we ever did."

We were both laughing, running down the street.

Luke had his arms stretched wide and was doing his happiness run, the one he'd used in the country, dipping and wheeling like a small plane or soaring bird.

We both knew where we were going first. Dunkin' Donuts.

Luke had already had a party at school, but he didn't care and neither did I. We drank a cup of coffee and made the waitress recite the list of doughnuts twice before we ordered.

The library. Past the fat librarian to the children's section. Back out before she was out of her chair. Luke didn't want a book today. Nothing to weight him down.

The corner store. We couldn't eat anything, but Luke told Dave, "I'm goin' into fourth. They skipped me."

The lipstick factory. The shed rebuilt. No sign of the fire. Luke couldn't find the hole where he had once kept his things.

The field. The mole hole was there. The six ducks' graves. Only three crosses still standing. Louisa Mae's was one.

The stream. Luke led us across, hopping from stone to stone, and this time I made it almost as quickly as he did.

The project. Luke unlocked the door with the key he still wore around his neck and shouted, "Hey, Ma! I passed. I'm going into fourth." Nobody was home, but we both knew his mother would be back by three. She always was these days.

Back outside. Only one place left.

"Shall we go to the mountain?" I asked.

We ran back across the field to my car parked across from the school, and drove away from Falls City, up to the woods, to the mountain.

Luke showed me where to park. Again, I would have missed it without his directions. Now we walked more slowly, tired from the excitement, as we climbed up toward the tower. There was no need to hurry now.

Luke's platform was still in place under the water tower. How many times had he been back? Would he come back next year? Now was not the time to ask.

It was cooler on the mountain and the storage tank formed an umbrella of shade above our heads. We sat together looking out over the city and the surrounding highways leading to New York and other parts of the country. We didn't talk. I didn't even try to guess what Luke was thinking. I let my own thoughts float free, trying only to experience, to make this water tower, this day, this boy, part of me forever.

Luke touched my knee. "Remember that deer? The one on the meadow?"

"Yes."

"He was just standing there. Quiet like now. But you know what, Mary? You know how I wished I'd seen him?"

I waited, listening hard.

"I wished I'd seen him running. I wished I'd seen him running beautiful and free."

I turned to face Luke, surprised by the poetry of his words, but he was no longer looking at me. He was looking out beyond the streets of Falls City.

"You will someday, Luke. I'm sure of that."

Beautiful and free. Luke's words reverberated around and around in my head.

I leaned back against the water tower and put my arm around Luke's shoulders. Together we looked at the world stretching out beyond Falls City. We'd done it. We'd gotten out from under and we were on our way.

33

It was the hottest day of the year, but it was also the final day of school for the kids at 23 and I had to go down.

It would be my last day there, too. My degree and certification in elementary and special education was safely filed in my drawer of important papers. I had accepted a job as supplementary teacher in a resource room in a public school beginning in the fall. It was only a part-time job, six dollars an hour. Not much to some, but more than I'd ever made before. What's more, I'd had to show my degree and teaching certificate to qualify. In the eyes of the law I was a "real teacher" now.

I had also been accepted in graduate school to work toward my master's and certification in learning disabilities this summer. I was determined to learn the techniques and tools of testing and evaluating as well as teaching. It would take another year and a half, but the courses were at night and there would be children every day at school.

When I was certified as a "learning disability specialist" (why couldn't they just call it learning specialist?), I planned to open my own practice so that I could work with children both in and out of school, with some like Luke, some with different needs. I wanted to continue to do the kind of educational therapy we'd been doing in School 23. I believed more strongly than ever that children's learning and emotional difficulties are inextricably linked. I was sure now that the most effective way to help children was to give them emotional support and at the same time teach them the skills they need to succeed academically and socially.

I had also come to understand that pain is never isolated. If the child is in trouble, the hurt will spill into the family, and vice versa. Parents must be included in, not out. In the long run, they are the real key to a child's success.

The clinic project may have staggered, through lack of funds or personnel, but the idea was right and that was what mattered. I couldn't be sure about Maureen or Louisa Mae, but Vernon, Milt, Bobby, and Luke had all grown and so had Hud and Shirley and myself, and that was a pretty good percentage. I hoped someday the program would have another chance. It deserved it.

★

I had bought a small gift for each of the children — a diary for Maureen, a fishing rod for Bobby, a new clock for

Luke, a toolbox for Harry. But when I got to school, Luke was absent. Uh, oh! What now? I hoped success hadn't gone to his head. I resolved to go over to the project and check up on Luke as soon as I'd seen the other children.

I said good-bye to Harry first, trying to use my Falls City cool, to remember all that the children had taught me, careful not to presume on our friendship. Harry thanked me for the toolbox, we wished each other good luck, and we were done.

It was harder than I had thought it would be. Maybe I had gone too fast, been too cool. I spent more time with Bobby. We had one last game of Black Jack and he invited me to go fishing with him and his brothers over the summer. He was sure the new rod would be lucky.

Maureen liked her diary, except, of course, actually she wished it was an autograph book. She was collecting autographs, she said. Finally she decided it was all right; she would use it as both an autograph book and a diary. She opened it to the current day.

"Sign it right here, Mary. Please."

"Okay. Fine." I started to write my name.

"No. Wait," she said. "Write what I say. All right?"

"Sure. Go ahead."

"All right. Write this." She spoke slowly, stopping at the end of each line.

> *"When the name that I write here*
> *is yellow with age,*
> *And the words that you see here*
> *grow dim on the page,*
> *Then think of me kindly*
> *and do not forget*
> *That wherever I am*
> *I'll remember you yet.*

"Now write 'Your friend, Mary MacCracken.' "

I did as she asked and then said, "Did you make up that poem, Maureen?"

She hesitated for a minute and then said, "Not exactly. My sister, the one in fifth grade, she's got it in her autograph book."

"Well, anyway, it's nice — and it's true. I surely will remember you."

I waved to Lisa from her classroom door. The kids were cleaning out their desks and throwing the stuff around the room.

"Call me when you get back from your trip. Let's have lunch," I called over the racket.

"Good," she shouted back. "Maybe I'll even take a course over at college."

★

Before I left for Luke's I packed the children's notebooks and whatever stories they had left behind. The rest could stay. Perhaps next year there would be someone who could use the clay and Magic Markers.

The door opened slowly, quietly, and then Harry's head appeared.

"Isss anybody here?" he lisped.

"Me."

"No. Anybody elssss?"

I shook my head.

Harry came all the way into the room. He was carrying his book bag. He put the book bag on the table and began unpacking. One book, two, three.

"Uh, Harry. I really can't . . ."

"Sssee. I didn't have time before. You were in sss — sss — anyway, a big hurry, and I couldn't get it unpacked."

I sat down. He was right. I had hurried him. I shook my

head. Just because I'd been afraid of my own emotions, hurrying to get out before I showed how I felt. Proud of my Falls City cool. Forgetting that these kids had enough cool for themselves and me too. Forgetting to be myself.

Harry had seven books on the table. "I had to put it down on the bottom ssso nobody'd sssee." He lifted out a square box wrapped in flowered paper and handed it to me.

"It'ss for you," he said.

Harry. Who would have guessed?

"Thank you." We were both embarrassed, but that was okay. I wasn't going to rush it this time. "Can I open it?"

Harry nodded and I carefully slit the pieces of Scotch tape and lifted off the paper. A bright pink box labeled Geranium Dusting Powder. Inside was a fat snowy puff on top of paper sealing in the powder. I poked in one corner of the paper and dipped my finger in the powder and rubbed it on the back of my hand.

Self-consciousness vanished in the scent of geraniums and I grabbed Harry and kissed him quick before either of us ran away.

"Hey," he objected, but he was grinning from ear to ear. "Do you really like it? I bought it for you with my own money."

"I love it," I told him. "It's absolutely perfect. You couldn't have picked anything nicer." I gave him one more kiss.

The door opened and Harry dove for his book bag.

It was the school secretary. "Mrs. Karras wants to see you before you leave."

"Okay. Be there in a minute."

Harry was already halfway down the hall. "Hey, Harry," I called. "Good-bye. Thanks for everything." He turned and waved, then scurried on, dragging the heavy book bag, empty now of its secret.

★

Mrs. Karras looked up from her desk. "What's this I hear about kissing in the music room?"

No wonder Harry buried his present under seven books. News traveled fast in School 23. "Couldn't help it," I admitted. I showed her the box of Geranium Dusting Powder.

Mrs. Karras smiled. "We've loved having you here, Mary. I wish we could keep you. Well — who knows? Maybe something will happen."

"You taught me something important," I said. "It's the principal who makes the school. You're the one who sets the mood, gives the encouragement, provides the material, becomes the model. No teacher can do it alone." I hugged her one last time. "Please stay in touch."

I ran down the grimy stone steps, waved at the yowling white dog, and drove to Luke's house.

I rang the doorbell and counted while I waited. One, two, three, four, five. I was about to ring again when the door opened slightly.

A stocky, black-haired man stood behind the half-open door. "Yeah. What is it?"

"I'm one of Luke's teachers over at the school. Is he all right?"

"Yeah. Sure." The door was starting to close.

"Chuck?" I asked. The door opened again.

"Where'd ya get my name?"

"Luke and his mother, too, mentioned you. I'm Mary MacCracken. This is my last day over at School Twenty-three and I just wanted to leave a good-bye present for Luke."

Chuck opened the door wider. "Listen. Sorry. I thought maybe you were one of those truant officers. See, I let the kids take the day off so they could go on up to Canada with their mother and my brother's family. We got a camp up there and I'm going up myself at the end of the week. But the kids have done so good, I thought I'd give 'em a break, and let 'em all go up in my brother's van. Come on in."

"No. No, thank you. I'm late already, but would you give this to Luke for me?"

"Sure. Sure I will. What was the name again?"

"Mary."

"Mary? Oh, sure. Now I know. Luke went up to the country with you. Right?"

I nodded.

"You know what Gloria, Luke's mother, that is, says? She says you worked a miracle on that boy."

"No. Don't say that. Luke did most of it himself."

"Well. Maybe. But I tell you, I'd never have believed that kid could do it. I mean get so smart and all." Chuck turned Luke's present awkwardly in his hands. "Could I ask you, I mean, would you tell me what you did to stop him from being some kind of stealing, cheating, bratty dumbbell?"

It was my turn to stand without speaking, shifting my weight from foot to foot in the Falls City sunlight.

What had I done? How could I put it into words for Chuck? I'd had my plan for helping Luke grow, teaching him academics, but I knew that what Chuck was really asking was how could he do whatever it was to keep on helping Luke.

It was a question I had longed to hear, and now I wasn't sure how to answer.

I did the best I could. "I'm not sure. I guess my part was showing Luke that he was smart, that the reading and

269

math weren't that hard — and listening to him. Luke needs someone to listen, so he can believe that words can make a difference." I hesitated, searching for words myself. "I guess we got involved with each other; anyway, I know I cared a lot about him.

"The rest Mrs. Brauer did here at home. She heard him read out loud and do his homework. She showed him she was proud of what he was doing, and when she really began to believe he could do it, then Luke believed it too."

Chuck put out his hand. "Well, I — uh — we thank you. And I'll tell you something. This summer up at the cabin, I'm gonna teach the kid to fish. I mean really fish. Wade the streams, cast, go after trout. A year ago I wouldn't have believed he could learn, but I'm pretty sure I can teach him how to do it now."

"I'm sure you can. Luke will love that. And remember, please call if I can ever help."

Chuck nodded and I shook his hand. Silence grew around us in the hot sunshine on the project stoop. I knew that I should go, but Luke had been such a large part of my life that it was hard to let him go for all time.

But he would be all right. I knew it. My part was done. It was foolish to stand there waiting for the right way to say good-bye. No words would ever be adequate.

I wrapped my heart in a cliché. "Give Luke my love," I called, as I ran down the project steps for the last time.

Appendix

When I began writing this book, I reviewed many old records and files that I had kept during my college years. One of the documents that I came across was "The Experimental Elementary School Mental Health Model." This was the model that was actually used for our initial training at the Mental Health Clinic. I was very excited to rediscover this program even though some parts were never implemented (the mother's group, for instance, p. 278). The plan had seemed good to me in 1970, and in 1980 it seemed even better. My excitement resulted in ninety hand-written pages describing each section of this model in detail, and the few training sessions we actually did have at the clinic in even greater detail.

Two drafts later I realized that the first ninety pages of my book were, in fact, very dull stuff. So I cut the ninety pages and began with Luke, who, of course, is the heart of the book.

Still, the idea haunted me that somewhere, someplace, there might be a teacher or psychologist or college professor who might want to initiate a program similar to that at School 23 — and this model could be a road map. (Actual names have, of course, been eliminated.)

So this Appendix is in lieu of those ninety pages. It is, I suppose, both a gift and a challenge to the network of people who truly care about children.

Experimental Elementary School Mental Health Model

It is clear that traditional models of diagnosis and treatment in Mental Health are totally inadequate in terms of available or projected manpower. Concepts of diagnosis and treatment that were accepted a decade ago are now under close scrutiny and as a result there has been a great deal of experimentation and innovation in order to design more efficient programs of prevention and amelioration. The public and private schools of our country offer the most fertile fields for the institution of programs which will eventually have a profound effect on our total population.*

Project Proposal

An experimental model for the expansion and intensification of mental health services in the schools.

Introduction

This pilot project was formulated through a series of discussions between personnel from the Department of Special Services of the School System and Personnel from the County Mental Health Clinic. Through these discussions it quickly became apparent that new and more radical approaches were needed to meet the ever increasing and overwhelming number of referrals for emotional disorders that were being made to the Department of Social Services and to the Clinic from School Personnel. These discussions indicated a need for more

---

* Proceedings of the thirty-seventh annual meeting of the Eastern Psychological Association, 1966.

immediate, intense and continual forms of help for pupil, parent and teacher within the structure of the school. Too often a child vegetates on someone's waiting list or never makes it for help. Too often the Clinic and the therapeutic process seemed divorced from those who have to work with and cope with the child in his daily crises. Hence, this project is an attempt, on the part of School and Clinic for Mental Health, to meet some of these needs by the use of new approaches by the Personnel of both Agencies.

Basic Rationale for the Project

The project proposal is based on the following assumptions:

1. Expansion and improvement of Mental Health Services in the schools will be introduced by using the school mental health specialist (social worker or psychologist) more as a consultant to those who work and live with the child. Furthermore, much of this consultative work will be facilitated by use of small group counseling techniques.

2. The majority of the school's referrals for emotional disorders can be treated on an immediate basis through a program of therapeutic counseling and tutoring at the school itself. Major stress is on the immediate problems of the child and the social context in which these problems are developing. The establishment of a program involving immediate intervention at the school should help forestall escalation of tensions and conflicts into more serious disturbances as well as easing teacher and parental frustration and concern. This program would also provide a means for extended observations and screening of what might be serious pathological disorders.

3. Major counseling contact with the child can be made by paraprofessionals or supplementary teachers who will be trained as therapeutic tutors and supervised by the school mental health specialist.

4. Substantial help can be extended to the child by working closely and continuously with the major figures in his immediate environment — teacher, parent, therapeutic tutor — without recourse to traditional, lengthy, time-consuming diagnostic and referral procedures.

Referral Procedure

All referrals initiated by teachers or parents will be processed by the school mental health specialist in consultation with the principal.

275

In cases involving learning handicaps believed due to emotional maladjustments or in cases of aggressiveness, hyperactivity, withdrawal, nervous symptoms, etc. wherein the child's classroom functioning is being seriously hampered, immediate placement would be made in the program. In cases of suspected retardation or serious neurological impairment, "quickie" psychological exams could be administered by the School Psychologist and if special class placement seemed indicated, a more complete and orthodox diagnostic evaluation would be undertaken by the Child Study Team. However, if space exists, the neurologically impaired or retarded child might be included in the program until special class placement is effected. As was pointed out, the program itself provides a means for continual, close diagnostic evaluation and when necessary referral to outside agencies can be made.

The Program

Essentially, the program is comprised of three interrelated parts involving the development of a sub mental health specialty, a teacher program, and a parent program.

THE THERAPEUTIC TUTOR   The first and most important phase of this program will be the development of the "therapeutic tutor." This individual would be a carefully screened part-time worker who might be a supplementary teacher, student teacher or paraprofessional. Screening will be done by a collaboration of the Clinic and the School. These individuals would receive in service training at the Clinic for Mental Health before entering the school program. The clinic training would focus upon the development of a "therapeutic attitude" and techniques of working with children. Further in service training, supervision and program coordination would require the "therapeutic worker" to attend a weekly group session involving the clinic consultant, the child study team member, the learning disability expert and, at times, the teachers of children in the program. These sessions would focus on therapeutic issues — the meaning of the child's actions and reactions, possible ways of handling future situations with the child, feedback information from home and classroom, evaluation of pupil progress as well as different learning materials and techniques that might be utilized. While the actual programming of learning materials or games and activities that would help develop academic skills needed by the child is the responsibility of the learning disability expert, the school's mental health specialist would be responsible for the supervision and coordination of the program.

276

The development of the therapeutic tutor role is predicated upon the belief that in the vast majority of school referrals, emotional and learning disorders are inextricably intertwined, and that both aspects of the problem should receive attention in a therapeutic program.

Educational therapy as defined in this project would require developing the tutor's capacity for creative listening — an alertness, sensitivity to, and an ability to reflect and clarify the child's underlying feelings and a strong empathy, honesty, and positive regard for the child coupled with some knowledge of reinforcement techniques. Therapeutic tutoring includes the area of increasing academic skills, but it is primarily concerned with reducing the anxieties disrupting the learning processes and it is concerned with increasing the child's basic self-esteem and motivation. Hence, much stress will be placed on creating a relationship between tutor and student and academic skills are viewed in terms of the child's personality dynamics.

In contrast to traditional psychotherapy, there would be no direct attempt to evoke unconscious material, offer analytic interpretation or attempt to reconstruct a personality. Stress will be on developing self-confidence, ego skills, and developing means of coping.

It is expected that the therapeutic tutor would see the child three times per week for approximately 50 minutes a session. As the program progressed and the children became better known to the personnel in the program, some of the children might be put in small groups for counseling and tutoring. The children would be seen during the school day.

TEACHERS' INVOLVEMENT   The second part of this project aims both to provide the teacher with more continual and intensive individual assistance in understanding and coping with the behavior of the referred child as well as offering a small group program to the staff designed to make them more sensitive to the developmental and psychological problems of their pupils and aware of their own reactions with regard to these issues. Teacher contact will be maintained through weekly classroom observations of the referred child by the mental health specialist (15 minutes) and by periodic small group consultations with the mental health specialist, therapeutic tutor, and learning disabilities expert.

In addition, the mental health specialist will keep a designated period of time free for weekly consultations with teachers concerning difficulties that they might be experiencing with their class or individual children.

Finally, an in service study group would be set up at the school for those of the staff who want to participate in the group. Group size would be 8–12 members, and the administrative staff would not be included. Group membership would be on a voluntary basis and the group would meet for 1½ hours after school. If sufficient members volunteer for the program, the program may be offered to several schools once a week for the duration of the program and would receive in service credit from the Board of Education for the course participation.

The initial focus of the group would be the study of the individual child. While the teacher would gather behavioral data with regard to a child in her classroom, the group itself would study as many children as there are teachers in the group. The purposes of this form of study would be to illustrate different means of observing behavior, how to make multiple hypotheses against further actions. As information is discussed within the group, the teachers should become more aware of the recurring patterns of behavior that are indicative of developmental stages as well as behavior patterns that suggest strong anxieties, compulsions, frustrations, aspirations, etc.

The main purpose of the group, however, is not just to gather ideas and insights with regard to the child, but rather to generate a greater empathy for and better relationship with children. As the group progresses, less structure would be imposed and more attempts would be made to help individual group members to gain insight into their underlying attitudes and anxieties with regard to the actions and problems of their pupils.

PARENTS' INVOLVEMENT   Parental contact and cooperation is obviously an important factor in any program attempting to effect change in the child's emotional attitude. It is felt that an open-ended mother's group should be set up at the school during or after school hours for the mothers of the children participating in this study. The purpose of the group would be to provide supportive situations where the mothers could face and deal with some of their problems, gain a greater understanding of themselves and their relation to their children and work out methods of effecting change in their child's behavior. If a mother, for various reasons, cannot become involved in the group, attempts will be made to meet the aforementioned purposes through periodic visits to the home by the Mental Health Specialist.

THE ORGANIZATION AND STAFFING OF THE PROJECT   The above-mentioned programs represent a pilot project to be tried in one

elementary school during the forthcoming school year. If upon evaluation, these programs or modifications thereof appear effective, the project programs would be expanded to include other schools in the succeeding year. It appears obvious that the success or failure of the project will depend to a large degree upon the capabilities and therapeutic skills of the school Mental Health Specialist. This individual is responsible for directing and coordinating the project which will entail supervision of the therapeutic tutors, heading an in service training group and mother's group, as well as consultations with teachers. Given these considerations, it was felt that the Clinic would aid the project best by supplying therapeutic consultation with regard to the aforementioned group programs. In short, the clinic consultant and the school Mental Health Specialist would work as co-therapists in the group programs. They would co-jointly evaluate and modify, if necessary, the group programs as well as evaluate and plan for the individuals within these programs. The Clinic will also collaborate with the school in the training of the therapeutic tutors.

The Clinic, during September and October, would provide in service training for the tutors. The in service training period of about 6–8 hours per week would include working with children at the Clinic under supervision as well as weekly sessions devoted to the discussion and evaluation of these experiences. The tutors would begin to work with children in the schools during the later part of October, after the Mental Health Specialist has had the opportunity to screen, with teachers, principal and other trained members, possible referrals for the program. The group work program would also be initiated at this time.

If these project programs prove viable and are expanded to include other schools in succeeding years, the Mental Health Specialist involved in the pilot project could assume the in service training functions for other school Mental Health Staff and the Mental Health Clinic's role in the project would be phased out, although always available on a consultative basis when needed.

The program as described should entail approximately three days work per week for the Mental Health Specialist:

(a) Weekly group consultation with therapeutic tutors, learning disability expert and occasionally teachers of the children involved in program = 3 hours.

(b) Brief periodic observations of children in classroom and tutoring sessions = 5 hours.

(c) Mother's group = 1½ hours.

(d) In service training = 1½ hours.

(e) Home visits = 4 hours.

(f) Time available for individual teacher consultation = 2 hours.

(g) Referral screening = 2 hours.

(h) Program preparation and evaluation with Clinic consultant = 2 hours.

PROJECT EVALUATION   This will be made by selected random sampling and when necessary will be made in cooperation with a central school. Tentatively, evaluation will be made in terms of the following program criteria:

1. *Does the program expand and improve mental health services?*
   Possible means of evaluation:
   Development of a teacher rating scale for effectiveness and comprehensiveness of Mental Health Services in the schools. Scale applied prior to and following project in control and experimental school.

2. *Does the program improve the mental health milieu of the School by making the teachers more sensitive and responsive to needs and conflicts of the child and better able to cope with the child's behavior in the classroom?*
   Possible means of evaluation:
   Measures of attitude change of teachers participating in group programs as compared to general faculty in experimental and control schools.

3. *Will relatively immediate treatment of the Problem and periodic consultation help the child change and improve?*
   Possible means of evaluation:
   Q-sorts by child in self-concept prior to and following treatment. Gains in academic and behavioral areas as measured by achievement tests, teacher rating and Q-sorts on child. These measures, again, would be compared with similar measures in a control school.

Obviously as the program unfolds, there would be areas requiring further survey and research in succeeding years.

PROJECT FUNDING   Prime areas of the project that would require funding are:

(a) Development of the research design for evaluating the project.

(b) Development training and supervision of the therapeutic tutors.